Festa

FESTA

Recipes and Recollections of Italian Holidays

HELEN BAROLINI

THE UNIVERSITY OF WISCONSIN PRESS

The University of Wisconsin Press
1930 Monroe Street
Madison, Wisconsin 53711

www.wisc.edu/wisconsinpress/

3 Henrietta Street
London WC2E 8LU, England

2   4   5   3   1

Printed in the United States of America

Library of Congress Cataloging-in-Publication Data
Barolini, Helen
Festa : recipes and recollections of Italian holidays / Helen Barolini
pp.   cm.
Originally published: San Diego : Harcourt Brace Jovanovich, 1988.
Includes index.
ISBN 0-299-17984-2 (pbk.: alk. paper)
1. Cookery, Italian. 2. Holiday cookery—Italy
3. Italy—Social life and customs.
I. Title
TX723.B245   2002
641.5′68—dc21   2002018051

Lascia ch'io ti prenda per mano . . .
Vieni! Saremo noi cinque . . . così come ai bei tempi

from *Viaggio col Veliero San Spiridione*
by Antonio Barolini

Acknowledgments

Were I to acknowledge each family member or friend who contributed to my culinary formation, I'd have a long list indeed—and even so might inadvertently overlook some. So let me say that I learned from many but will name only the foremost.

Among these is my late husband, Antonio Barolini, who first educated me in the lore and love of the Italian kitchen. Others are my mother, Angela Mollica, and my mother-in-law, who is nonna Lucia in this collection: signora Vita Cusumano Parrino; Rosetta of our Strambino days; and my daughter Susanna and her mother-in-law, Cleofe Mengacci, in Urbino.

Some recipes have been transmitted through such a long span of years from person to person that it is hard to trace their origin—as, for instance, the recipe for Sausage Bread, which comes from Barbara Bailey but before that from someone else, back to who knows where or when. Mrs. F. Pezzano, a reader of my novel *Umbertina*, wrote me from Albuquerque, New Mexico, and included a recipe for her Easter Pie, which proved so irresistible that I have since made it a part of my own Easter dinner. And Mary K. Mazotti, whose charming story "La Ciramella" appears in my collection of writings of Italian-American women, *The Dream Book*, shared with me her recipes for Christmas cookies, which come from the same part of Italy as did my grandmother but had the advantage of being written down, not transmitted orally.

To all these generous people, I give my thanks and my best wishes in turn for *Buone feste!* And many of them.

Contents

A Personal Introduction

I intended to ask Italo Calvino to write the introduction to *Festa*. He was a friend of my late husband's and mine and still at the beginning of his fabulous career when, some twenty-five years ago, I translated for him the first lecture that he gave in this country (prophetically titled "The Novel of the Future"). I went on to translate stories of his because of the great delight they gave me; his metaphors of reality, his layered use of probing reflection, his fine-tuned irony, inspired my own work as a writer. To everyone's loss, Italo Calvino died in Italy in September 1985, just before he was to come over to lecture at Harvard.

When I first became possessed by the idea for this book, it seemed foreign territory. Yet as I delved into the traditions that the foods and festas of Italy represented, I began to feel connected to the same body of traditional lore that Calvino preserved in his *Italian Folktales*.

Also, Italo Calvino was the first guest entered in the book of menus and occasions that I began to keep some years into my marriage. It was Thanksgiving Day 1959. My husband, Antonio, and our daughters and I lived then in a big old gray stucco house in Croton-on-Hudson, within commuting distance of New York. At that time Antonio was the U.S. correspondent for *La Stampa* of Turin and, as an Italian author, was a very active part of the Italian literary scene. It was natural that visiting Italian writers who came over would look him up. Italo Calvino was on his first trip to the States, and his book *The Baron in the Trees* had just been published here. He was an elegant, handsome young bachelor who delighted my daughters first by giving them a copy of his *Fiabe italiane* (many years later translated as *Italian Folktales*) inscribed with the hope that through it they would learn to read Italian well, and then by saying that he must have imagined his baron in just such trees as grew in Croton. I still have the book in which he wrote, *a Helen, mia prima lettrice tra gli alberi di Croton.*

He was thoughtful, too, about ritual and food; he pondered the American dishes, unfamiliar to him, which I had prepared for that quintessential American holiday. He liked it all except pumpkin pie, but that was to be expected. I have never met an Italian who did like pumpkin as a dessert rather than in gnocchi. And that included Antonio, who was, nonetheless, served it each Thanksgiving. For even when we lived in Rome, I'd declare, "You can't have Thanksgiving without the smell of pumpkin and spices in the air."

The menu for that Thanksgiving in Croton was straight American of the times; the only concession to Italian taste was an appetizer of black olives and finocchio—served, however, I'm startled to see as I consult my old guest book, with eggnog. I wish now I had done it differently, with Punt e Mes, say, or Bitter Campari as the aperitif. The fact is that Thanksgiving became progressively better as I *did* Italianize it—bread stuffing gave way to one of sausage and chestnut; pumpkin now shows up with herbs as a first course, *gnocchi di zucca.*

The big old stucco house became celebrated in Antonio's poem "La casa di Croton," part of his Croton Elegies collection, which, fittingly enough, I've always thought, was to win one of those literary prizes with culinary background in which Italy abounds. Italian writers frequently meet in excellent eating places to discuss literature; *Elegie di Croton* was honored by the first and foremost of such groups, the Premio Bagutta, which emanates from Milan's excellent Bagutta restaurant, where, on the plaque in the entrance, Antonio's name and work is recorded for 1960.

We eventually left the Croton house; by 1965 Antonio's work had returned us to Italy, and we were living in Rome. Italo Calvino was in Rome, too, at that time, a newlywed, living near Campo Marzio with his wife, Chichita. Before they left for a long period in Paris, we had dinner one night in a modest trattoria on Via dei Portoghesi near their apartment. I remember Chichita remarking on the Italian love for pasta. "It is the food of a poor society," Italo explained. "It fills the stomach; it seems endless, abundant. It costs little, it lends itself to the imagination. It is simple and honest; it reminds us that we keep a humble table."

How right he was. He was memorializing not only pasta, but a whole way of living and eating. One of the catchwords Italians use over and over to laud what is best in food and dining is *genuina*— what is genuine, authentic, undoctored by extravagant sauces or disguises: good bread, good pasta, excellent oil and wine, absolutely fresh vegetables and salad stuffs, the best fish of the sea, the sun-blessed fruits of the earth. Italo Calvino knew and valued what was genuine in all things. He connected me to my own family background and the frugal and imaginative use of all things edible.

Italo Calvino is no longer here to add his words to this present celebration of festas. But I think he would have liked the idea of the book. It's intended in the same spirit as his great retelling of the Italian folktales—a salvage operation in order, as he wrote in his foreword to the collection, "to ensure the survival of the race" through preserving its heritage. So, too, this offering as a bond with tradition, a keeping of the past for future celebrants.

Helen Barolini
Hastings-on-Hudson, New York

A Personal Introduction

Festa

Italy is as close to me as appetite. Indeed, my first memory of the country is gastronomic. It's September 1948. I'm coming into Italy on a train from Cannes, and at a station stop in Ventimiglia, on the Italian side of the frontier with France, I push down the window in my third-class coach. From among the crowds of milling people and porters on the platform, I unerringly single out the food vendor from whom, with gestures only, I buy my first Italian food, a *panino*—crusty bread around paper-thin slices of smooth white-flecked mortadella, that noble, venerable, and fragrant sausage of Bologna which is considerably debased in this country as baloney. The good air, the animation of the people, the fact of being in Italy, and the taste of that basic, fundamental food delivered me into the kind of transcendent exaltation I once experienced long before, as a child, at the solemn moment of First Communion.

Arrival in Italy *was* communion; it underscored my sense of Italy as the base of my identity and bloodline; the place where all my grandparents, and everyone before them, had been born. My desire for Italy had surfaced on its own thrust, breaking through layers of family repression wherein Italy and all things Italian had been put out of sight and mind, tinged as they were with indefinable feelings of shame and embarrassment. The family fervor was to be "American."

But receptiveness is all: this arrival was something I seem to have longed for before I could even name it as *l'Italia*. And somehow it became focused in the then almost totally WASP world of Wells College. There we were, three students in Miss Grether's advanced Latin class: Mary Jean Wells (named like our college founder, the Henry Wells of Wells Fargo fame), Joan Borden (called Jinx), and

I, the odd one with the unpronounceable Italian surname. We were reading the elegiac poets of Rome, and it was Catullus, Tibullus, Propertius, *et al* who awakened in me longings for the Mediterranean world my grandparents had departed from.

Although my parents, children of immigrants, had eagerly wanted to be melted down in the common pot, when it came to food, they could not quite do it. We ate American, but there were some wonderful exceptions: each night my father brought home from the Columbus Bakery on Syracuse's Italian North Side a loaf of fresh bread, his allegiance inviolate to the staff of life, which, in his estimate, was insulted by the spongy stuff we disparagingly called "American bread." Pasta, which was known only as "spaghetti" and always *was* spaghetti, we had on Sunday. Christmas meant Grandma Cardamone's filled cookies, and the strict observance of the fish courses on Christmas Eve. But it was at my grandmother's house in Utica that I had my first truly foreign foods: *braciole*; ravioli; Italian vegetables from her backyard garden, such as pole beans, escarole, broccoli, and zucchini, which were not then eaten in American homes. And Grandma herself was foreign, always dressed in black with her hair in a straggly knob, and always standing and stirring pots of sauce at her big black wood-burning stove, which wafted odors strikingly different from those in my mother's remodeled kitchen, with its all-white cabinets and the allure of a hospital. Generally, I was not interested in food; what we ate at home and in the school cafeteria, and what I was taught to prepare in my home economics class—welsh rarebit, blancmange, tuna casserole—was what being American meant in those days before we discovered the world.

Once in a while my mother would have me accompany her to the North Side to get cheese (which, as I recall its strong, pungent odor, I now think must have been romano—certainly not parmesan) in an import store which I hated to enter because of the smells—

smells that were Italian and which intensified my own determination not to be. I hated the fish store on the North Side because of the revoltingly un-American eels and squid that were displayed there. I even hated Josie's pastry shop because Josie, who made all those foreign-looking cookies, was fat and foreign looking herself, with black circles under her eyes and an uncorseted figure—not at all the image of life I was seeing each Saturday afternoon at the movies.

Nonetheless, I was ready for Italian food the moment I leaned out the train window at Ventimiglia and had my first taste of it on Italian soil. My gastronomic celebration of Italy started there and went on: at the springs of Clitunno (which Propertius had praised in odes) I had trout just netted from the clear waters and broiled with garlic and sage and served under an arbor with liters of Umbrian wine; on a Tuscan hillside at the stone house where Leonardo was born, there were fresh figs with country prosciutto. There was also the taste of free-ranging, not cooped, chicken roasted on the open hearth of a farm in the Appenines; the delectable, woodsy taste of those large, fleshy mushrooms, *funghi porcini*, which appear each fall and can be grilled like steaks; the exquisite aroma of white truffle being thinly grated over fresh, homemade tagliatelli. In Taormina at Easter, I had my first experience of true *cassata alla siciliana*. In each Italian town there was the sight, smell, and sound of every marketplace—sensational, fulfilling, humanizing.

That my memories and ties to Italy would be gastronomic seems to have been forecast from the start. The word *recipe* itself is Latin— the imperative form of the verb meaning "to procure"—and takes me back to that Latin class at Wells College, where my voyage to Italy seems to have been decided. In my case destiny saw to it that I arrived in Italy not knowing anyone and armed only with the name and address of one Antonio Barolini, an author and journalist living in Milan. I was in Europe as an exchange student at the University of London and, having gotten that far, I had determined to reach

Italy. I was writing features for the Syracuse *Herald-Journal* and was glad when a fellow student in London provided the name of a journalist to contact in Milan.

I did meet signor Barolini. He did not speak English, nor I Italian. My other language at Wells was Spanish, taught with the Castillian lisp which considerably limited my courage to speak it. After college I had started teaching myself Italian by following words in the libretti as I played opera records and sang along with Tosca, Violetta, Mimi, and Gilda. This I implemented by studying verbs once a week with a patient Italian typesetter who worked for *La Gazzetta*, Syracuse's Italian-language weekly newspaper. But I hadn't gotten very far, so when we first met, Antonio Barolini and I spoke a lingua franca of French, Spanish, and Latin until he found that the true common language between us was food.

I was courted with the exquisite strategem of dining well and often. In Milan he'd head for an elegant bar like the Sant'Ambroeus (which, mirabile dictu, I have seen reincarnated these forty years later on Madison Avenue in New York City). He introduced me to Rabarbaro, a rhubarb-based aperitivo which he said unaccountably (for our acquaintance had just begun), would be good for my liver; Cynar, of the artichoke, would fortify me against the rigors of modern living. Bitter Campari was good for the character.

Or we'd take tea with, to me, an extravagance of new and wondrous pastries. Dinner might be at the Biffi Scala with Antonio's writer friends, a group that included two future Nobel Prize laureates, Salvatore Quasimodo and Eugenio (but called Eusebio) Montale; the poet Maria Luisa Spazziani; novelists Guido Piovene and Marise Ferro; and artists Italo and Nini Valenti. I didn't know enough Italian for conversation; I looked, listened to the brilliant pyrotechnics of dialogue whirling about me, and ate—tasting my first *ossobuco*, the elegant simplicity of the *paillard di vitello*, and the Milanese veal cutlet which is a large, sumptuous chop completely unlike the American version. It was at the Biffi that Montale re-

4

marked concerning my quietness, *"È molto serena"*—"She's very serene." Years later, when Antonio and I were traveling by train with him and Mosca (the woman companion who fostered his career and whom he was to marry in their old age) and chatting in Italian, he recalled that early impression of serenity and said, "But now you've found your tongue."

Montale was quiet and dour, timid and fearful, often sarcastic, but a man of great intellect and artistic sensibility. He was not only a world poet; he also had a fine musical talent from having been trained as a singer in his youth, and he delighted in drawing with pastels. When Antonio and I married, Eusebio gave us a gift of one of his delicate floral compositions. This is a drawing that is always with me and that I look at every day, remembering.

That first year of mine in Italy, when Antonio knew I would be alone for the holidays, he invited me to spend Christmas at his mother's home in Vicenza, where he would join me from his post in Milan. In 1948, trains were still few. I was lucky to get on one, literally, for the trip north; it was so packed, I stood all the way, jammed in the corridor amid other holiday travelers for the seven- or eight-hour trip. In a coincidental and Orwellian transposition of figures, in 1984, I again made a journey to Vicenza, this time comfortably seated in the crack *rapido* called Freccia della Laguna to visit the memorial dedicated to my now deceased husband by his city.

On a June day, I stood in the sunshine in Via Santa Lucia, reading the plaque affixed to the wall of an old palazzo. There the city fathers recorded that in that dwelling Antonio Barolini had written his first volumes of poetry and the novel called *Giornate di Stefano*, which was the first work of his that I was to read in my newly acquired Italian. I remembered the shivery time I had spent at Christmas all those years ago in the top-floor apartment of the converted palazzo, where we sat in the kitchen around the stove to conserve heat. There signora Lucia, Antonio's mother, had prepared her famous *strudel di gris*, a long roll-like preparation of spinach and ricotta encased in pasta and served as a first course for Christmas. And there the serious deliberations had taken place about where to get the festive panettone and how large it should be. The purchase was made at the aristocratic Caffè Meneghini on Vicenza's Piazza dei Signori, its tiny quarters meant to accommodate only the precious few, while across the way the hugely democratic Caffè-bar della Repubblica had room for all the others. I still remember that Christmas dinner with its (to me) exotic accompaniments of *mostarda*, *cotognata*, and *mandorlato*.

Antonio was not only a man of great humor and humanism; he was also deeply centered in his traditions and in family. Montale, reviewing Antonio's stories in *Our Last Family Countess*, which had appeared first in my English versions and then were translated back into Italian, wrote, "Barolini was not born modern, that much is known and reveals nothing. More interesting to ascertain is that he has not moved a finger to become so." In fact, it was that perduring, tradition-rich air about him that was also so compelling an attraction to me in my longing for a family past.

In time I learned Italian, as well as my *italianità*. And then I married Antonio Barolini and learned to cook. Antonio introduced me to many things, from the poetry of Leopardi and Montale, to the polenta of his Veneto region and the classic torte of Horace; living in Italy taught me the rest. My Italian marriage even had a beneficial effect on my mother's cooking. For, won over by Antonio's charm from the moment he first kissed her hand and called her Mamma, she started resurrecting her own buried southern Italian heritage.

Actually, after the end of World War II, Italy started becoming fashionable and right. Soon my mother was dredging from her memory foods from her own mother's Italian kitchen: handmade manicotti, stuffed shells, calamari in red sauce, delicious fritters of minced celery leaves, and the wonderful summer vegetable stew known as *giardiniera*. The first Christmas after my return from Italy, we were photographed for the Syracuse *Herald-Journal* making Italian Christmas sweets—*cannoli, cuscinetti, amaretti, biscotti all'anice*—the whole repertoire! Starting in her kitchen, my mother found her way back to her heritage, and this, I suspect, happened for many Italian-American families who were rescued from lives of denial by the "ethnic" explosion of the sixties.

Since I had felt the pull toward Italy while reading the Roman poets, it was altogether fitting that the first thing Antonio and I ever cooked together was what he called *la torta oraziana*, or Horace's torte. It is also known as the cake of two flours, for it incorporates white flour and yellow cornmeal. I remember it clearly, on a summer day in my mother's American kitchen in Syracuse while everyone else was out playing golf. To distract and entertain me (for I was pregnant with our first child then) and to satisfy his own nostalgia for his distant birthplace Antonio said, "I will make you a sweet from Horace's own recipe!" My mother later eyed it skeptically and noted the great quantity of her butter and almonds it had taken, but ever after I was enthralled by Antonio's gay improvisation in the kitchen and learned that cooking is also of the heart as well as the book. Years later I recognized the torte in Daniela Sacco's *Sbrisolona*.

After Linda Lucia was born, we returned to the north of Italy, to the Piedmont region and a small country village called Strambino. It was some 5 kilometers from Ivrea, where Adrianno Olivetti had created a kind of duchy of Weimar of contemporary enlightenment, calling to his headquarters at the plant where typewriters and business machines were manufactured the intellectuals, artists, and authors of Italy. While Antonio, as cultural emissary, implemented Adrianno's community program throughout the region, I kept house and children and table with the aid of a comely young woman named Rosetta, and something called *Il Libro della Casa*—an annual house book of food lore, maxims, advice, and pages for daily entries for keeping accounts. In it I recorded observations, menus, where I shopped, and how much was spent.

Antonio had also equipped me with an Italian cookbook called *Il Cucchiaio d'Argento*—literally, "The Silver Spoon." Its only fault is that it was published too soon after the war, when the grade of paper was so bad that it has browned and fragmented, and I doubt that it will last to be passed on. He inscribed the book to me in these translated words: "The devourer of Italian foods to the promising preparer . . . to Helen, so that our daily food may become spiritual energy . . . with a kiss from ex-cook, Antonio." In fact, Antonio, as a bachelor, had been a cook, and I kept on learning from him all through our married life.

Antonio and I lived part of our marriage in the States. We settled in Westchester, and he became a commuter to New York while I became the English translator of his Italian stories, those delicate reminiscences of his Veneto boyhood which began to appear regularly in *The New Yorker*. And for him then, as for me now, food was the medium of his memory. There were stories about the great bird barbecues on the lands of his grandfather Gregorio; the veritable recipe for the holy broth of Pope Pius IX, which was part of the legend of zia Gegia; the extravagances of cousin Lisetta; the tale of the Pepper Man—all the bittersweet memories of other times and ways, the feasts and harvests of people long gone.

We lived first in Croton-on-Hudson, then in the neighboring town of Ossining. Our Ossining home, in an area that still remains rural, was a converted barn, which we bought from Aaron Copland. No one was aware, it seemed, that he lived in Ossining, and I remember my awe, first at stepping into the magnificent space of that structure and then upon meeting its owner, the eminent composer. Genial and urbane, Aaron Copland amiably wondered aloud how we, a family of four, would fit into his bachelor home, barn though it was. We not only did, but in conformance with the old

Italian maxim that a new home brings a new child, we increased the family to five with the birth of our last child, Nicoletta, while we lived there. It always seemed to me destined that Niki would be, as she is, an artist, for our barn home resonated with the wonderful sensations of the creative people who had lived and worked and visited there—not only Aaron Copland, whose baby grand piano seemed almost inconspicuous in the space of the great room, but also Antonio himself. I remember our life at Shady Lane Farm as a time of burgeoning creativity in our writing for both of us, and I feel it had much to do with the beauty of the setting and the sensations the house itself unleashed in us. I still think of it as my dream house, the place in which Antonio and I would greet our grandchildren, while apples from the backyard trees baked in a pie.

Our neighbors over the hill were John and Mary Cheever who, having spent a year in Italy, were delighted to speak Italian with Antonio. John often took long walks with his Labrador dog and would come down over the adjoining hill and through our place to get over onto the Croton Aqueduct walkway. Often he'd stop in for a drink and a chat, and I well remember the day when he recounted a story he had imagined as he walked—of a man, seeking home, who swam his way across the county from pool to pool. That turned out to be the beautiful story, "The Swimmer."

The Cheevers had brought back from Rome with them an Italian nursemaid, Jole, who made wonderful fresh pasta for their dinner parties. And occasionally Antonio, too, would cook. He was deeply involved in his journalistic work, with daily deadlines to meet, and also in his writing of stories and novels. But every so often, he'd feel a great nostalgia for some food from his past and decide to create a *pasticcio di macaroni* with squab, or a *risotto* of seafood. Many things recalled his childhood to him, and he wove those memories into his stories, verbal and written. Once, driving through New Mexico, we stopped at a little village to buy peaches, and I remember vividly the gasp of joy as he bit into a peach and said it

Prelude

was identical to those famous peaches grown near Lake Garda, which he had never dared hope to taste again.

At Shady Lane Farm I started the Christmas season with the observance of Santa Lucia's Day on December 13, both in remembrance of Antonio's mother and as the name day for our first child, Linda Lucia. All the symbolism was meaningful: Linda, as I, had been born in Syracuse, New York; Santa Lucia was born in Syracuse, Sicily, of which she is patron. But the saint's relics now rest in the Church of San Geremia, Venice, a bonding between north and south Italy, which, I felt, had overtones for my own marriage. According to my jesting husband with his thousand-year-old Veneto heritage and kinship with the nobles of Vicenza, the only way a gentleman of Verona, or anyplace else in the north, could marry someone of southern and Sicilian lineage, such as I, was thanks to a purging (or melting, as with the pot?) of peasantry by three successful generations in America. The sea change was all. So the day of Santa Lucia was well observed in my household for many reasons, and year by year the tradition evolved. From the time she was eight years old, Linda Lucia would arise early and bake Lucia buns for the rest of the family. That evening there would be a special dinner, and Linda Lucia would be the queen of the occasion, donning a headpiece in which candles had been set, for Lucia (whose name derives from the Latin for light), recalls the light in that darkest part of the year.

We lived happy years at Shady Lane Farm, with occasional trips back to Italy, as when Antonio was given the Bagutta Literary Prize. Some years later, while in Italy, a designer friend of ours from Croton made a special trip to the Bagutta restaurant and pointed out Antonio's name on the wall to the waiter; she said she was treated exceptionally well.

In 1965, however, Antonio's work took us away from Shady Lane Farm and back to Italy. We settled in Rome, which is where, in 1971, he suddenly died. I returned to the States and became immersed in working and starting again. The children grew and left for college. Then their lives took them farther and farther away, in marriage or in their work. There were fewer and fewer occasions for the old traditions and feasts. When I finally got myself to revisit Shady Lane Farm, I found our old house empty and forlorn, acquired by a greatly expanded General Electric Corporation across the way and earmarked to be torn down for a volleyball court.

Somehow it was not until the summer of 1984, when I went back to Vicenza to see the plaque that had been dedicated to Antonio by the town of his birth, that I recovered my old sense of connection with the place that had been so fundamental to my life and growth. Years before, on a gray day in February, the town walls had been covered with the notice of Antonio's death, and I was there to follow the coffin to where it would rest in the part of the cemetery reserved for Vicenza's illustrious citizens. Near his fellow poet, Giacomo Zanella; the Count Rossi, who had started the wool industry in that part of the Veneto; and other notables, Antonio, too, was interred. I deposited his papers in the venerable city library, la Bertoliana, and said good-bye to Italy.

The summer of 1984, however, I was glad to get back, glad to have all the good memories intact. Vicenza was a delight—flourishing, busy, beautified, filled with the colors of flowers as I'd never seen it. And then I realized why: I had always been there in the season of its gray fogs and damp or during its postwar austerity. Even our wedding in the chapel of San Nicola had taken place in a bleak November.

I walked through the old historic center to the Ponte degli Angeli. When I first knew the surrounding quarter, it had been wardamaged, dilapidated, and down on its fortunes. The Bridge of the Angels ends in a square esconced on each side with a noble seventeenth-century building, and there begins Via Santa Lucia, an old, old street of arcades. Toward the beginning of the street is the venerable palazzo where Antonio's grandmother, Caterina Crivellari, had grown up. Caterina's recipe book, in her own beautiful hand, is with me now, a gift of my sister-in-law, Arcangela. Farther down, next to the grand entrance of Palazzo Faccioli, an imposing building with balustraded windows and impressive archways, was the tiny entrance to the apartments that had been carved out of the back part of the palazzo. And on the top floor lived Antonio's mother, Lucia, and Arcangela, in an apartment opening onto the courtyard; next to them, in a veritable garret, was a distant cousin, Gilda Faccioli. Her husband had been of the noble family whose notable palace still graces the center of town, but before his death, he had gone through his fortune, and war had done the rest.

In the entrance to signora Lucia's apartment was the beautiful walnut credenza that is now here with me in my American home; in the dining room, which also served as salon, were the nineteenth-century lady chairs and nonna Lucia's chaise longue, which also became part of my home. Then there was a kitchen, a larder opposite it, three bedrooms off the long corridor and, at the end of it, a bathroom with gas boiler above the tub to heat water. Bookcases in the corridor housed what was left of Antonio's once huge library, most of which, along with other furnishings, had been lost in an American bombing of the city.

There is no one, now, of the Barolini family who lives in the old historic center. Antonio's widowed sister lives in a modern apartment on the newly developed outskirts of town, with her great joy, an American kitchen. At Number 44 of Via Santa Lucia, the plaque that records that Antonio Barolini lived there from 1924 until 1951 is affixed. And, in a new part of town, there is a middle school, the Scuola Media Statale Antonio Barolini, where, I like to think, students are reading his stories.

I rediscovered Italy and with it the nostalgia for all those family feasts Antonio and I had engaged in, the cooking and eating we had done, and I thought with some sadness and sense of loss about the complications of living, of the distances (geographical and otherwise) that now keep me from setting a family table. I thought of the disquieting cracks now perceptible in what had been, I thought, the everlasting structure of our family rituals, of family itself. I thought, what a shame if those customs and cookery are not recorded for our daughters . . . and for all those Italian-descended families in America.

One Christmas Eve my New England son-in-law sat at my Italian table, a table that had come from a country kitchen of Antonio's ancestors—a vast kitchen of other times. In good sport my son-in-law wondered aloud if I weren't inventing that whole rigmarole of the seven fish courses that I served on Christmas Eve. "Is this another of your new traditions?" he asked jokingly, as if I had made it up on the spot. Certainly it was not what he, not a fish lover anyway, knew about Christmas from his background, and that was to be understood. But what gave me pause was my daughter—that same Linda Lucia of the Santa Lucia childhood rituals—who began to abet her husband and call into doubt the tradition of the seven fish.

Doubt the seven fish dishes of Christmas Eve? Good Lord, even if everything else goes by the board, that is one occasion that is solemn in any Italian household. Even my watered-down Italian-American childhood records Christmas Eve as special and traditional and Italian. One might as well—as I never did and still do not—doubt Antonio's words that the torte of two flours was the great lyric poet Horace's own recipe. (Naive! naive! cry my three daughters.)

That's when it occurred to me that these menus and memories should be set down or else, indeed, they would first be doubted and then lost for good.

Mangiando, ricordo. My memory seems more and more tied to the table, to a full table of good food and festivity; to the place of food and ritual and celebration in life. Yes, I believe in good food and in festivity. Food is the medium of my remembrance—of my memory of Italy and family and of children at my table. As a friend said of me, "You're like my mother—anything for a party."

One

DECEMBER

Toward the end of every November, the sound of the nutcracker was heard in my childhood home: I can picture my mother, just after Thanksgiving, at work on mounds of Brazil nuts, hazelnuts, pecans, almonds, and walnuts. They were all in the shell, and all had to be cracked, opened, lightly roasted, and chopped for the great filled-pastry enterprise known as Grandma's Christmas cookies, the recipe for which was one of few possessions Grandma Cardamone had brought from her native Calabria when she emigrated a century ago. This cookie is known in several regions by various dialect names—just as *pignolata* seems to have myriad names but is always recognizable as the same basic pinecone-shaped sweet (that reminds me of the giant bronze cone from antiquity, which stands imposingly in the Vatican's Pigna Court and whose size Dante remarked on in the *Divine Comedy*). I can recognize Grandma's cookies in, for instance, artist Ed Giobbi's *calgionetti*, *Italian Bouquet's pitte con niepita*, or Aunt Josephine's Filled Cushions, and in the sweets known as *mustazzoli*, *cuccidate*, *nepitelli*, *cucitate*, and *cuscinetti di teramo*.

The other Christmas cookie I can remember vividly is the plain sand tart for cutouts. As a child I loved making all those figure cutouts and decorating them with colored icings, sprinkles, coconut, cinnamon drops, nuts, and chocolate. It's a simple recipe for a dough that can repose in the refrigerator for several days and then be rolled out at intervals for baking, so I was amused to find in Artusi (the great master, who is to Italian cooking what Brillat-Savarin is to French) a recipe for sand tarts that begins, "Don't be alarmed to hear that they require 2 hours of uninterrupted kneading in a place protected from air currents, and stirring with the wooden spoon constantly in one direction. Ladies who are by nature patient . . . will not be dismayed by this. . . ." Even in my childhood, ladies were busy women with things to do besides stirring patiently in one direction for hours, so my mother's sand tarts were quickly made. It was the cutting and decorating that took time, but that could be spaced over days, and with several children participating, it was always fun. My daughters still remember with affection the "nut test" I gave them to identify the different kinds of nuts in their shells by name.

Actually, however, the Christmas season began not with my mother's Advent nut-cracking, but with the earlier preparation of grape juice conserve (which Artusi refers to as *sapa*) left from the fall wine making that my father's family engaged in. As in most Italian-American families, there was in ours a curious rivalry in the "mixed marriages" (partners were "mixed" if they came from different regions of Italy) as to which provenance was superior, and thus which spouse outranked the other. My mother's family came from Castagna, a hill town in Calabria surrounded by forests of chestnut trees; *castagna* means chestnut, which gave rise to my father's jest: "Castagna is where all the nuts come from." His family, on the other hand, was from the Sicilian fishing village of Spadafora, which translates into "unsheathed sword" and probably provoked off-color jokes in kind. As my father told it, the Sicilians bested the Calabrians because of the English blood that had mingled with Sicilian when twelfth-century Crusaders, led by King Richard the Lion-Hearted, had stopped off on the island on their way to the Holy Land. My mother would counter that her father had been a tall, blue-eyed shepherd, which clearly bespoke his own Norman blood and his likely descendance from the feudal lord who had built the Norman castle now lying in ruins outside Castagna. These were the family legends, with their ingenuous pretensions to spurious nobility, that were told and retold in the boasting matches I remember as part of every holiday reunion.

I took part in making Grandma Cardamone's Christmas cookies, but I never saw the grape conserve being made. My father's cousin Grace Pizzuto Fahey has described it to me, referring to the conserve, however, as *mostarda*, which it isn't. *Sapa* was prepared after the first pressing of grapes for wine. The unfermented run-off juice was boiled down to the thickness of honey and made into a grape pudding with chopped orange, walnuts, cinnamon, cloves, and grated lemon rind. The mix was stirred and boiled until thick, then poured into dishes to cool and finally stored in canisters until it was time to use it as filling for Christmas cookies.

I was fascinated by Grace's misnomer of the grape conserve as *mostarda* because the true one is the fruit confection from Cremona that I became familiar with through my husband's northern Italian tradition. The rigmarole I sang to my babies, starting with the first, was *"Mostarda, mostardon/Butta la Linda* (or Susi, or Niki) *giù dal balcon!"* At my first Christmas in Italy, dinner in Vicenza had featured those luscious whole fruits—kumquats, seckel pears, apricots, figs, plums, and cherries, plus pieces of peach, melon, and pineapple!—candied in a thick golden mustard-flavored and spicy conserve the wonder of which has stayed with me ever since.

I never knew until years later that that first Christmas dinner at the home of Antonio's mother and sister had been boycotted by their closest relatives, zia Giulia and zio Giuseppe Gavazzo, the sister and brother-in-law of signora Lucia. The *zii*, as they were called collectively, had objected to an intimate family occasion being violated by the presence of a stranger—me. And they had good precedent in the Italian saying, *"Natale festeggia coi tuoi/Capo d'anno con chi vuoi"*—"Celebrate Christmas with your own, New Year's with whom you please." Signora Lucia, on the other hand, with the tolerance and good nature which was to distinguish her son, my future husband, felt that Christmas was exactly the right time to invite a stranger who would otherwise be alone in a strange country on that day.

But what I did learn on that cold day in war-scarred Vicenza so many years ago was that in some ways an Italian-American of southern background would be as much, if not more, a stranger in a northern Italian household as an American of non-Italian heritage. I didn't seem to recognize anything familiar in the food preparations signora Lucia and her daughter, Arcangela, went through in their tiny kitchen; nothing reminded me of the foods of Grandma Cardamone's kitchen across the ocean in Utica, New York. My first lessons in Italian cooking were northern; later I reintegrated parts of the southern; now my own kitchen is, as my children are, a combination of north and south Italy.

I had been at the University for Foreign Students in Perugia long enough to learn that my maiden name, Mollica, meant the soft inner part of the bread loaf. A crumb, I asked myself, that's what I am—

a crumb? And I wanted to know from Antonio what "Barolini" meant. Surely from Barolo, he teased—a diminutive of the strong red wine of that name; we're the makings of Communion: bread and wine. Or, I answered, the title of Ignazio Silone's novel. I became glad to have a nomenclatural association with bread, the staff of life. My father's bringing home the fresh Italian loaf each evening had kept a link to tradition and heritage; to bear the name of something so basic and so rooted in my family pleased me. And didn't an English economist, David Ricardo, say that all human history is really the story of bread? In Spain, it's said, bread dropped on the floor is picked up and kissed before being put back on the table. In Italy a meal without bread is unthinkable, and it is bread that, if no longer homemade, is bought fresh each day, sometimes twice a day.

I never made a practice of baking bread at home, and the only person in Italy I know who bakes bread at home is Susi, my American-educated daughter of the "back-to-basics" seventies, who makes an atypical whole wheat loaf in her Urbino home. Bread from bakeries has been a highly developed art in Italy since Roman times; the epicure Apicius makes no mention at all of home baking. As Galen noted from antiquity, "Bread baked in large ovens . . . excels in all good qualities, for it is well flavored, good for the stomach, easily digested, and very readily assimilated." And to this day, I cannot see bread wasted. Bread is sacred, a miracle of human ingenuity and resource, and to Italians, "Give us this day our daily bread" means, literally, "Give us for another day the gift of life." To discard bread wantonly in the kind of waste many Americans indulge in would be to blaspheme, to invite misfortune. Instead, one makes bread crumbs, twice-baked slices for dunking in the morning caffè-latte, bread puddings, and croutons; stale bread is excellent dipped in a hot *fonduta*, and leftover bread can be toasted for use in soups or salads.

Bread exalted to great heights is what the Christmas *panettone* is—it means, literally, "great bread." And once all cakes, cookies, tarts, and pastries were thought of as forms of bread. It is said that the special baking of the Christmas season derives from the celebration of the winter solstice, observed as a feast of thanksgiving for the grain harvest, when fine cakes and breads were offered to the deities. So this book of festive occasions begins, as it should, with the Advent baking of cookies—sweet breads—for the holidays.

Advent

Advent (from the Latin *adventus*, "the coming"), a moveable feast beginning on the Sunday closest to the last day in November, begins the liturgical year. It is the season which precedes and prepares the way for Christmas. Just so, our holiday food preparations for Christmas begin in Advent, when twelve varieties of cookies, one for each of the Twelve Days of Christmas, are prepared. When we lived at Shady Lane Farm, I'd make up little trays of these assorted cookies, which Linda and Susi took to our neighbors.

For Niki there began the custom of the Advent calendar, in which, day by day, right through December 24, she'd open a flap window or door on the calendar to see how many more days were left until Christmas. Our dining table (a remarkable symbol in itself, for it once stood in the great country kitchen of Antonio's grandparents) was permanently set for the holidays with the Advent wreath, a circle of greenery in which four candles, one for each week of Advent, were placed and lit for Sunday dinners. The Advent wreath is a first, and very lovely, holiday decoration, with its symbolism of anticipation and lights connected to ancient light customs. "The light in darkness" (at the darkest period of the year) is the meaning of the Advent candles and the general illumination of homes and cities with Christmas lights, and is related to ancient customs of recovering light at the time of the winter solstice.

The other seasonal wreath that I loved to prepare was the della

Robbia, clusters of fruit in a circular garland, inspired by the terra-cotta originals of that Florentine family of artists. I remember my mother first fashioning these wreaths to hang over the fireplace, and my thinking as a child that they were in honor of my father, a fruit wholesaler, whose birthday is Christmas Day.

Advent, as a preparatory season, started in Rome during the sixth century as a joyful season; then the "Frankish" influence of the North gave it a penitential character. By the twelfth century, a compromise was effected so that it became a time of "joyful penance," and the first Sunday of Advent came to initiate the Church's liturgical year. It was a time of pondering, of modest treats of fruits and sweets (the first tangerines, or an exotic pomegranate), of anticipation, quite different from the deafening exhortation and orgiastic shopping and weariness of today's great marketing event. Above all, it has remained expectation, as children know it, an opening, day by day, of another window or door leading to the long-awaited, joyous moment of Christmas festivity.

Saint Nicholas's Day, December 6

December 6, the feast of Saint Nicholas, is our Niki's name day and a candy-making day for all children, for whom Saint Nicholas is the special patron saint. In Rome we lived on a steep street off Piazza Bernini named for another, less-familiar sainted Nicholas, Saint Nicholas of Tolentino, an Augustinian friar who lived from 1245 to 1305 and spent the last thirty years of his life in the central Italian town of Tolentino, where he preached and did good works and was known as a miracle worker on account of the great number of graces obtained through his intercession. Often, driving to the Marche region, where we had a little vacation house, we'd stop in the main piazza of Tolentino to view the stupendous basilica raised to him and conserving his tomb. The sun with rays is his emblem, and he is often depicted with this attribute on his breast. A glorious sunburst appears over the fine main portal of the church and is said to represent the star that beckoned him to follow until he reached Tolentino, where he was to found his church. Since Saint Nicholas of Tolentino is famed as a powerful intercessor, his sanctuary is the center of the grandly styled Pious Union of the Souls in Purgatory. At home we used his sunburst emblem in our cutout Christmas cookies and in decorations for the tree.

The more famous Saint Nicholas, who is the ancestor of Santa Claus, was a fourth-century bishop of Myra in Asia Minor in the region today of southern Turkey. His tomb, however, is in the Norman basilica built in his honor in Bari, in the southernmost Apulia region of Italy. Intrepid Italian mariners seemed to have developed a speciality of making off with the remains of saints and reentombing them in Italian churches with the long-sighted view, perhaps, to the festival occasions attendant on honoring the saints in situ. In the case of Saint Nicholas, Bari sailors in the eleventh century brought back the body of the saint before the heathens could burn down the church in which it was hidden.

An exquisite altarpiece by Fra Angelico in the Vatican Pinacoteca depicts events from the life of Saint Nicholas, and in one scene he is represented tossing three purses of gold into the room of three sleeping maidens to portray his generosity in providing dowry money for each of those dowerless sisters whose impoverished father was contemplating selling them into prostitution. This incident is said to be the connection between Saint Nicholas and the giving of gifts. In Europe it was the custom to give children gifts on Saint Nicholas's Eve, December 5. Young women boarders in convent schools would leave their stockings at the door of the abbess, with notes recommending themselves to the generosity of Saint Nicholas, and these are said to be the forerunners of notes to Santa Claus. The next day the stockings would be filled with sweetmeats of nuts and dried fruits.

Saint Nicholas's Day precedes Christmas, and it is incongruous that his imitation, the department store figure dressed in red with cotton-batting beard, has become the unique symbol of the Christmas season. Saint Nicholas's Day is a feast unto itself, a forerunner in a particularly endearing way of the major feast to come.

Santa Lucia's Day, December 13

I began to love these festivals and saints' days for what they revealed to me of a rich heritage and family lore. Inevitably, a festa motif would recall something in the family—a trait, a name, an appearance or idiosyncrasy. And festa meant food, special foods. So it was inevitable, festa and family and food were all entwined. Festas were all kinds of holidays—family anniversaries and birthdays, saints' days, secular holidays, seasonal foods, or harvest festivals. Anything for a party!

The day of Santa Lucia recalls both Antonio's mother, who shared the saint's name, and my mother's Cardamone family, whose kitchen, during Santa Lucia's Day became redolent with the gingery spice known as cardamom (sometimes spelled cardamon). Is there a connection between that spice of tropical Asia and my mother's family name of Cardamone? It's not too farfetched a notion, for cardamom was known to the Arabs, and in the melting pot of the classical world, traders and mariners reached Italian ports with all kinds of goods. In the ancient world what is known today as Calabria was part of a more extensive area called Magna Graecia, and it is very likely that its thriving cities of Crotone and Sibari carried on trade with the East. In any case, cardamom spice is definitely part of our Christmas cooking, from Lucia muffins to mulled wine, or even a bit of the ground seeds in caffè espresso for a pungent aroma.

Saint Lucy invokes the festival of lights: in Sweden cakes are flavored with saffron, which imparts the yellow color of sunlight, or with cardamom, whose delicious scent flavors the air during the baking of Lucia buns. In our time Sweden seems to have taken over the celebration and customs of Santa Lucia, but both the saint and the festivity are of old Sicilian origin. We Sicilians did, however, adopt the Swedish custom of having the eldest daughter of the household wear a white gown and a crown of lighted candles (symbolizing the crowns that martyrs are said to wear in heaven), and serve the rest of the family the special breakfast buns she has prepared. In our case, the eldest daughter was truly a Lucia.

Linda Lucia has gone on to become a Dante scholar, and of course, the Paradise cantos, that sublime celebration of the light of human reason reaching to God, has as one of its honored figures the ascendant Santa Lucia. Santa Lucia's eyes figure prominently in the legends about her, perhaps because of her name and the connection between eyes and light. She was said to have gouged out her eyes because their beauty attracted a heathen suitor; or, alternatively, her eyes were plucked out by her torturers. In the duomo of Syracuse, Sicily, which is her titular church, there is a stone statue of Lucia resembling a Greek goddess and holding her eyes in a chalice; other times her statue is furnished with a platter on which supplicants for her grace and intercession place clay or wax effigies of eyes. In a most elegant painting by Francesco Del Cossa that hangs in the National Gallery of Art in Washington, she is shown holding a long quill in her right hand and delicately, between thumb and index finger of her left hand, a stem on which grow two leaves and two half-opened buds encasing a pair of eyes. She receives the special devotions of those whose sight is afflicted and is the patron saint of street lamp lighters, if any such remain. Her name itself derives from *lux, lucis*, the Latin word for light; Lucy became a favorite Christian name, inspired by Saint Paul's text on Christians as "children of the light." She is often depicted holding a lamp and is, endearingly, the patron of scribes who may also be said to bring light.

Dante himself was said to have been cured of grave damage to his sight (brought about through tears shed at the death of Beatrice) through the intercession of Santa Lucia, whom he frequently invoked. Certainly Santa Lucia is present in each of the divisions of his *Divine Comedy*, and her presence within the Candid Rose of the elect in Paradise shows his regard for her and the strong symbolism she manifests in her name.

On December 13, which Sicilian peasants say is the shortest day of the year because it is the anniversary of when she was made blind, torch processions and bonfires are lit for Santa Lucia, virgin and martyr, the patron of Syracuse in Sicily. The feast day's bonfires and torches and emphasis on light have to do with the shortening of days and the old pagan winter solstice, which took place at the shortest time of the year, when the forces of darkness prevailed in northern Europe. Before the reform of the calendar, December 13 actually *was* the shortest day of the year, giving rise to an old saying:

> Lucy-light, Lucy-light
> the shortest day
> and the longest night.

Thus, the whole theme of light and sight and renewed hope symbolized by the Christian saint came to substitute for the pagan rituals meant to assure the sun god's return, and Santa Lucia took on special meaning for the dark northern countries, for she has survived there in the popular imagination despite the Protestant Reformation of the sixteenth century.

Antonio and I were married in Vicenza, where his mother's family lived, but he never stopped reminding me that on his father's side he was of Venetian stock—sea merchants who had been entrusted, no less, with transporting the gold *zecchini* of the Serene Republic. We often went to Venice by train, and close to the station is the Palladian-style church of San Geremia, where Santa Lucia reposes in a side chapel, her own namesake church having been demolished in 1860 to make way for the railroad. We went to visit her church. Above her altar is an inscription, which, translated, reads:

Lucy
Virgin of Syracuse
Martyr of Christ
Rests
In This Temple
For Italy and The World
Implore
Light   Peace

The saint's story, as related in the booklet sold to us by the custodian priest, is a fascinating and disquieting one. Santa Lucia was born in Syracuse in A.D. 283 and, having been denounced for her Christian beliefs by pagan informers, was killed in A.D. 304 during the severe religious persecutions of the Roman emperor Diocletian. Her remains have not rested in peace. Though venerated for many years in Syracuse in the basilica built above her sepulcher, fear of an Arab invasion of Sicily in 878 caused her body first to be hidden in a secret place, then to be claimed by Greek mercenaries who liberated Syracuse from the Arabs and wanted the saint's body to give as a gift to the Byzantine emperor. Lucia's body lay in Constantinople until 1204, when the Venetians won it and carried it off. In Venice, through the centuries, she was moved from church to church until her own was built in 1611. But first that sanctuary was closed under the Napoleonic suppression, then demolished.

Her latest abduction, from the church of San Geremia on the Grand Canal, occurred on November 7, 1981, when two youths burst into the chapel and, before the startled eyes of the priest and a visiting honeymoon couple, broke open the glass urn containing the saint's robed skeleton and made off with it before they could be stopped. Lucia's remains were found in a plastic bag in a hunting lodge outside Venice and, authenticated by the patriarch of Venice, returned to their place in the altar. On her feast day in December, it is said that the gondoliers of Venice sing the very Neapolitan song "Santa Lucia" in her honor.

Legend relates that during a great famine the Syracusans went to their cathedral to invoke the assistance of Santa Lucia. While they were praying, a ship carrying grain came into the harbor and saved the city. A wheat dish is traditionally eaten on December 13 to recall the miracle, and the Santa Lucia dinner recalls this in the Gnocchi di Semolina dish, for semolina is milled from wheat.

As for the Roast of Pork Arista, it's called that from the Greek meaning "best." It's a specially seasoned roast loin of pork, and Artusi attributes the name to the time of the Council of Florence in 1439, when Cosimo de' Medici, truly and well termed *Pater Patriae*, invited the council of prelates and scholars who were trying to unite the Christian church of Rome with that of the East to convene in Florence after their meetings in Ferrara were disbanded. On that occasion bishops and their retinues were served the pork roast, which they applauded with the Greek exclamation, "Arista, Arista!"—the best! Ever since, that word has accompanied this excellent roast. And from that meeting of Greeks and Italians in Florence, with its illuminating exchange of language and manuscripts, some historians are inclined to date the Italian Renaissance.

The day after Santa Lucia's feast, December 14, is the feast day of the little-known Saint Spiridion, a fourth-century anomaly: he was both a married rustic shepherd and a bishop, both humble and eloquent. In her book *Saint Watching*, Phyllis McGinley records that Saint Spiridion, having once interrupted a gang of thieves attempting to carry off his sheep, not only let the thieves go, but gave them a ram "lest they should have been up all night for nothing." Saint Spiridion lived on Cyprus, and his relics rest in Corfu, of which he is patron saint. Perhaps because of his association with those Mediterranean islands, around which the Barolini sea merchants plied their trade, one of their vessels was named the San Spiridione. He is also present in the title of Antonio's first volume of collected poetry, *Voyage with the Sailing-Ship St. Spiridion*. I like to think of Saint Spiridion as the proper guiding spirit for poets because he was said to believe in the power of the Holy Spirit above the words and arguments of pedants, believing also that no precepts (ecclesiastical or otherwise) should bind unreasonably. His attribute is the spike with which his eyes were said to be put out, which allies him closely with Santa Lucia.

Twelve Days of Christmas

Christmas was not always merry when I was growing up in Syracuse, and it took years for me not to feel deprived about that—to realize that Christmas was essentially a reflective holiday and not an extravaganza of faked goodwill and redundant gifts. I think it was when I got to Italy and experienced Christmas during the postwar austerity of 1948 that I realized that Christmas, as festa, had another richness and extension that did not depend on the whipped-up commercial frenzy of gift-giving on December 25, followed by the inevitable let-down until more forced jollity on New Year's Eve. In Italy I began to realize the value of simplicity. The family gathering was good unto itself—the special foods, the ritual of the panettone purchase, the respite from the daily routine, and the time to greet friends.

Christmas in Vicenza in 1948 was simple and full at the same time. The city still showed the ravages of wartime bombing and postwar shortages; gasoline was in short supply for the few automobiles on the road at the time, and fuel for homes was greatly reduced, curtailing the use of ovens for long baking and the use of hot water as well. People walked, and the Corso was still the main street for vehicles—not, as now, off bounds to a hugely increased volume of traffic. Vicenza had the look and feel of a small provincial city and the sense of a people who could make do with little and make that little memorable.

I had always remembered Christmas Eve as a fast night—fish

night—in preparation for the great feast of the following day. And Christmas was always special because it was my father's birthday. His middle name, Salvatore, commemorates the birth of the Savior, and I thought it wonderful and mysterious that our family had been singled out for this honor. But perhaps just because that was his special day, his celebrations began early the day before, and I can often remember him sleeping off the effects while my mother, with us children, struggled to put up the tree, lay the tracks for the electric train, do the baking, and prepare the dinner.

During my childhood Christmas was a quick orgy of toys. My brothers and I woke up as early as we could, unwrapped everything, and by noontime, it seemed, it was all over. In Italy I learned a new rhythm. I learned that the twelve days of Christmas was not just the title of a Christmas carol, but a span of observance from the day of Christ's birth until the Epiphany of January 6—the day he was made manifest to the Three Wise Men, who came bearing gifts for the child. And *that* was the day for the exchange of gifts! Befana, a corruption of the Italian *epifania*, became the broom-riding witch who bestowed gifts according to one's merits—sweet oranges and toys for the good, lumps of coal for the bad.

December 25 as the feast of Christ's natal day is retained in the Italian word *Natale* and started being observed toward the middle of the fourth century. By medieval times the Nativity was known in English as the Mass of Christ, or Christmas. It is so joyful and popular because it is so intimately associated with home life and children. Also from the Middle Ages is the custom of keeping the twelve days from the Nativity to the Epiphany, with their own particular symbols and customs all blending into the main celebration, as the festive season.

The Christmas storefronts I saw in Vicenza were filled with panettone and Befana's licorice-flavored lumps of sugar coal. Later, when I lived in Rome and shopped on the Via della Croce for Christmas delicacies, I'd find sweet Zibibbo grapes baked in their

29

leaves to plump raisins and sent up from Calabria, and huge, tender figs stuffed with a mince of orange, chocolate, and cinnamon. Blood oranges arrived from Sicily, *mandorlato* from Venice, *mostarda* from Cremona, *panforte* from Siena. Each Italian home had a miniature manger scene modeled after the first *presepio*, which was created by Saint Francis near Assisi more than 750 years ago. Most Italian families treasure their manger figures, and they are handed down through the generations; Antonio's family preserved an exquisite tiny, hand-carved Christ child, which, in our family, each child took turns laying in the crib each year. My own favorite manger scene is Tintoretto's *Il Presepio* in the Scuola Grande di San Rocco in Venice, which is also one of John Ruskin's three great sights in Italy.

Italian manger scenes are absolutely marvelous. The full range of Italian life in all its aspects, high and low, is portrayed along with the Holy Family and rejoicing angels. There are figures of farmers, merchants, market vendors, shoppers, schoolchildren, ladies and gentlemen, rogues and drunkards—everyone—and all against backgrounds of real life. There is the tavern, the bakery, the fishmonger's, the bishop's palace. All this is depicted with the Italian genius for realism, and pieces to add to family scenes can be purchased each season in the Piazza Navona's great Christmas bazaar. Papier-mâché creations duplicate everything from an exquisite miniature tray of many-shaped breads to a magnificent model of a whole hill town with bridges and streets, farmhouses and shops, mountains and forests selling for a million and a half lire, about $1500. And in the *presepio*, a grotto among the hills will be the sacred scene of Christ's birth with the shepherds approaching. The figures of the Magi are still far off, being moved across the landscape, day by day, until by Epiphany they have reached their destination at the manger.

All throughout Italy, churches vie with one another in creating fabulous manger scenes. The figures created for them are not only cherished heirlooms, handed down in families over many generations, but have even become sought-after objets d'art. In Rome we used to visit the *presepio* in the Franciscan church of Ara Coeli, at the top of a long flight of steps (a stairway built in 1348 in thanksgiving for delivery from the pestilence of the Black Death), on the highest point of the Capitoline Hill.

Now things have changed. The last Christmas I spent in Rome, a few years ago, I was riding in a cab through Piazza Venezia when I spotted a tall, skinny, rather abject pine tree in one of the square's grassy parterres. "A tree!" I exclaimed. The driver, taking me for a tourist (not recognizing in my Italian a former resident of Rome), said without a pause, "It's always been there." But most assuredly it had not. Nor had the clumps of white plastic ferns affixed to storefronts on Via Quattro Novembre, nor the Styrofoam angels dangling over Via Giulia. Tinsel decorations began being hung on Via della Croce while I was still in Rome in the early seventies; now more is more.

Santa Claus has come to town with northern reindeer and fir trees, displacing the Saint Nicholas of Italian tradition, while even Befana seems less and less present. The old traditional *ceppo*, a triangular wood frame in which the manger scene was displayed at the base, gifts placed on the graduated shelves on two or three other levels, sides ornamented with candles, and the top of the triangle decorated by a star—that has all but disappeared. The *zampognari*, itinerant shepherds wearing rough white sheepskins and leather foot wrappings, still come down from the Abruzzi mountains to Rome and play on their bagpipes those dirgelike songs that tell of Christ's coming during the days preceding Christmas; and a spectacular *presepio*, or Nativity scene, is mounted on the Spanish Steps. Yet somehow it doesn't seem the same.

The festival atmosphere is inherent in the Piazza Navona, the most picturesque square of Rome, since in antiquity it was the site of the emperor Domitian's stadium and continued to be the scene of historic festivals, jousts, horse races, and celebrations. Today it retains its popular carnivalesque air, even with the grandiose architecture that surrounds it, and it is perfectly suited to the booths and toy sellers and candy makers that cram it from Christmas through Epiphany. It is said that the place has been the site of fairs since the Saturnalia of pagan times and that no other place demonstrates as well the Roman genius for taking what comes and adapting to change. Everything survives together: the traditional *presepio* figures along with plastic toys, space suits, American rock cassettes and T-shirts. Sadly, today the place is full of drug pushers and their customers. A few raggle-taggle Santas wander aimlessly about, ogling the women and waiting for the occasional child who still wants a photo taken with *"Babbo Natale."* But by January 6, the square offers pretty poor pickings.

Still, some things persist, and one of these is the fast night of Christmas Eve. How did it ever become the night of the seven-fish dinner? Is it in commemoration of the Church's seven sacraments or Christ's seven utterances from the cross? Of the Gospels' seven works of mercy? Or the illuminating seven gifts of the Holy Spirit, which are wisdom, understanding, counsel, fortitude, knowledge, piety, and fear of the Lord? Is it in honor of the so-called seven champions of Christendom: Saints Andrew of Scotland, Anthony of Italy, David of Wales, Denis of France, George of England, James of Spain, and Patrick of Ireland? Or, whimsically, does it stand for the seven prevailing winds of Italy, the seven hills of Rome? Who knows?

I respect the tradition of the seven fish (for seven is a powerful number), but I am not observant when it comes to including eel among the fish dishes, even though it is usually the pièce de resistance of the Christmas vigil. The fact is that the only eel I like is encased in Montale's superb poem *L'anguilla*: "... l'anguilla, torcia, frusta,/freccia d'Amore in terra ..." (which Robert Lowell translated as "the eel, a whipstock, a Roman candle, love's arrow on earth").

The day following Christmas is the feast of Saint Stephen, who, as the first Christian martyr, is termed the "protomartyr" and holds a unique place in the lives and legends of the saints. As a deacon of the early Christian church, Saint Stephen was accused of blasphemy by the Jewish elders of the judicial tribunal in Jerusalem and was stoned to death in A.D. 36. His life and martyrdom inspired some of Fra Angelico's most sublime painting: the frescoes in the chapel of Pope Nicholas V in the Vatican, which show scenes from the legends of Saint Stephen and Saint Lawrence.

One of the most interesting churches of Rome is San Stefano Rotondo ("Saint Stephen Round," from its circular shape), built in the fifth century on what is perhaps the loveliest of the seven hills of Rome, the Coelian Hill opposite the Caracallan Baths, an area that fulfills the nineteenth-century description of Rome as "a classical landscape with churches." Still somewhat secluded from the road-way and framed in the green of a shady garden, the church of Saint Stephen was originally built in a series of concentric circles. Though greatly overbuilt in succeeding centuries, it still possesses the feeling of tranquil seclusion that must have affected Palestrina when, in the sixteenth century, he was living nearby and composing the sacred music that Pius IV described as "concerts of the angels."

Outside Rome, in the hill towns and countryside, Saint Stephen's feast was once commemorated by chopping down a chestnut tree and setting it up in the main piazza as a festive focus for music and dancing following the ritual blessing. While that rite is no longer practiced, the chestnuts associated with Saint Stephen, the beloved roasted chestnuts (*caldarrosti*) of the Italian winter season, certainly endure and are still eaten on December 26. And because he was the patron saint of horses, bread shaped like horseshoes is some-times still found on that day.

It always seemed especially appropriate, after the great quantities of food consumed on Christmas Eve and Christmas Day, to have the respite of roasted chestnuts and mulled wine on Saint Stephen's Day. The wine, which goes so well with the roasted chestnuts when friends gather during holiday calls, is actually part of the remembrance of the feast of Saint John the Evangelist (the apostle known also as Saint John the Divine, the "beloved disciple"), which takes place on December 27. On that day the Catholic Church provides a special blessing of wine in the liturgy in recognition of Saint John's surviving a poisoned wine that had been served him. He is represented in art with a chalice from which a serpent issues, an allusion to his driving the poison from the wine.

On Saint Stephen's Day we remember my father's mother, Stefana, who died while her children were still young and whose memory is kept alive as her name is passed on in succeeding generations in either the masculine or feminine version. From the simple rustic *castagnaccio* of Tuscany, which is made with chestnut flour and rosemary, to the elegant and rich Monte Bianco, made to resemble Mount Blanc, it fits naturally with the season, with tradition and legend, to have chestnut desserts during Christmas week. And it all seems to recall the Cardamones of Castagna.

DECEMBER RECIPES

Advent
Italian Lemon Drops
Grandma's Filled Cookies
Anise Slices
Lemon Wafers
Bici
Fig Fruitcake
Wine Cookies
Almond Drops
Bow Knots
Honey Balls
Mother's Sand Tarts
Florentines
Candied Orange Peel

Saint Nicholas's Day
Italian Garlic Bread
Bean Soup with Escarole
Saint Nicholas Sweetmeats
Italian Brittle Candy

Santa Lucia's Day
Lucia Muffins
Roman Gnocchi
Roast Loin of Pork Arista
Aunt Mary's Eggplant Rissoles
Fried Artichoke Hearts
Endive and Arugula Salad
Sicilian Cassata
Orange Pound Cake

Christmas Eve
Mussels in White Wine Sauce
Chicory and Arugula Salad with
   Anchovy Dressing
Sardine Spread with Celery and
   Crostini
Crostini
Spaghettini with Red Calamari
   Sauce
Spaghettini with White Clam
   Sauce
Roasted Red Peppers
Broccoli with Oil and Lemon
Broiled Shrimp
Poached Whiting
Cauliflower Salad
Sliced Blood Oranges

Christmas Day
Cardamom Wreath
Tortellini in Broth
Roast Suckling Pig
Potatoes Roasted with
   Rosemary
Puréed Beans
Fennel and Endive Salad

Christmas Week — Saint Stephen's Day
Roast Chestnuts
Mulled Wine
Chestnut Dessert

Christmas Week — Anytime
Mixed Boiled Meats and
   Vegetables
Quince Conserve
Green Sauce
Norma's Potato Torta

ITALIAN LEMON DROPS
YIELD: 2½ DOZEN

1 tablespoon baking powder

4 tablespoons sugar

2 cups sifted all-purpose flour

4 tablespoons butter

½ cup milk

1 egg

1 teaspoon lemon extract or fresh lemon juice

ICING

⅓ cup butter

2 cups confectioners' sugar

Heated milk, approximately ¼ cup

Nuts, coconut, or colored sprinkles

Preheat the oven to 375° F.

1. Grease a baking sheet.

2. Add the baking powder and sugar to the flour, and sift into a bowl. Cut in the shortening. Add the milk, egg and lemon extract or juice. Blend thoroughly.

3. With floured hands, roll the dough into 1-inch balls.

4. Place on the baking sheet 1 inch apart, and bake for 10 to 15 minutes, until golden.

5. Make the icing by cutting the shortening into the sugar. Then add milk, 1 tablespoon at a time, until the icing is of spreading consistency.

6. Ice the cookies, and sprinkle with nuts, coconut, or colored sprinkles.

GRANDMA'S FILLED COOKIES (*Cuscinetti*)

Preheat oven to 350°

Dough:

> 2 cups all-purpose flour
> ½ cup sugar
> ¼ teaspoon baking powder
> ¼ teaspoon salt
> 8 tablespoons unsalted butter
> 2 lightly beaten egg yolks
> ⅓ cup water
> 1 tablespoon lemon juice

1. In a large bowl sift together the flour, sugar, baking powder, and salt. Cut in the butter with a pastry blender until pea-sized particles are formed.

2. Add water and lemon juice to the egg yolks, and add this mixture to the dry ingredients. Mix well until a soft ball of dough is formed. Chill.

Filling:

> 2 cups chopped and toasted mixed nutmeats
> 1 cup seedless raisins
> 1 cup Welch's grape jam (not jelly)
> freshly grated rind of one orange
> ½ cup light olive oil
> Cinnamon
> colored sugar sprinkles
> lightly beaten egg whites

1. Grease two baking sheets.

2. In a bowl mix the nuts, raisins, grape jam, and orange rind.

3. On a floured surface or pastry cloth, roll out small amounts of dough. Cut into rounds with a 3-inch cutter and place on a greased baking sheet, not too close together.

4. Use a pastry brush to brush each round lightly with olive oil, then sprinkle the round with cinnamon. Place a spoonful of the filling on the lower half of each round, fold over the top half and press the edges together with the tines of a fork. Brush the top with egg white, and top with sugar sprinkles.

5. Bake 15 minutes, cool on racks. Store in air-tight container.

ANISE SLICES (*Biscotti*)
YIELD: 2 DOZEN

> *½ cup unsalted butter, softened*
> *1 cup sugar*
> *1 tablespoon baking powder*
> *1 tablespoon anise or fennel seeds*
> *1 teaspoon anise extract*
> *3 eggs*
> *3 cups sifted all-purpose flour*
> *1 cup hazelnuts chopped in large pieces*

Preheat oven to 375°; line 2 baking sheets with brown parchment.

1. Cream together the butter and sugar until light and fluffy. Add the anise or fennel seeds and anise extract. Beat in the eggs.

2. Sift together the flour and baking powder into another bowl and add the nuts.

3. Add flour mix to the creamed mix.

4. Divide dough into two parts, one on each baking sheet. Shape each part into a loaf about 12 inches long and 2 inches wide. Bake about 30 minutes, until slightly risen and beginning to crack on top.

5. Remove loaves from oven but do not turn off oven. Let loaves cool about ten minutes.

6. Transfer to cutting board and use a serrated knife to cut loaves into ½ inch thick slices on a diagonal. Lay slices close together on baking sheet and bake another 15 minutes until dry and crisp.

Variations: use 1 tablespoon grated lemon rind and 1 teaspoon lemon extract, or ¼ cup cocoa powder and 1 tablespoon vanilla extract in place of anise flavorings. (For a different flavor, use 1 tablespoon grated lemon rind and 1 teaspoon lemon extract rather than the anise. Or use chocolate chips rather than nuts with 1 teaspoon vanilla extract as flavoring.)

LEMON WAFERS (*Pizzelle*)
YIELD: 4 DOZEN

> 12 eggs
> 3 cups sugar
> 1½ cups olive oil, finest grade light extra-virgin
> 6 tablespoons fresh lemon juice
> Freshly grated rind of 4 large lemons
> 4 cups all-purpose flour
> ½ teaspoon baking powder

1. Beat the eggs until they are lemon in color. Add the sugar gradually and beat well to incorporate each addition. Add the olive oil, lemon juice, and lemon rind. Beat until smooth.

2. Gradually add the flour and baking powder, again beating until well blended.

3. Chill the batter overnight or for several days to enrich its flavor.

4. Grease both grids of a heated *pizzelle* iron, and spoon batter into the center of the bottom grid. Close the iron, and cook until golden brown on both sides.

Note: It may take several runs to get batter amounts and length of cooking time correct.

BICI

> 13 tablespoons unsalted butter
> 1/4 cup sugar
> 1/4 teaspoon cinnamon
> Freshly grated rind of 1 lemon
> 1 tablespoon unsweetened cocoa
> 2 cups cake flour
> 1/3 cup fine cornmeal
> 1 egg plus 2 yolks

1. Cream the butter and sugar until light and fluffy. Add the cinnamon, lemon rind, and cocoa. Mix well. Add the flour, cornmeal, egg, and yolks. Mix well.

2. Chill the dough 24 hours.

3. Preheat the oven to 350° F. Grease a baking sheet.

4. With floured hands, break off pieces of dough, and roll them into walnut-size balls. Place them on the baking sheet and flatten slightly.

5. Bake 15 minutes on the middle rack of the oven.

Note: These cookies keep well in a tightly covered tin.

FIG FRUITCAKE (*Frustingolo*)
YIELD: 8 TO 10 SERVINGS

> 3 cups (1 pound) dried figs
> 1/2 cup sherry
> 1 1/2 cups water
> 1/2 cup white seedless raisins
> 1/3 cup semisweet chocolate bits
> 1/2 cup blanched almonds, chopped

40

½ cup walnuts, chopped

¼ cup Candied Orange Peel, chopped (see recipe,
  page 48)

½ cup sugar

1½ cups unseasoned breadcrumbs

½ cup olive oil, finest grade light extra-virgin

¼ teaspoon nutmeg

⅔ cup honey

1 tablespoon pine nuts (pignoli)

1. Soak the figs overnight in water to cover.

2. The next day, in the same water, add the sherry and bring to a boil. Simmer over low heat until soft. Let cool; drain. Set the figs aside.

3. Plump the raisins in hot water to cover.

4. Preheat the oven to 375° F. Grease a 10-inch tube cake pan.

5. Combine the chocolate, almonds, walnuts, Candied Orange Peel, sugar, breadcrumbs, olive oil, nutmeg, and honey in a bowl.

6. Chop the figs, and add to the nut mixture. Drain the raisins, add to the nut mixture, and blend.

7. Pour the batter into the prepared pan. Sprinkle with the pine nuts.

8. Bake 45 minutes on the middle rack of the oven, or until the cake is firm and a toothpick inserted in the center comes out clean.

9. Cool the cake in the pan on a rack. Turn out onto a plate, cover with another plate and flip so the *pignoli* are on top. Cool completely before serving.

WINE COOKIES (*Turdilli*)
YIELD: 4 DOZEN

> 2 ½ cups flour
> ½ teaspoon baking powder
> pinch salt
> grated rind of 1 orange
> ¾ cup sugar
> 2 eggs
> ½ cup olive oil
> ¾ cup dry red wine

1. Preheat oven to 375°. Combine the dry ingredients and orange rind. Beat the eggs with the oil and wine. Fold the liquids into the dry ingredients and mix well. If dough is too stiff, add a bit more wine.

2. Drop by rounded teaspoons onto a greased cookie sheet and bake 12–15 minutes, until lightly browned. Let cool on rack.

ALMOND DROPS
YIELD: 2½ DOZEN

> 1 cup lightly roasted almonds
> 1⅓ cup sugar
> 1 cup all-purpose flour
> 1 teaspoon almond extract
> 3 large egg whites

Preheat oven to 325°.

Grind almonds in a food processor until very fine. Transfer to bowl and add sugar and flour, blending together. Add almond extract and egg whites, and mix until a dough is formed. With floured hands shape dough into small balls and place on greased baking sheets.

Bake 30 minutes or less, until crisp on outside and soft inside. Let cool on racks.

ALMOND HONEY CAKES (*Mostacciuoli*)
YIELD: 8 DOZEN

> *8 cups all-purpose flour*
> *½ cup sliced toasted almonds*
> *Freshly grated rind of 1 orange*
> *½ teaspoon cinnamon*
> *1 egg*
> *One 2-pound jar dark honey*

Preheat the oven to 375° F.

1. On a flat surface or in a large bowl, mix flour, almonds, orange rind, and cinnamon. Form a well in the center.

2. In a small bowl mix the egg and honey together, then pour into the well in the dry ingredients. Gradually draw in the flour, and mix thoroughly. The dough should be smooth. If it is sticky, add more flour, as necessary.

3. Take a piece of the dough and, with floured hands, roll it into a rope 8 inches long and 2 inches thick. Make 24 ropes in all. Flatten them slightly, and put them on ungreased baking sheets.

4. Bake 20 minutes.

5. Cool on racks. Wrap individually in foil and store in the refrigerator.

6. Slice each rope diagonally in 1-inch-wide pieces before serving.

Note: These cookies are hard when freshly made but soften after being kept some time.

BOW KNOTS (*Taralli*)

>*4 cups all-purpose flour*
>*4 teaspoons baking powder*
>*½ teaspoon salt*
>*6 eggs, lightly beaten*
>*1 cup sugar*
>*½ cup olive oil, finest grade light extra-virgin*
>*1½ teaspoons lemon extract*

LEMON ICING

>*1 pound confectioners' sugar*
>*Juice of 2 lemons*
>*Candied fruit*

Preheat the oven to 400° F.

1. Grease 2 baking sheets.

2. Sift the flour, baking powder, and salt into a large bowl.

3. Blend in the eggs, sugar, olive oil, and lemon extract.

4. Knead the dough until it is soft and smooth.

5. Break off pieces of dough about the size of a walnut. On a floured board roll each piece with your hands into a rope about 4 inches long. Tie each dough rope into a knot. Place on the prepared baking sheets.

6. Bake about 15 minutes.

7. Cool on a rack.

8. Make the icing by blending the sugar and juice to a runny consistency. Add more juice, if necessary.

9. Ice the cookies and decorate them with candied fruit.

HONEY BALLS (*Pignolata*)

2½ cups all-purpose flour
4 eggs plus 1 egg yolk
¼ cup butter
½ tablespoon sugar
Dash salt
½ teaspoon freshly grated lemon rind
2 cups peanut oil, for frying
1½ cups honey, preferably orange blossom honey
1 teaspoon freshly grated orange rind
1½ tablespoons colored sprinkles

1. Place the flour on a flat surface or in a large bowl. Make a well in the center.

2. Put the eggs, butter, sugar, salt, and lemon rind into the well. Mix well to make a dough. Knead the dough with the heel of your hand until smooth.

3. Shape the dough into marble-size balls.

4. Heat the oil in a deep skillet until very hot. Fry the balls, a few at a time, until they are golden brown. Remove with a slotted spoon, and drain on paper towels.

5. Heat the honey in a wide saucepan. Remove from the heat, and stir in the orange rind.

6. Stir the fried balls in the honey mixture until they are well coated. Remove them with a slotted spoon to a platter.

7. Chill at least 2 hours.

8. On a large serving platter, arrange the balls in a cone shape to resemble a Christmas tree.

9. Shake the sprinkles over the cone.

MOTHER'S SAND TARTS
YIELD: 6 DOZEN

½ cup unsalted butter
1 cup sugar
2 eggs
1 teaspoon vanilla extract
⅛ teaspoon salt
2⅛ cups cake flour
1½ teaspoons baking powder
Double recipe Lemon Icing (see recipe, page 44)

1. Cream the butter and sugar together until light and fluffy. Add the eggs, vanilla, and salt. Beat 2 minutes with an electric mixer. Add the flour and baking powder. Chill for at least 1 hour.

2. Preheat the oven to 350° F. Grease several baking sheets.

3. Roll the dough out very thin on a floured board. Use Christmas cookie cutters dipped in flour to cut out the cookies.

4. Arrange them on the baking sheets 1 inch apart. Bake 10 minutes.

5. Cool the cookies on a rack.

6. Decorate them with Lemon Icing, tinted with various food colors, and any of the following: colored sprinkles, chopped nuts, cherries, coconut, or cinnamon drops (red hots).

ALTERNATE TOPPING

1 egg white, beaten
½ teaspoon cinnamon
1 tablespoon sugar
½ cup slivered almonds

1. Follow steps 1 through 4, using a doughnut cutter instead of cookie cutters.

2. Mix the egg white, cinnamon, sugar, and almonds. Spread on the cookies.

3. Arrange on baking sheets 1 inch apart. Bake 10 minutes. Cool on a rack.

FLORENTINES
YIELD: 2 DOZEN

1/2 cup sugar
1/3 cup heavy cream
1/3 cup honey
Dash of salt
1 1/2 cups sliced, unblanched almonds
1/3 cup finely chopped Candied Orange Peel (see recipe, page 48)
6 tablespoons flour
6 ounces semisweet chocolate
1 teaspoon shortening

Preheat oven to 325° F.

1. Combine sugar, cream, and honey in a saucepan. Bring to a boil, stirring, then gently boil to 238° F (soft-ball stage).

2. Remove the saucepan from heat. Stir in the salt, almonds, orange peel, and flour.

3. Drop by level tablespoons 3 inches apart onto foil placed on a cookie sheet. Flatten cookies slightly.

4. Bake 10 to 13 minutes, or until cookies are golden brown around the edges and done in center.

5. Cool thoroughly on foil, then peel off and invert cookies on wire rack.

6. Melt the chocolate in the top of a double boiler. Stir in the shortening.

7. Spread the mixture over the flat bottoms of the cookies.

CANDIED ORANGE PEEL
YIELD: ½ CUP

Peel of ½ orange
Pinch of salt
4 tablespoons sugar

1. Cut peel into strips. Put in saucepan, add salt, and cover with cold water. Boil 15 minutes. Pour off water and add fresh water. Boil 20 minutes. Change water again and boil another 20 minutes.

2. Drain thoroughly and cover with 3 tablespoons sugar and 2 teaspoons water. Simmer, stirring continuously until all syrup is boiled away.

3. Spread on cookie sheet and roll each piece in remaining 1 tablespoon of sugar. Cool.

Saint Nicholas's Day

ITALIAN GARLIC BREAD (*Bruschetta*)
8 SERVINGS

1 loaf Italian bread, cut in thick slices
2 cloves garlic, lightly crushed
Olive oil
Salt and freshly ground black pepper, to taste

1. Toast the bread slices on both sides until brown.

2. Rub at once with garlic; brush lightly with oil. Salt and pepper to taste.

3. Serve hot.

BEAN SOUP WITH ESCAROLE
8 SERVINGS

1 pound dried navy beans
6 cups beef stock
2 bay leaves
¼ pound lean salt pork, cut into ¼-inch cubes
1 cup minced onion
3 cloves garlic, minced
1 large head escarole
Salt and freshly ground black pepper, to taste
Grated Parmesan cheese to pass at table

1. Soak the beans overnight in water to cover by 2 inches. Or, cover with water, bring to a boil, boil 5 minutes, and soak, covered, for 1 hour.

2. Put the beans and their soaking water, the beef stock, and bay leaves in a large kettle. Bring to a boil, reduce the heat, and simmer for 1 hour, or until the beans are tender.

3. While the beans are cooking, put the salt pork in a large skillet and brown over moderate heat. Add the onions and garlic, and cook them in the rendered fat, but do not let them brown. Stir frequently. Remove the mixture with a slotted spoon, and add it to the soup.

4. Wash the escarole thoroughly, and tear it into 2-inch pieces. When the beans are cooked, add the escarole. Simmer 5 minutes or until soft. Season to taste, keeping in mind the fact that Parmesan cheese is salty. Serve at once, with a bowl of grated Parmesan cheese.

SAINT NICHOLAS SWEETMEATS
YIELD: 10 DOZEN

> 1 pound mixed unsalted nuts, such as peanuts,
>   cashews, and walnuts
> 1 pound mixed dried fruit, such as dates, raisins,
>   and figs
> 1 pound candied fruits, such as orange, lemon, and
>   pineapple
> Few pieces crystallized ginger
> ¼ cup brandy
> Sugar for coating

1. Put the nuts, all the fruit, and the ginger through a food grinder.

2. Moisten the mixture with the brandy, 1 tablespoon at a time, until a dough forms. (You may not need all the brandy.)

3. Break off pieces, shape them into balls, and roll them in the sugar.

ITALIAN BRITTLE CANDY (*Croccante*)
YIELD: 4 DOZEN PIECES

> 1½ cups blanched almonds
> 1 cup sugar
> Juice of 1 lemon

Preheat the oven to 450° F.

1. Spread the almonds on a baking sheet. Toast in the center of the oven until lightly brown, about 6 minutes.

2. Chop the almonds very fine.

3. Put the sugar in a small, heavy saucepan, and cook over moderate heat until the sugar melts. When it becomes pale blond in color, add the almonds and lemon juice. Stir with a wooden spoon until

the color turns dark blond. Watch very carefully; caramel can burn in an instant.

4. Remove the saucepan from the heat. Quickly pour the mixture out onto a baking sheet or marble slab moistened with half of a lemon. Spread to a thickness of ⅛ inch. Before the candy cools, cut it deeply into diamond shapes.

5. When the candy is cool, wrap it in aluminum foil, and store it in a jar. The candy keeps for a long time.

Note: To make a topping for ice cream or custard, crush the candy in a mortar, blender, or food processor, and sprinkle over each serving.

Santa Lucia's Day

LUCIA MUFFINS
YIELD: 1 DOZEN

> *2 cups unbleached all-purpose flour*
> *2 teaspoons baking powder*
> *½ teaspoon salt*
> *10 tablespoons unsalted butter*
> *¾ cup sugar*
> *1 egg, beaten*
> *¾ cup milk*
> *1 teaspoon vanilla extract*
> *¼ cup honey*
> *2 tablespoons brown sugar*
> *¼ cup finely crushed walnuts*

Preheat the oven to 350° F.

1. Grease two 6-cup muffin tins.

2. Combine the flour, baking powder, and salt in a small bowl.

3. In a large bowl cream 8 tablespoons of the butter with the sugar until light and fluffy. Stir in the egg, milk, and vanilla. Add the dry ingredients, stirring until smooth.

4. Spoon the mixture into the muffin tins, filling them ⅔ full.

5. Warm the honey in a small saucepan over low heat. Add the brown sugar and the remaining 2 tablespoons of butter, stirring until the sugar dissolves. Add the nuts.

6. Spoon the honey-nut mixture over each uncooked muffin.

7. Bake 20 minutes. Serve hot.

ROMAN GNOCCHI
6 SERVINGS

> 1 cup semolina (1¼ cup Cream of Wheat
>   breakfast cereal)
> 3¾ cups milk
> 1 teaspoon salt
> ⅛ teaspoon pepper
> ¼ teaspoon nutmeg
> 2 eggs, slightly beaten
> 11 tablespoons grated Parmesan cheese
> 4 tablespoons unsalted butter, melted

1. In a bowl, combine the semolina with 1¼ cups of the milk.

2. In a large saucepan bring the remaining 2½ cups of milk to a boil; add the salt, pepper, and nutmeg. Stir in the semolina mixture, and continue to stir until it is thick, about 5 minutes.

3. Remove from the heat. Beat in the eggs and 6 tablespoons of the Parmesan cheese. Turn onto a lightly greased cookie sheet, and spread to a thickness of about ½ inch.

52

4. Chill until firm, about 1 hour.

5. Preheat the oven to 375° F. Using a biscuit cutter about 1½ inches in diameter, cut the dough into rounds, and place them in overlapping layers in a shallow greased baking dish 8 × 10 inches or 9 × 12 inches.

6. Drizzle with the melted butter, and sprinkle with the remaining Parmesan cheese.

7. Bake 25 minutes, or until the top is browned. (If necessary, put under the broiler for a minute or two for browning.)

Note: To prepare ahead of time, cover the gnocchi mixture with plastic wrap, and refrigerate overnight. Cut and bake the gnocchi the next day.

ROAST LOIN OF PORK ARISTA
6 SERVINGS

1 cup (about ½ pound) pitted prunes
½ cup dry red wine
1 tablespoon chopped fresh fennel leaves or heaping
    ¼ teaspoon crushed fennel seeds
1 teaspoon chopped fresh rosemary or heaping ¼
    teaspoon dried rosemary
⅛ teaspoon chopped fresh oregano leaves or pinch
    dried oregano
½ teaspoon chopped fresh sage leaves or pinch dried
    sage
6 slices chopped lean bacon
2 cloves garlic, crushed
1 tablespoon olive oil

3 pounds boned pork tenderloin, pocket cut for
   stuffing
Salt and freshly ground black pepper, to taste

1. In a small mixing bowl, soak the prunes in red wine for 1 hour.

2. Preheat the oven to 350° F. Add the herbs, bacon, garlic, and olive oil to the prunes. Mix well, and stuff the pocket in the meat with the mixture. Close the opening with stuffing pins or skewers.

3. Place the pork in a roasting pan; season it with salt and pepper. Bake 2 hours on the middle rack of the oven, or until well done.

4. Slice the roast, and serve it with its own juices scraped from the pan.

AUNT MARY'S EGGPLANT RISSOLES
6 SERVINGS

2 medium eggplants
2 tablespoons unsalted butter
½ cup seasoned breadcrumbs
1 garlic clove, minced
1 egg
⅓ cup freshly grated Parmesan cheese
Salt and freshly ground black pepper, to taste
1 recipe Basic Tomato Sauce (see recipe below)

Preheat the oven to 350° F.

1. Cut the eggplants in half from top to bottom. Put them in a shallow baking dish, cut side down, with a small amount of water, about ⅛ inch deep. Bake 1 hour on the middle rack of the oven, or until soft.

2. Scoop out the pulp, and combine it in a medium bowl with the butter, breadcrumbs, garlic, egg, Parmesan cheese, salt, and pepper.

If necessary, add additional breadcrumbs so the mixture will hold together.

3. Shape the mixture into 2-inch balls, and arrange them in an oiled baking dish just large enough to hold them comfortably. Spoon half of the Basic Tomato Sauce over them. Bake 25 minutes, or until browned.

4. Serve the *rissoles* with the remaining sauce on the side.

BASIC TOMATO SAUCE
YIELD: 3½ CUPS

> *4 tablespoons unsalted butter*
> *2½ tablespoons olive oil*
> *1 small onion, chopped*
> *1 stalk celery, chopped*
> *1 carrot, chopped*
> *1 clove garlic, minced*
> *1 cup beef broth*
> *One 28-ounce can peeled Italian plum tomatoes*
> *   (pelati)*
> *1 tablespoon chopped parsley*
> *3 fresh basil leaves*
> *½ teaspoon salt*
> *Freshly ground black pepper, to taste*

1. Put the butter and oil in a large, heavy skillet over moderate heat. When it is sizzling, cook the onion, celery, carrot, and garlic until they are soft but not brown.

2. Add the beef broth, tomatoes, parsley, basil leaves, salt, and pepper.

3. Put the lid on askew, and cook 45 minutes, stirring often.

FRIED ARTICHOKE HEARTS
6 SERVINGS

>1 tablespoon freshly chopped parsley
>1 cup unseasoned breadcrumbs
>2 eggs
>Pinch salt
>24 small, fresh artichoke hearts, cleaned and rinsed,
>   or 2 9-ounce packages frozen artichoke hearts,
>   thawed
>¾ cup peanut oil

1. Combine the parsley and breadcrumbs in a small bowl.

2. In another bowl lightly beat the eggs and salt.

3. Dip the artichoke hearts into the beaten egg, let the excess drip off, then roll them in the breadcrumb mixture.

4. Place the oil in a large skillet over medium-high heat. When it is sizzling, cook the breaded artichoke hearts approximately 3 minutes on each side. Cook them in batches, if necessary; do not crowd the pan. Drain cooked artichoke hearts on paper towels, and serve immediately.

ENDIVE AND ARUGULA SALAD
8 SERVINGS

>2 large bunches arugula (rughetta)
>1 bunch curly endive
>Basic Salad Dressing (see recipe opposite)

1. Wash the arugula thoroughly, removing all dirt and sand. Cut off the ends. Dry.

2. Wash the endive, dry it, and tear it into pieces.

3. Toss the greens in a bowl with the Basic Salad Dressing.

BASIC SALAD DRESSING
YIELD: 1 CUP

> 1/2 cup olive oil
> 1 tablespoon red wine vinegar
> 1/2 teaspoon light soy sauce
> 1 teaspoon dry mustard
> 1 clove garlic, crushed
> 1/4 teaspoon dried oregano

Put all the ingredients in a blender container, and mix thoroughly.

SICILIAN CASSATA
8 SERVINGS

> 1 pound ricotta cheese
> 2 tablespoons heavy cream
> 1/4 cup sugar
> 3 tablespoons Candied Orange Peel (see recipe, page 48)
> 2 ounces semi-sweet chocolate chips
> 1/4 cup pine nuts (pignoli), chopped
> 1 loaf Orange Pound Cake (see recipe below)
> 3 tablespoons orange-flavored liqueur, such as Grand Marnier

FROSTING

> 12 ounces semisweet chocolate
> 3/4 cup espresso coffee
> 1/2 pound unsalted butter, cut into small pieces

1. Put the ricotta into a large mixing bowl and beat until smooth. Add the cream and sugar, beating until smooth.

2. With a rubber spatula, fold in the fruit, chocolate, and nuts.

3. With a sharp serrated knife, slice the pound cake horizontally into ¾-inch-thick slabs.

4. With a pastry brush spread the liqueur evenly on the slabs.

5. Put the bottom slab of cake on a plate, and spread it generously with the ricotta mixture. Carefully place another slab of cake on top of it, keeping the sides and ends even, and spread it with more of the ricotta mixture. Repeat until all the cake slabs are assembled and the ricotta mixture is used up. Finish with a plain slab of cake.

6. Gently press the loaf to make it as compact as possible but without letting the filling ooze. Wrap it in plastic wrap, and chill for a minimum of 12 hours.

7. To make the frosting, melt the chocolate in the coffee in a small, heavy saucepan over low heat, stirring constantly.

8. Take the pan from the heat and beat in the butter, 1 piece at a time, until all the butter is incorporated and the mixture is smoothly blended.

9. Chill the frosting until it thickens to spreading consistency, about 30 minutes.

10. With a metal spatula, spread the frosting over the sides and top of the loaf, in a swirling motion.

11. Cover the loaf loosely with plastic wrap and chill for a minimum of 24 hours before serving.

ORANGE POUND CAKE
YIELD: 1 LOAF

> ½ pound butter
> 1⅔ cups sugar
> 5 eggs
> 2 tablespoons orange juice
> 2 cups cake flour

Preheat oven to 300° F.

1. Grease and flour a 9-inch loaf pan.

2. Cream the butter with an electric beater. Add the sugar; then add the eggs one at a time. Finally, add the orange juice.

3. Fold in the flour with a spatula.

4. Pour the batter into the loaf pan, and bake for 1½ hours.

Note: The cake improves if it is stored for a day.

Christmas Eve

MUSSELS IN WHITE WINE SAUCE
6 TO 8 SERVINGS

6 pounds fresh mussels
3 tablespoons olive oil
½ cup minced onion or shallots
2 cloves garlic, minced
1 bay leaf
8 parsley sprigs
Freshly ground black pepper, few twists of the mill
½ teaspoon dried thyme
1½ cups dry white wine
½ cup chopped parsley

1. Scrub the mussels with a rough brush under running water. Scrape off the beards with a small knife. Set the mussels in a basin of fresh water to cover for 1 hour to rid them of any sand.

2. Lift the mussels from the water, place them in a colander, and rinse them again.

3. Pour the olive oil into a large pot. Over moderate heat sauté the onion and garlic until the onion is translucent, stirring constantly. Add the mussels, bay leaf, parsley sprigs, pepper, thyme, and wine. Cover and steam over high heat until the shells open, about 5 minutes. Discard any unopened mussels.

4. Lift the mussels from the pot with a skimmer, and place them in a large bowl. Let the liquid in the pot settle so that any sand will collect on the bottom. Ladle the liquid over the mussels, and sprinkle them with the chopped parsley.

5. Serve in soup bowls, accompanied by crusty bread.

CHICORY AND ARUGULA SALAD WITH ANCHOVY DRESSING
8 SERVINGS

> *1 bunch chicory*
> *1 bunch arugula* (rughetta)
> *1 clove garlic*
> *2 anchovy fillets, chopped, or 2 tablespoons anchovy*
> *paste*
> *2 tablespoons red wine vinegar*
> *6 tablespoons olive oil*
> *Salt and freshly ground black pepper, to taste*

1. Wash and dry the greens, and tear them into pieces. Place them in a salad bowl.

2. Put the remaining ingredients in a blender, and blend well. Pour the mixture over the greens, and toss.

SARDINE SPREAD
8 SERVINGS

2 tins boned, skinless sardines in oil
4 tablespoons unsalted butter
1 tablespoon lemon juice
2 tablespoon Dijon mustard
1 tablespoon chopped parsley
salt and pepper to taste
1 tablespoon capers, drained
celery, cut in short lengths
Crostini (see recipe below)

1. Put contents of sardine tins in blender. Add butter, lemon juice, mustard, and parsley and blend until creamy. Add salt and pepper if desired.

2. Spread on celery or crostini and top with capers.

CROSTINI
YIELD: 2 TO 4 DOZEN PIECES

6 slices white bread
1 to 2 tablespoons olive oil
1 small clove garlic, crushed
Salt, to taste

1. Cut each slice of bread into 4 lengths or 8 squares.

2. Heat the oil in a large skillet; add the garlic and lightly brown, then discard it. Add the bread and toss until it is golden brown. Sprinkle it with salt, if desired.

3. Drain *crostini* on paper towels.

Note: Crostini can be served with a variety of toppings, or used in soups.

SPAGHETTINI WITH RED CALAMARI SAUCE
4 TO 6 SERVINGS

¼ cup olive oil
1 clove garlic
1 medium onion, sliced
1 medium carrot, grated
1 stalk celery, chopped
One 28-ounce can peeled Italian plum tomatoes
3 fresh basil leaves or ½ teaspoon dried basil
Salt, to taste
¼ teaspoon crushed red pepper
1 tablespoon minced parsley
1 pound spaghettini
2 pounds cleaned squid (calamari), main body cut
*   into rings, the rest in pieces*

1. Heat the olive oil in a large saucepan. When it is sizzling, cook the garlic until golden, pressing it down into the oil with the back of a wooden spoon. Discard the garlic.

2. Add the onion, carrot, and celery; reduce the heat to low and cook until the vegetables are soft.

3. Add the tomatoes, breaking them up into small pieces with the back of a wooden spoon.

4. Add the basil and cook slowly, about 1 hour.

5. Season with salt, crushed red pepper, and the parsley.

6. Begin cooking the pasta in boiling, salted water. At the same time, add the squid to the tomato mixture, and cook 8 to 10 minutes.

7. When the pasta is tender but still somewhat firm, or al dente, drain it and toss with the calamari sauce.

SPAGHETTINI WITH WHITE CLAM SAUCE
4 TO 6 SERVINGS

1 pound spaghettini
½ cup olive oil
2 cloves garlic, halved
1 pound minced clams
¼ cup dry white wine
1 cup bottled clam juice
¼ teaspoon salt
¼ teaspoon freshly ground black pepper
¼ cup finely chopped parsley

1. In a large pot filled with salted water, begin cooking the spaghettini according to package directions.

2. Put the olive oil in a large skillet over moderate heat. When it is sizzling, cook the garlic quickly, stirring; do not let it brown. Flatten the garlic pieces with the back of a wooden spoon, pressing them into the oil. Discard the garlic.

3. Add the clams, wine, clam juice, salt, and pepper. Cook, uncovered, until the wine evaporates and the liquid is somewhat reduced, less than 10 minutes. Stir in the parsley, mixing well.

4. Drain the pasta, and toss it in a warmed serving bowl with half the clam sauce. Spoon the remaining sauce over individual portions.

ROASTED RED PEPPERS
6 SERVINGS

6 large red sweet peppers
2 tablespoons thinly sliced garlic
⅓ to ½ cup olive oil

Preheat the oven to 350° F.

63

1. Put the peppers in a roasting pan, and roast them, turning often, until the skin begins to blacken, about 15 minutes.

2. Remove the peppers from the oven, put them in a brown bag, and let them stand for 15 minutes.

3. One by one peel, core, and seed the peppers. Cut them into strips.

4. Lay the peppers on a platter, cover them with the garlic, and pour on the olive oil. Cover the platter, and refrigerate overnight.

5. Serve at room temperature.

BROCCOLI WITH OIL AND LEMON
4 SERVINGS

> *1 pound broccoli*
> *¼ cup olive oil*
> *2 cloves garlic, halved lengthwise and stuck with*
> *   toothpicks*
> *2 tablespoons fresh lemon juice*
> *Salt and freshly ground black pepper, to taste*

1. Wash the broccoli, and break it into florets. In a small amount of water, steam the broccoli over moderate heat until it is cooked but still firm, about 6 to 8 minutes.

2. Pour the olive oil into a skillet over moderate heat. When it is hot, brown the garlic halves, remove from heat. Add the lemon juice, and stir well. Season with salt and pepper, and stir well.

3. Put the broccoli in a bowl, and pour the olive oil mixture over it. Cover and chill for several hours.

4. Before serving, discard the garlic.

BROILED SHRIMP
6 SERVINGS

2 pounds jumbo shrimp
8 tablespoons unsalted butter
½ cup olive oil
1 tablespoon fresh lemon juice
2 tablespoons minced garlic
5 tablespoons minced parsley
Lemon wedges, for garnish

Preheat the broiler.

1. Wash and shell the shrimp, leaving the tails on; devein them.

2. Put the butter in a flat baking dish, and heat under the broiler until the butter is melted. Stir in the olive oil, lemon juice, and garlic. Add the shrimp, turning to coat it with the oil mixture.

3. Broil 3 inches from the flame or element for 5 to 10 minutes, until lightly browned and firm to the touch.

4. Transfer the shrimp to a heated platter, and pour on the sauce. Sprinkle with the parsley and serve immediately, with lemon wedges.

POACHED WHITING
6 to 8 SERVINGS

2 pounds (3 to 4) whiting, or hake
½ teaspoon salt
1 small onion, sliced
½ lemon, sliced
6 whole black peppercorns
¼ teaspoon whole cloves or whole allspice
2 tablespoons olive oil
Juice of ½ lemon
2 tablespoons chopped parsley

65

1. Put the fish in a skillet, and cover it with cold water. Add the salt, onion, lemon, peppercorns (crushed just enough to open), and cloves or allspice.

2. Slowly bring to a boil, and simmer about 10 minutes.

3. Mix together the olive oil, lemon juice, and parsley.

4. Carefully transfer the fish to a platter, pour on the oil mixture, and serve.

CAULIFLOWER SALAD
4 TO 6 SERVINGS

> *3 tablespoons chopped scallions*
> *2 cloves garlic, chopped*
> *1 teaspoon dry mustard*
> *4 anchovy fillets, drained and chopped*
> *¼ cup fresh lemon juice*
> *1 tablespoon red wine vinegar*
> *⅓ cup olive oil*
> *2 tablespoons capers, drained*
> *1 head cauliflower, washed, trimmed, and cut into*
>   *florets*
> *Salt and freshly ground black pepper, to taste*

1. Combine the scallions, garlic, mustard, anchovies, lemon juice, vinegar, and olive oil in the container of a blender or food processor. Process just until finely chopped; do not make a smooth purée.

2. Stir in the capers.

3. In a small amount of water over moderate heat, steam the cauliflower until tender but still crisp, about 8 minutes.

4. Season the cauliflower with salt and pepper, and transfer it to a serving dish. Pour on the dressing. Let stand for 1 hour to let the flavors blend and develop. Serve at room temperature.

SLICED BLOOD ORANGES
8 SERVINGS

8 blood oranges
Freshly grated rind of 1 lemon
½ cup fine granulated sugar
Juice of 2 blood oranges
Juice of 1 lemon

1. Peel the oranges, removing all white membranes. Slice the oranges and put them into a shallow serving dish.

2. Add the grated lemon rind, sugar, orange juice, and lemon juice. Turn the orange slices over a few times to coat.

3. Cover and refrigerate. Serve chilled.

Christmas Day

CARDAMOM WREATH
YIELD: 2 WREATHS

2 envelopes active dry yeast
½ cup warm water
3½ cups all-purpose flour
½ cup milk
10 tablespoons unsalted butter
⅓ cup sugar
1 teaspoon salt
1½ teaspoons ground cardamom
3 eggs
1 cup raisins
1 cup candied citron
1 cup slivered almonds

1. Dissolve the yeast in the warm water.

67

2. Sift 2 cups of the flour into a large bowl.

3. Put the milk, 8 tablespoons of the butter, the sugar, salt, and cardamom in a small saucepan, and heat over medium-low flame until the mixture is warm and the butter melted.

4. Stir the milk mixture and the yeast into the flour. Beat 2 minutes with an electric mixer at medium speed. Add the eggs; beat well. Add 1 more cup of the flour, and beat 3 minutes. If necessary, add more flour to make a stiff dough. Stir in the raisins, citron, and ½ cup of the almonds.

5. Turn the dough onto a floured work surface, and knead 8 to 10 minutes.

6. Put the dough in a greased bowl, turning to coat it. Cover and let rise in a warm place 1½ hours, or until doubled in bulk.

7. Punch the dough down, and let it rest 10 minutes.

8. Divide the dough in half, then divide each half into 3 equal pieces. Roll the 6 pieces into 15-inch-long strips. Take 3 strips and weave them into a braid; curve the braid into a wreath, and place it on a greased baking sheet. Repeat with the remaining 3 strips.

9. Let the braids rise, lightly covered, in a warm, draft-free place for 45 minutes or until doubled in bulk.

10. Preheat the oven to 350° F. Sprinkle the wreaths with the remaining almonds, and bake 35 to 40 minutes.

Note: To freeze, wrap each wreath in aluminum foil, then put it in a plastic bag. Thaw 1 hour at room temperature.

TORTELLINI IN BROTH
YIELD: 180 TORTELLINI
10 TO 12 SERVINGS

> *¼ pound skinless turkey or chicken breast*
> *1 tablespoon unsalted butter*

68

¼ pound lean loin of pork, in one piece
¼ pound lean veal, in one piece
¼ pound sliced prosciutto
¼ pound mortadella (available in Italian groceries)
8 eggs
1¼ cup freshly grated Parmesan cheese
½ teaspoon salt
¼ teaspoon freshly ground black pepper
¼ teaspoon freshly grated nutmeg
6 cups all-purpose flour
1½ tablespoons olive oil
1½ tablespoons tepid water
3 quarts chicken broth

1. Remove the tendons from the turkey or chicken breast.

2. Put the butter in a medium skillet, over moderate heat. When the butter is sizzling, add the turkey or chicken breast, pork, and veal. Cook the turkey or chicken breast on both sides until it turns white, then remove it; continue to cook the pork and veal until they are browned. (The pork should be thoroughly cooked.)

3. Grind the turkey or chicken breast, pork, veal, prosciutto, and mortadella in a meat grinder until the texture is very fine.

4. Put the mixture in a large bowl. Add 2 eggs, ¼ cup of the Parmesan cheese, the salt, pepper, and nutmeg. Mix well into a thick paste. Refrigerate, covered, until ready to use.

5. Mix the flour, the remaining eggs, olive oil, and water. Knead into a smooth dough.

6. On a floured work surface, roll the dough out very thin. Cut it into small circles 1½ to 2 inches in diameter. Using the back of a small spoon, place a tiny mound of filling in the center of each circle. (The trick to making tortellini is to put as much filling as possible into dough circles that are as small as one can manipulate, so that you taste more stuffing than wrapper.)

69

7. Double the dough over the filling, making half-circles, and pinch the edges together. Take the 2 "points" of the dough, fold them around your index finger, and press them together firmly. The resulting ringlets must not ooze stuffing.

8. Bring the chicken broth to a boil in a large kettle. Add the tortellini; when the broth boils again, lower the heat and simmer for at least 15 minutes. The tortellini must be well cooked, or the folds will be tough.

9. Serve with the remaining Parmesan cheese, and freshly ground pepper.

ROAST SUCKLING PIG
10 TO 12 SERVINGS

1 10- to 12-pound suckling pig, cleaned and oven-
     ready
Salt and freshly ground black pepper, to taste
½ tablespoon dried sage or thyme
1 whole apple or orange
Olive oil or melted unsalted butter, for basting

STUFFING

4 cups chopped onions
½ cup chopped celery
12 tablespoons unsalted butter
6 cups dry breadcrumbs
2 eggs, beaten
Salt and freshly ground black pepper, to taste
½ cup chopped parsley
1 to 2 tart apples, peeled and chopped
2 cups chicken stock or white wine

GARNISH

   1 lady apple for mouth
   Grapes for platter

Preheat the oven to 450° F.

1. Rub the inside of the pig with salt, pepper, and sage or thyme.

2. To make the stuffing, sauté the onions and celery in the butter over moderate heat until the onions are soft and translucent but not brown. Add the breadcrumbs, eggs, salt and pepper, parsley, chopped apples, and chicken stock or wine, and mix thoroughly but lightly. Taste for seasoning.

3. Fill the pig's cavity with the stuffing. Close with skewers, and lace with string. Place the apple or orange in the pig's mouth.

4. Place the pig on a rack in a large roasting pan. Tuck the hind legs under the rump, and the front legs forward. Rub the pig with oil or butter. Baste every 30 minutes with pan juices.

5. Roast 30 minutes, then reduce the oven temperature to 350° F. Roast about 20 minutes to the pound, or approximately 3½ to 4 hours. (A meat thermometer will register 185° F when the pig is done.)

6. Remove the pig to a heated platter. Remove the skewers, string lacings, and stuffer in mouth. Put the lady apple in the mouth, and the grapes around the pig on the platter.

7. Skim the fat from the pan drippings, and serve the juices with the roast pig. The Italian fruit chutney, *Mostarda di Cremona*, is also well suited as an accompaniment.

8. To carve, first remove the forelegs and hind legs. Cut down the center of the back, and remove the rib chops.

POTATOES ROASTED WITH ROSEMARY

6 SERVINGS

> 20 to 24 (4 pounds) new potatoes
> ½ cup olive oil
> 2 tablespoons chopped fresh rosemary
> Salt and freshly ground black pepper, to taste

Preheat the oven to 350° F.

1. Scrub the potatoes and slice them thinly (do not peel). Put them in a 9 × 13-inch baking pan.

2. Coat the slices with the olive oil, and sprinkle with the rosemary, salt, and pepper. Bake 45 to 60 minutes, until potatoes are crisp and lightly browned.

PURÉED BEANS

6 SERVINGS

> 2 cups dried white kidney beans (or two 17-ounce
>   cans cannellini)
> ¼ cup olive oil
> ¼ cup unsalted butter
> 3 tablespoons chopped fresh sage, or 1 teaspoon
>   ground sage
> 1 teaspoon chopped parsley
> ¼ teaspoon salt
> Freshly ground black pepper (a few twists of the mill)

1. If dried beans are used, soak them overnight in water to cover. If canned beans are used, drain them.

2. Drain the soaked beans, and place them in a pan with water to cover. Bring to a boil, and simmer them, partially covered, for 45 minutes. Do not let the beans open.

3. Heat the olive oil and butter in a skillet over moderate heat. Add

the beans, sage, parsley, salt, and pepper and cook for 10 minutes.

4. Put the mixture through a food mill to purée.

5. Serve at room temperature with Roast Suckling Pig, or any roast meat.

FENNEL AND ENDIVE SALAD
8 SERVINGS

> *2 large heads fennel* (finocchio)
> *1 bunch curly endive*
> *Basic Salad Dressing (see recipe, page 57)*

1. Cut off the feathery fennel leaves, most of the stalks, and any bruised parts of the heads. Wash them, then cut them horizontally into very thin slices.

2. Wash and dry the endive, and tear it into pieces.

3. Put the fennel and endive in a salad bowl, pour on the dressing, and toss. Serve immediately.

Christmas Week—Saint Stephen's Day

ROAST CHESTNUTS
8 TO 10 SERVINGS

> *2 pounds fresh chestnuts*

Preheat the oven to 425° F.

1. Cut 2 crisscross slits on the flat side of each chestnut.

2. Place the chestnuts in a shallow baking pan, slit side up. Roast them 25 to 30 minutes.

3. Serve warm.

MULLED WINE
8 TO 10 SERVINGS

1 bottle dry red wine
3 whole cloves
¼ teaspoon ground cardamom
2 two-inch cinnamon sticks
½ teaspoon freshly grated nutmeg
2 cups water
2 tablespoons sugar
Pared rind of an orange

Pour the wine into a large nonaluminum saucepan, and add the remaining ingredients. Bring to a boil and heat 5 minutes. Serve hot.

CHESTNUT DESSERT (*Monte Bianco*)
6 TO 8 SERVINGS

1½ pounds fresh chestnuts
3 cups milk
6 ounces semisweet chocolate
1 cup powdered sugar
1 cup heavy cream
¼ cup Cognac

1. Cut a crisscross on the flat side of each chestnut. Put the chestnuts in a saucepan, cover them with water, and bring to a boil. Simmer 15 minutes.

2. Drain and peel them, and remove the inner skin.

3. Return the chestnuts to the saucepan, add the milk, and cook over medium heat for 45 minutes.

4. Meanwhile, melt the chocolate in the top of a double boiler, over simmering water.

5. Drain the chestnuts, then put them through a food mill and into a bowl. Mix with the sugar and chocolate, and pass the mixture through the food mill again.

74

6. Put the mixture into serving dishes, mounding it into cone shapes. Chill 1 hour.

7. Whip the cream, and fold in the Cognac. Cover the mounds with whipped cream.

Christmas Week—Anytime

MIXED BOILED MEATS AND VEGETABLES
6 SERVINGS

> *1½ pounds top round or brisket of beef*
> *1 small bunch parsley*
> *Shells of 2 or 3 eggs*
> *1 large tomato, cut in half, or 5 plum tomatoes*
> *6 to 8 stalks celery, scraped and washed*
> *1 medium onion, stuck with 4 cloves*
> *Salt, to taste*
> *5 whole black peppercorns*
> *One 2- to 3-pound soup chicken*
> *2 pounds veal rump roast*
> *6 to 8 small white onions, peeled*
> *10 to 12 small potatoes, washed and peeled*
> *4 carrots, scraped, washed, and cut in half*
> *½ pound green beans, washed and trimmed*
> *Quince Conserve (see recipe below)*
> *Green Sauce (see recipe below)*

1. Bring 6 quarts of water to a boil in a large pot. Add the beef, parsley, egg shells, tomato, 1 stalk of celery, the onion with cloves, and salt. Crush each peppercorn just enough to open it, and add to the water. Reduce the heat to low and simmer, uncovered, for 30 minutes.

75

2. Add the chicken and veal to the pot; cook about 20 minutes, or until tender.

3. When the beef, chicken, and veal are cooked, remove them and discard the remaining solids. Strain the broth. Return the broth to the pot, then add the white onions and potatoes. Bring to a boil, then cook 20 minutes over moderate heat.

4. Add the carrots. After 5 minutes, add the green beans and the rest of the celery. Cook 10 minutes. Test the vegetables for doneness; do not overcook. When the vegetables are tender but still firm, remove them and set them aside.

5. Preheat the oven to 350° F. Cut the veal and beef into slices. Cut the chicken into serving pieces.

6. In a baking dish that can also be used as a serving dish, arrange 6 slices of beef, 12 slices of veal, and 6 pieces of chicken. Cover the meats with some of the strained broth. Place on the middle rack of the oven for 5 minutes.

7. Arrange the vegetables in a separate baking dish, and cover them with 1 cup of the broth. Put in the oven for 5 minutes.

8. Before serving, drain all but ½ cup of broth from the meats and all but ⅓ cup from the vegetables.

9. Serve the meat with Quince Conserve or Green Sauce. Serve the vegetables in a separate dish.

Quince Conserve (*Cotognata*)
YIELD: 2½ to 3 PINTS

> *2 pounds quinces, peeled and cored*
> *2 cups cider vinegar*
> *1 cup water*
> *2½ cups sugar*
> *2 cinnamon sticks*

1 tablespoon whole cloves
¼ cup sliced, peeled fresh ginger

1. Cut the quinces into slices, and put them in a saucepan. Cover them with water, bring to a boil, and cook until they are almost tender. Drain.

2. Boil the vinegar, water, sugar, cinnamon sticks, cloves, and ginger for 5 minutes.

3. Add the quinces and cook over low heat just until the quince slices are clear and tender. Cool. Serve with boiled meats.

GREEN SAUCE
YIELD: 1½ CUPS

1 cup Pesto Sauce (see recipe below)
4 tablespoons olive oil
2 tablespoons red wine vinegar
6 chopped anchovies
1 teaspoon minced capers

Put all the ingredients in a blender container and mix well. Serve with boiled meats.

PESTO SAUCE

2 cups pack fresh young basil leaves
½ cup olive oil
½ cup grated Parmesan cheese
1 clove garlic
½ cup pine nuts (pignoli)
pinch of salt
3 tablespoon butter, melted

Use young basil leaves, since large older leaves develop too strong a taste.

1. Toast pignoli in 350° oven for 5 minutes.

2. Slice garlic into blender, add basil, pignoli, salt, and oil and blend together.

3. Transfer to bowl and add cheese and melted butter.

Before tossing pesto with pasta, dilute the pesto with a tablespoon or two of the water in which the pasta has cooked.

Note, to freeze pesto, omit garlic and cheese and add them at time of using the sauce.

NORMA'S POTATO TORTA
6 TO 8 SERVINGS

>*1 pound (3 medium) potatoes*
>*2 tablespoons unsalted butter*
>*2 tablespoons milk*
>*½ cup shredded mozzarella cheese*
>*3 ounces Bel Paese cheese, cut in pieces*
>*½ cup grated Parmesan cheese*
>*1 cup ricotta cheese*
>*2 eggs, lightly beaten*
>*½ teaspoon salt*
>*Freshly ground black pepper, to taste*
>*Freshly grated nutmeg, to taste*
>*1 tablespoon chopped green bell pepper*
>*½ cup chopped scallion, including green part*

1. Peel the potatoes and boil them in lightly salted water until tender.

2. Preheat the oven to 350° F. Grease a 1½-quart baking dish.

3. Mash the potatoes with the butter and milk. Add the remaining ingredients, and mix well.

4. Put the mixture into the prepared baking dish.

5. Bake 1 hour, or until puffed and lightly browned.

Two

JANUARY

New Year's Eve

In antiquity, Janus, the two-faced deity of classical Rome, was the god of light who opened the sky at daybreak and closed it at sunset. He presided over all beginnings and endings, all entrances and exits. Doors and openings fell under his protection, and he was said to keep the gate of heaven. Thus, he is represented with one face forward and one backward and, by his power to see past and future, gives his name to the first month after the winter solstice,

---

79

when one makes up the balance sheet of the past year and resolves to get rid of the dross and look forward to an improved future.

Even today Romans take this backward-forward view of the New Year very literally, welcoming the chance to get rid of past mistakes. At some private parties, upon the stroke of midnight on New Year's Eve, the host may take a broom and figuratively sweep out the old year, throwing open windows to let the new one come clamoring in with the sounds of thousands of car horns, whistles, and bells. From windows and balconies all over town, the junk of the past year is tossed into the streets below: old pots and pans, broken dishes, ugly lamps, even furniture. It's not a time for strolling! Still, the last time I was in Rome on a New Year's Eve, in 1987, there seemed much less throwing away of old things. Times are harder, I was told; people are holding onto their possessions.

New Year's Eve is also a time for replenishing one's wealth by eating lentils. Some have said that lentils are eaten because their shape vaguely resembles coins, and the more lentils you eat, the more money will accrue to you, which is somewhat ironic since lentils (and beans in general) are a poor people's staple. Others give an earthier interpretation, focusing on the cathartic value of the lentils, which better fits the ribald Italian temperament and is consistent with Italian traditions of naming and eating certain foods according to the beneficial results they produce. In Italy abundance, luck, and riches have always been associated with the natural functions, and there is no primness or embarrassment about the association.

One year, when my cousin Donna Cardamone Jackson was a Fulbright student of Renaissance music in Italy, we took a trip to the temples of Paestum and ended up in Pompeii on New Year's Eve. Somehow it was appropriate; not only was the place free from the usual tourist hordes and so was immediately visible and accessible in all its secrets, but even more telling, it was imbued with the *feeling* of ancient divinity. What a bounty of deities of all kinds that trip revealed to me in statuary and wall paintings! My strong impression was of the omnipresence of Silenus, the satyr; of fauns, nymphs, bacchantes, sileni, Pan, Bacchus, Priapus, and all those symbols of revelry and sensuality depicted over and over again as divine forces in life. They were important in the classical view and are the joyous reverse of the penitential and punitive aspect of religion.

New Year's Eve is known in Italy as San Silvestro, for it falls on the feast day of Saint Sylvester, who was pope from A.D. 324 to 335, during the reign of Constantine, who effected the turning point in Christianity by giving it legality. San Silvestro is a very familiar name to those of us who have lived in Rome, for it marks the central downtown square, where all the bus lines converge and the main post office is located. There, too, is the church of San Silvestro in Capite, erected in 752 on the remains of an ancient temple to the sun. The feast of San Silvestro is, as so many holidays are, a blend of old rites and Christian ones, which did not so much supplant as reinterpret pagan rituals in order to fit them into Church liturgy.

The word *pagan* derives from *paganus*, "a country dweller," and as Phyllis Williams has pointed out in *South Italian Folkways in Europe and America*, modified versions of ancient beliefs are more likely to be preserved among country folk, while Christianity, a social innovation, found more acceptance in towns and cities. Indeed, Carlo Levi confirms in his book of exile among the southern Italian peasants, *Christ Stopped at Eboli*, what Williams maintains: that peasant conversion was gradual and only superficial; pre-Christian beliefs still persist and can be seen in the veneration of statues and relics; in the attribution of specific powers to individual saints, much like those ascribed to the old pantheon of gods and goddesses; and the transformation of old pagan festivals into semi-religious observances. Many are the folk saints who never appear in the writings of the Church fathers and are substitutes for the old classical spirit world. The guardian angel of each Italian child is a transformation of the Roman tutelary spirit.

The celebrating and noisemaking of New Year's Eve is a relic of the ancient Roman revels, when merrymaking all through the night was thought to drive away demons and salute the New Year. So, accompanying the lentils is the Saint Sylvester punch bowl for laughter and merriment. This is the night our silver punch bowl is set out on the old credenza, flanked by brass candle holders that have been passed down through generations of Barolinis. The long refectory table from Calabria holds the makings of the buffet supper. This is a celebration, I've always thought, really made for home and hearth, for fun among friends.

The last time I was in Italy for the Christmas holidays I spent Christmas with my daughter Susanna's family in Urbino. For New Year's Eve, however, I was in Rome with my friends Daniela and Beppe Sacco, and we spent San Silvestro at their friends' country place in Palestrina, a town that, approached at night from the *auto-strada*, displays a splendidly lighted outline of its triangular construction on the old Roman ruins of a temple to the goddess Fortuna. Anciently called Praeneste, the town was a great center for predicting the future, a fortune-telling mecca. In a charming country house redone in the former stables of an estate, we dined on lentils with sausage and a roast baby lamb with all the trimmings—(*i contorni*). At midnight, after toasting, our host led us outside into the cold, crisp starry night and set off fireworks and sparklers as his children applauded and shouted, and dogs barked.

Daniela, a feminist and activist with a busy life, had earlier told me that she had cut down on time-consuming specialties for the holidays: *"Non vale la pena,"* "It isn't worth the pain," she explained. (And yet it was she who had contributed the traditional lentil dish and the *sbrisciolona*, a shortbread, for the evening's feast.) In Urbino Susi's smart sister-in-law, Maria, had said much the same about the old traditions. "Everyone works now," she explained when I had apprehensively asked if she were preparing eel. "No one has time."

Still, she and her mother-in-law, Cleofe, had produced the traditional Christmas Eve meal and, for Christmas, hundreds of handmade meat-filled *cappelletti* for the broth course. In that region they
have a saying: "Long noodles and short bills." When noodles are
made too short, they reflect the maker's lack of skill; only bills to
be paid are better short than long. In other words, a skillful hand
at pasta is still esteemed; some things will always be worth the pain.
I think that both women were reflecting the idea that traditions and
feasts are too precious to give up, so they are made more manage-
able with less food and less fuss than in earlier times. As Tancredi
astutely said to the Prince in *The Leopard*, "If you want things to
stay the same, they have to change."

New Year's Day

There is a nice custom in Italy of giving friends New Year's gifts of
mistletoe and calendars. These gifts are called *strenne*, a word that
derives from the goddess Strenia, of Sabine origin. Strenia presided
over the gift-giving that ushered in the new year; it was from her
grove that sacred twigs were carried in procession along the Via
Sacra on the first day of Janus's month, January. In ancient times
sprigs of mistletoe were hung over doorways to ward off illness.
Now they either embellish one's entrance or hang inside for luck
in everything, not only love.

When we lived in Rome, I remember that New Year's Day was
always heralded by Mr. O. K.'s dive into the Tiber. Mr. O.K. was a
Belgian expatriate—a tall, bald, oldish man who, decked in a swirling cape, used to lead reporters and onlookers to the Cavour Bridge,
from which, with a great deal of fanfare, he'd plunge into the chill,
yellowy swirling waters and swim to the river bank. It was a ritual
that was always reported in the papers—the beginning of a New
Year certified by Mr. O. K. Now well into his eighties, Mr. O. K. has

retired from the plunge, and it's said that his place has been taken by two young *romani*, Mr. O. and Mr. K.

The pagan revels of the New Year were said to be so licentious and excessive that the early Christians deliberately omitted the holiday from Christmastide festivities and observed January 1 as a strict fast day. It wasn't until the sixth century that the Church decided to recognize the day and incorporate it into the season by sanctifying it as the Feast of the Circumcision, which marked the initiation of Jesus into Judaism and, by analogy, was meant to focus attention on the initiation of persons into Christianity. Since 1970, when a major calendar revision took place, the Church has recognized the day as the Solemnity of Mary, Mother of God.

The New Year's Day dinner presented here is not as elaborate as some, but it does include the traditional Sicilian lasagne made with ricotta cheese, which the unsurpassed scholar and author, Salvatore Salomone-Marino, a nineteenth-century collector of Sicilian traditions, recorded chidingly as *lasagne cacate*, or "shitty noodles," making it known that their being "uniformly called throughout the Island by a nasty name . . . does not detract from their being relished and eaten eagerly and avidly, even in cities, and in spite of their name. . . ." In fact, as Salomone-Marino explains, *lasagne cacate* is beneficial, and not just for a day, according to the saying:

> Shitty noodles and wine by the jug
> Make good blood the year round.

The proverb reflects the popular feeling and conforms to the ancient usage of the early Romans who held that the first day of the year is a festive and sacred day, a day that determines what is to follow in the remaining 364. Salomone-Marino continues, "From this inveterate and universal belief stems the constant care to begin it rightly and luckily, to avoid all nasty encounters, all displeasures, in short, everything that can bring regret—therefore the care to studiously practice everything pleasant, to bring joy and comfort to the soul, health and prosperity to the body." Consequently, one does everything to assure a happy day, with abundant food and wine and jokes. There is no way to put the significance of the *lasagne cacate* delicately; it is, after all, a fact of life that good eating should be followed by good elimination as a sign of good health. The right food provides a good start on the year, and so the auspicious name of the lasagne.

When I first heard of Salomone-Marino's *lasagne cacate*, I was, in fact, reminded of one of Antonio's stories of the Veneto, in which an important bowel movement is celebrated. "It is told," he wrote, "that on the occasion of a certain sovereign's passage through the Veneto during the time of the Austrian dominion over that part of Italy, the officials of Vicenza went to pay their respects to their ruler during his stopover in their city. And on this particular occasion, they were made to wait for their audience for an unaccountably great length of time. There was a royal emergency, it seems, due to some rather intemperate eating of game the night before at the villa of Stra, near Padua, from whence the entourage was proceeding toward Verona.

"The sovereign, plagued with a condition that threatened to ruin the pleasure of his trip, was finally relieved in Vicenza. Entering the great hall where the dignitaries had awaited their audience for hours, and feeling himself well and happy once more, the sovereign is reputed to have said, 'Sirs, noble or not, you have not waited in vain. . . . As many of you as are here gathered, as many of you as have awaited our presence patiently and faithfully, so many of you shall from this moment be counts of our royal household by our proclamation!'

"And so the attendants were exalted, the august guest enabled to continue on his way, and a dozen new counts given to the people of the Veneto, who immediately labeled them the 'counts of the Imperial B.M. . . .' "

The converse to ensuring good luck for the whole year by beginning January 1 happily is the idea that no chore or small task which is under way in the last days of December should be left incomplete when midnight sounds on New Year's Eve. For if that should happen, the task will remain incomplete the whole year, no matter how hard one tries to complete it.

Epiphany

In England Twelfth Night, the eve of Epiphany, was celebrated with a great feast to mark the end of the holiday season. In earlier times in the Italian countryside, great bonfires were kindled, and amid the dancing around them, predictions for good or bad weather were made for the coming year according to the direction in which the smoke blew. In Rome it is the last chance to splurge at Piazza Navona before the stalls and candy makers and hawkers close up and leave for another year. The great sense of merrymaking that used to reign in Piazza Navona on Twelfth Night, or Epiphany Eve, has found expression in Respighi's musical composition titled "Feste Romane." The Befana (Epiphany) segment is a great sounding and mixing of instruments to mark the clamor and joyousness of that holiday, and it echoes in its rhythms the crowds of Piazza Navona, the strains of a barrel organ, the calls of the barkers, and the rustic motifs congruous to the crowds of yesteryear.

Closure of the holiday season is supposed to take place on January 6, the day of the Befana. According to distant sources, the little old woman known as la Befana was sweeping her house when the Three Kings came by looking for the Christ Child to present their gifts to. When she was asked to accompany them, she said she was too busy with her sweeping. Later, when she finished, she set out to find the Child but lost her way and is still searching. Each year, it's said, she passes through Italy, leaving pretty gifts for children who are good and bits of charcoal for the naughty. Hispanics in the United States still exchange gifts on this Day of the Three Kings in memory of the Magi, who bore presents to Christ.

Epiphany, like so many other Christian feasts, was apparently established to compete with a pagan festival, this one to offer an alternative to the manifestation of the sun god. Thus, the early Christians instituted a feast to honor the manifestation of the true Savior.

My youngest daughter's birthday falls just a week from Epiphany. Niki is the artist of the family, enamored of colorful objects and pattern, so the Befana cake became hers to decorate as she pleases. The cake itself is baked with a lucky almond (as a substitute for the bean, which, at the Roman Saturnalia, was used to designate the master of the rites). Whoever gets the almond in his or her piece becomes the ruler of the feast. Niki cuts a piece of cake and calls out the name of whoever at the table gets it, thus creating suspense as to where the almond will end up. The cake is frosted and decorated with colored candies, chocolate bits, gold and silver dragées, gumdrops, or whatever comes to Niki's mind to make the cake resemble (somewhat) a jewel-encrusted crown in remembrance of the arrival of the Three Kings.

Although we don't celebrate it in any particular way, we also like to remember that January 20 is the feast day of Saint Sebastian, that handsome youth with whom Renaissance painters were so taken and who is so beautifully remembered in this passage of Thomas Mann's *Death in Venice*: "For to be poised against fatality, to meet adverse conditions gracefully, is more than simple endurance; it is an act of aggression, a positive triumph—and the figure of Sebastian is the most beautiful figure, if not of art as a whole, at least of the art of literature."

Sebastian was an officer of the Praetorian Guard under the emperor Diocletian, when Christians were severely persecuted. Learning that he was one of the detested sect, the emperor ordered him bound to a tree and shot through with arrows, as he is depicted in so many paintings. One of the arrows that pierced the martyr is said to be conserved in his namesake church on the Via Appia Antica. Sebastiano is a frequently occurring name in the Barolini family, and stories are told of a formidable Donna Sebastiana, who actually took charge of a ship during some terrible storm and brought it safely through the peril. Thereafter, the men in the family were named for her, and each generation of Barolinis has had a Sebastiano, though not, as yet, a Sebastiana.

The evening after Saint Sebastian's feast day is Saint Agnes Eve, the night on which young women go supperless to bed in order to dream of their intended love. John Keats recounts the legend in his long narrative poem, "The Eve of St. Agnes," which he wrote in a few days during the January of 1819:

> how, upon St. Agnes' Eve,
> Young virgins might have visions of delight,
> And soft adorings from their loves receive
> Upon the honey'd middle of the night.

Saint Agnes, virgin and martyr, is thought to be particularly indulgent to romantic young girls. The poem greatly stirred me as a young girl. And though I fasted and hoped to see my intended as I slept on that eve, I never did picture Antonio Barolini in my imagination or in my dreams. But now I sometimes think how strange it is that his death came on January 21, Saint Agnes Eve.

JANUARY RECIPES

New Year's Eve
Punch Bowl Wine
Bagna Cauda with Raw
  Vegetables
Lentils with Cotechino
Celeriac Salad
Cardamom Cake

New Year's Day
Holiday Lasagne with Ragu
  Sauce
Chicken Rosetta
Fried Cauliflower
Caramelized Oranges

Epiphany
Pasta Ring with Mushrooms
Chicken with Fennel
Wilted Spinach
Orange Sponge Cake

New Year's Eve

PUNCH BOWL WINE
24 SERVINGS

> *1 quart freshly brewed tea*
> *¼ cup rum, light or dark*
> *¼ cup Cognac*
> *Juice of 2 lemons*
> *2 bottles Lambrusco sparkling wine*
> *1 cup sugar syrup (optional)*

1. Cool the tea to room temperature.

2. Add the rum, Cognac, and lemon juice, and chill.

3. When you are ready to serve, pour the mixture into a punch bowl. Add ice, and stir in the Lambrusco.

4. If desired, sweeten with sugar syrup. (Make the syrup by boiling 1 cup of water with 2 cups of sugar for 5 minutes.)

BAGNA CAUDA
8 SERVINGS

> *1 cup olive oil*
> *6 anchovy filets*
> *4 cloves garlic*
> *freshly ground pepper*
> *grissini (Italian bread sticks)*
> *fresh raw vegetables in bite-size pieces: carrots, whole*
> *mushrooms, broccoli florets, fennel and celery,*
> *pepper strips, scallions, etc.*

1. Mash anchovies and their oil with the garlic. Put in a fondue pot and heat with the olive oil until anchovies have dissolved and blended into the sauce. Add several twists of a pepper mill.

2. Dip bread sticks and vegetables into the fondue pot.

LENTILS WITH COTECHINO
6 SERVINGS

> 1 cup dried lentils
> 1/4 pound salt pork, cut in cubes
> 1 medium onion, chopped
> 1 clove garlic
> 2 tablespoons tomato paste
> 2 cups chicken or beef broth
> Salt and freshly ground black pepper, to taste
> 1 tablespoon minced parsley
> Cotechino (see recipe below)

1. Soak the lentils overnight in water to cover. Drain and rinse.

2. Render the salt pork in a saucepan. Add the onion and garlic, and cook 2 minutes. Discard the garlic before it is brown.

3. Stir in the tomato paste and lentils. Add the broth and bring the mixture to a boil. Partially cover. Simmer 25 to 30 minutes until the lentils are tender.

4. Add salt and pepper to taste.

5. Put the lentils on a serving plate, top with the parsley, and accompany with *cotechino*.

COTECHINO

> *2 pounds* cotechino *(Italian fresh pork sausage)*

1. Prick the skin all over with a fork. Place *cotechino* in a large pan of cold water to cover.

2. Bring the water to a boil; boil gently for about 3 hours. (Add more boiling water, if necessary.)

3. Drain and cut into 1/2-inch rounds. Serve with lentils.

CELERIAC SALAD

2 large celeriacs (celery roots)
1 cucumber
¼ cup balsamic vinegar
2 tablespoons fresh lemon juice
2 tablespoons Dijon prepared mustard
1 teaspoon dried tarragon
2 tablespoons minced parsley
½ cup olive oil
Freshly ground black pepper, to taste
3 Belgian endives, washed and slivered
1 head of romaine lettuce, washed and shredded

1. Peel the celeriacs, and slice them into fine strips. Put the strips in a bowl of acidulated water.

2. Peel the cucumber and slice it into thin rounds.

3. Whisk together the vinegar, lemon juice, mustard, tarragon, and 1 tablespoon of the parsley (or use a blender to combine). Add the olive oil; blend well. Season with pepper. Drain the celeriac, pat dry, and combine with the cucumber. Pour on the dressing, and mix well. Refrigerate overnight.

4. Drain the excess dressing from the celeriac-cucumber mixture, and reserve it.

5. Add the endive and lettuce, and toss together.

6. If needed, replace some of the reserved dressing.

7. Sprinkle with the remaining parsley, and serve.

CARDAMOM CAKE
8 SERVINGS

> 2²/₃ *cups all-purpose flour*
> *1 tablespoon ground cardamom*
> *2 teaspoons cinnamon*
> *2 teaspoons ground cloves*
> *2 teaspoons ground ginger*
> *1 teaspoon baking soda*
> *¹/₂ teaspoon salt*
> *1 cup unsalted butter, softened*
> *2 cups sugar*
> *6 eggs*
> *2 cups sour cream*
> *Confectioners' sugar, for dusting*

Preheat oven to 325° F.

1. Grease a 3-quart bundt pan.

2. Sift the flour with the spices, baking soda, and salt into a bowl.

3. In the large bowl of an electric mixer, cream the butter, gradually adding the sugar and continuing to beat until the mixture is light and fluffy. Add the eggs 1 at a time, beating well after each addition.

4. Stir the flour mixture into the butter mixture, alternating with the sour cream. Mix well.

5. Spoon the batter into the prepared bundt pan. Bake 1 hour on the middle rack of the oven or until a toothpick inserted in the center comes out of the cake clean.

6. Cool the cake 10 minutes on a rack, then turn it onto a rack. Dust with confectioners' sugar.

HOLIDAY LASAGNE WITH RAGU SAUCE
8 TO 10 SERVINGS

> *1 recipe Ragu Sauce (see recipe below)*
> *1 pound Italian sausage, cut in small pieces*
> *1½ pounds ricotta cheese*
> *4 eggs*
> *¼ cup minced parsley*
> *1 pound fresh lasagne noodles*
> *½ pound mozzarella, sliced thin*
> *¾ cup grated Parmesan cheese*

Preheat oven to 350° F.

1. In a medium skillet over moderate heat, cook the sausage pieces until brown, stirring often. Drain and set aside.

2. Combine the ricotta cheese, eggs, and parsley in a medium bowl and mix well. Set aside.

3. If using packaged lasagne, cook it in boiling water. (If you have fresh pasta, cooking is not necessary.)

4. Spread a thin layer of sauce on the bottom of a 10 × 13-inch shallow baking pan. Follow with a layer of lasagne, then layers of the ricotta mixture, sausage, and mozzarella. Cover with some of the sauce, and sprinkle with some of the Parmesan cheese.

5. Repeat the layering, ending with sauce and grated Parmesan cheese. Bake 40 minutes on the middle rack of the oven. Let the lasagne stand 10 minutes before serving.

2 ounces dried wild mushrooms, such as porcini
1 tablespoon olive oil
1 pound lean ground beef
½ cup dry white wine
4 tablespoons unsalted butter
1 medium onion, chopped
1 carrot, chopped
2 stalks celery, chopped
2 cloves garlic
2 tablespoons chopped parsley
1 teaspoon salt
¼ teaspoon white pepper
⅛ teaspoon freshly grated nutmeg
One 16-ounce can Italian plum tomatoes
1 cup homemade or canned beef broth

1. Soak the mushrooms in lukewarm water to cover for 30 minutes; drain, rinse, and chop.

2. Heat the oil in a medium skillet over moderate heat. Brown the meat in the olive oil, stirring often. Add the mushrooms; cook 5 minutes. Add the wine, and cook 5 minutes more.

3. In a large, heavy saucepan heat the butter, and sauté the onion, carrot, celery, and garlic over medium-low heat until soft, about 15 minutes. Do not let the vegetables brown.

4. Stir in the parsley, salt, white pepper, tomatoes with juice, and the broth. Break up the tomatoes with a wooden spoon. Add the meat mixture. Cover and simmer 2 hours over low heat.

5. Remove the garlic cloves before using.

CHICKEN ROSETTA
6 SERVINGS

¼ cup olive oil
2 cloves garlic
Branch of fresh rosemary
2 broiler chickens, 2½ to 3 pounds in all, cut in
  pieces
1 cup dry white wine
Salt and freshly ground black pepper, to taste

1. Heat the oil in a large skillet over moderate heat. Sauté the garlic cloves until golden.

2. Put in three chicken pieces, and brown all over, turning with tongs. Remove the browned chicken to a dish while sautéing the second batch of chicken.

3. Return all chicken to the skillet, sprinkle with salt and pepper, and add the branch of rosemary.

4. Pour the wine over the chicken, raise the heat, and burn off the alcohol quickly, then lower the heat, cover tightly, and cook for 15 minutes.

5. Uncover the skillet, discard the garlic cloves and the rosemary, and cook the chicken another 10 minutes, turning. Serve the chicken with the pan juices.

FRIED CAULIFLOWER
6 SERVINGS

½ cup all-purpose flour
1 tablespoon olive oil
½ cup warm water
1 egg, beaten
½ cup grated Parmesan cheese

96

Salt and freshly ground black pepper, to taste
Oil for deep frying
1 medium cauliflower, washed and broken into
florets

1. Sift the flour into a shallow bowl. Stir in the oil, water, and egg. Mix until smooth. Add half the Parmesan cheese, the salt and pepper, and mix thoroughly. Set aside 1 hour at room temperature.

2. Heat the oil. (For deep-frying instructions, see Apple Fritters recipe, page 327.)

2. Dip the florets into the batter and fry, a few at a time, until golden. Drain on paper towels, and sprinkle with the remaining Parmesan cheese.

CARAMELIZED ORANGES
6 SERVINGS

6 oranges
1 cup sugar
1¼ cups water
2 teaspoons of orange-flavored liqueur, such as
Grand Marnier

1. Peel the oranges, removing all the pith. Cut the peel as thin as possible and then cut it into fine strips. Plunge the peel into boiling water, and cook about 7 minutes. Drain and set aside.

2. Put the sugar, water, and liqueur in a pan and cook over medium heat, stirring constantly, until a thick syrup forms.

3. When the syrup is thick, dip the oranges into it, turning them to cover completely; leave them in the syrup for 2 to 3 minutes. Remove them to a large dish.

4. Put the orange peel in the syrup, and cook until the peel starts

to become translucent. Remove the caramelized peel, and place over the oranges.

5. Chill and serve.

Epiphany

PASTA RING WITH MUSHROOMS
8 SERVINGS

 ½ cup unseasoned breadcrumbs
 1 pound ziti cut (pasta tubes)
 1 tablespoon unsalted butter
 2 tablespoons all-purpose flour
 1½ cups milk
 1 tablespoon whipping cream
 2 eggs, beaten
 ½ cup grated Parmesan cheese
 Salt, freshly ground black pepper, and grated
   nutmeg, to taste

FILLING

 ¼ cup olive oil
 4 tablespoons unsalted butter
 2 pounds mushrooms, washed, stems trimmed and
   sliced
 Salt and freshly ground black pepper, to taste
 ½ cup dry white wine
 2 tablespoons fresh lemon juice
 1 tablespoon chopped parsley

Preheat the oven to 350° F.

1. Grease a 3½- to 4-cup ring mold. Coat it with the breadcrumbs.

2. Cook the pasta al dente, and drain it.

3. While the pasta is cooking, melt the butter over moderate heat, and blend in the flour. Add the milk and cream, and stir until the mixture thickens. Stir in the eggs, cheese, and seasonings.

4. Add the mixture to the pasta, and fill the prepared mold. Set the mold in a pan of boiling water that comes halfway up the sides of the mold, and bake until set, about 20 minutes.

5. To make the filling, put the oil and butter in a skillet large enough to hold the mushrooms. Over high heat cook the mushrooms until they are wilted; add the salt, pepper, wine, lemon juice, and parsley, and cook 3 minutes, stirring.

6. To serve, unmold the pasta ring on a serving plate, and put the filling in the center.

CHICKEN WITH FENNEL
8 SERVINGS

> 2 chickens, cut into serving pieces
> Salt and freshly ground black pepper, to taste
> 1/4 cup all-purpose flour
> 3 tablespoons olive oil
> 4 large garlic cloves, sliced
> 1/2 cup onions, sliced
> 1 1/2 cups fresh trimmed fennel, cut in thick slices,
>   plus some of the feathery leaves
> 2/3 cup dry white wine

1. Wash and dry the chicken pieces.

2. Season the chicken with salt and pepper, then dredge it in the flour.

3. Place the olive oil in a large skillet over moderate heat; when it is sizzling, brown the chicken pieces, turning them often. Remove them from the skillet.

4. Add the garlic and onion, and cook until tender. Stir in the fennel slices and cook 1 to 2 minutes. Return the chicken to the skillet, season with salt and pepper to taste, and pour in the wine.

5. Cover the skillet, reduce the heat to low, and cook slowly for 30 minutes.

6. Serve garnished with chopped fennel leaves sprinkled over the chicken.

WILTED SPINACH
6 TO 8 SERVINGS

> *3 pounds fresh spinach, well washed*
> *½ teaspoon salt*
> *4 tablespoons olive oil*
> *1½ tablespoons fresh lemon juice*

1. Cook washed spinach, with only water left on the leaves, on high heat briefly until wilted.

2. Spread the spinach on a platter. Sprinkle with the salt, olive oil, and lemon juice. Serve hot or cold.

ORANGE SPONGE CAKE
8 SERVINGS

CAKE

> *3 eggs, separated*
> *¼ teaspoon cream of tartar*
> *1 cup sugar*
> *2 teaspoons freshly grated orange rind*
> *⅓ cup freshly squeezed orange juice*
> *1¼ cups cake flour*

1½ teaspoons baking powder
¼ teaspoon salt
1 blanched almond

FILLING

¼ cup sugar
1½ tablespoons all-purpose flour
¼ teaspoon salt
2 teaspoons freshly grated orange rind
½ cup freshly squeezed orange juice
1 egg yolk
2 teaspoons unsalted butter
1 teaspoon fresh lemon juice

ICING

2 tablespoons unsalted butter
¼ cup freshly squeezed orange juice
1 cup confectioners' sugar

Preheat the oven to 325° F.

1. To make the cake, in a large bowl beat the egg whites with the cream of tartar until they form stiff peaks. Add the egg yolks 1 at a time, beating well after each addition. Add the sugar gradually, beating constantly.

2. Add the orange rind and juice, stirring.

3. Sift together the flour, baking powder, and salt. Fold into the egg yolk mixture with a rubber spatula.

4. Pour the batter into two 8-inch unbuttered cake pans. Slip the blanched almond into one of them. (The person who gets the slice with the lucky almond rules the feast.)

5. Bake 18 minutes on the middle rack of the oven, or until a toothpick inserted in the center of a cake comes out clean. Cool on racks, then turn out.

6. To make the filling, put the sugar, flour, and salt in the top of a

double boiler over simmering water, and mix thoroughly. Add the orange rind and juice. Stir in the butter and egg yolk, and cook until the mixture is smooth and thick.

7. Remove from the heat and beat in the lemon juice.

8. To make the icing, melt the butter in a small pan over moderate heat. Mix in the orange juice; add to the confectioners' sugar, and mix well.

9. To assemble the cake, spread some of the filling on 1 cake layer. Place the second layer on top, and ice the entire cake.

Three

FEBRUARY

Carnival Season

When we lived in Italy, no sooner did we recover from Christmastide
than Carnival began. Some say Carnival lasts from December 26 to
Mardi Gras night. Others locate the beginning at Epiphany, or in
mid-January. As for me, we were always into February before I began
to take real notice of the costumes in store windows and the pastry
shops filled with temptations. This is a time of indulgence before
Ash Wednesday signals penance and fasting; *Carnevale*, in the Ital

ian, means literally "farewell to flesh" and is the long lead time before Lent.

Depending on the date of Easter, which is a moveable feast, the whole month of February, or most of it, can be devoted to Carnival. The festivities of the last days are the most intense as they culminate in Fat Tuesday (Mardi Gras). Carnival is general all through Italy, and every city, town, and village celebrates its own version. Interspersed in the overall calendar of Carnival there are several saints' days in February that are of special significance.

February 2, Groundhog Day in the States, is known as Candlemas Day elsewhere. There is a parallel between the two:

> If Candlemas Day be fair and bright
> Winter will have another flight.

The groundhog's seeing his shadow in sunlight and going back underground because winter will be prolonged is similar to the couplet's expression of winter still having rule over the land. In the Catholic Church it's the occasion for blessing all the candles that symbolize Christ as "the light of the world" and that are used throughout the year's services.

On February 3, crossed candles are used to bless throats. Saint Blaise is the patron of this part of the body because it is said that while in prison he healed a boy who had a fish bone stuck in his throat. San Biagio, as he's called in Italian, was a fourth-century bishop of Armenia who suffered the terrible martyrdom of being torn to pieces with iron wool combs. His relics were brought to Italy by Christians fleeing persecution in Asia Minor, and since 732 they have rested in a shrine at the summit of Monte San Biagio on the heights above Maratea. It is because we once had a small place by the sea in Maratea that I know of this saint at all. Since then I have learned of a little village in Cornwall called Saint Blazey, after Saint Blaise, where he is invoked against toothache—a spin-off, perhaps, from the contiguous throat area under his protection?

Rome's splendid Renaissance street, Via Giulia, has a little church called forthrightly San Biagio degli Armeni (Saint Blaise of the Armenians) but popularly known as *della pagnotta* (Saint Blaise of the loaf) because on his feast day, after a choral mass according to the Armenian rite, small loaves of bread are given out. (Having once gotten a fish bone stuck in my throat and dislodging it by eating a small loaf of bread, I can attest to the appropriateness.)

Saint Blaise means Maratea to me, which survives in my memory as a secret place of ineffable beauty. To have been there at all now seems a moment of grace. And to remember, in the middle of February, the whitewashed sanctuary of San Biagio on a precipice set off by yellow *ginestra* and looking out to the cobalt sea is like a special blessing in itself. It was later, from anthropologist Carla Bianco in Rome, that I learned that hard biscuits are eaten on this saint's feast day, perhaps to make sure that all is well with one's throat. Since then I have always put aside from the Christmas baking enough hard almond-honey biscuits (*mostacciuoli*) to make sure we'd have them for February 3.

Saint Agatha's Day

On the fifth of February, Saint Agatha, whose breasts were severed in her martyrdom, is honored through bread baked in round loaves. Some feel that old traditions such as these are best left unexplored because of the unpleasantness of their imagery. Still, every culture has them, and Saint Agatha cookies are no more repugnant than, say, the Purim sweet called "Haman's Ears"; as in fairy tales, the long span of time and the constancy of custom wipes out the horrific, and what is left is an innocent vision of virtue and faith just as it was depicted by Giotto, Fra Angelico, Gentile da Fabbriano, and so many other early Italian masters. These artists made scenes of atrocious torture into works of exquisite candor and beauty, transcending the fact and honoring the spirit. Dante, recounting Inferno's pains and punishments, is remembered for the sublime poetry of the telling. So, I think, all the saints who were torn or pressed or dragged or boiled or grilled deserve to be honored even if so humbly as through the shape of a loaf of bread.

In Saint Agatha's birthplace, Catania in Sicily, and elsewhere in the region, little rounded marzipan confections meant to simulate breasts are also eaten on her day as special treats. Again, there are no overly delicate feelings about their being too vivid a recollection of bygone suffering. Carlo Levi, in his *Words Are Stone*, tells of the Catanese nuns who make the sweets, called *minne de vergine*, and reflects on "the obvious fact that the Breast of Saint Agatha is none other than Mount Etna, that great breast of the earth." Don Fabrizio in Lampedusa's *Leopard* also reflects on the obvious sexuality evoked by the sweets called "breasts of the virgin." Why, he wonders, didn't the Church forbid these cakes—Saint Agatha's sliced-off breasts, sold by convents, and devoured at worldly social occasions? The answer is the Church's own worldly wisdom.

Since Saint Agatha is patron of Catania, the Catanese pay her homage in a rich three-day festival. *Candelora*—or enormous tapers—are tied together and placed on platforms carved with scenes from the saint's life and paraded through the streets by guildsmen in costume shouting out, *"Evviva Sant'Agata!"* Oral tradition has endowed Saint Agatha with shadings of her pagan predecessors, and her legend contains the familiar story of the unwelcome suitor. She held him off by asking him to wait until she finished weaving a ceremonial cloth. Like Penelope, she wove by day and undid by night. She died a virgin and martyr and is the patroness of weavers, as well as the protector of nursing mothers. A cloth attributed to her was believed to have stopped an eruption of Mount Etna when the city fathers of Catania paraded it toward the smoking volcano.

Again this legend harks back to the ingrained quid pro quo way the Italian peasant treats his saints, which scholars have related directly to the pagan worship of the pre-Christian gods and spirits and which has never entirely been replaced by the official Church. Some of these special devotions to saints, and the pretext they give for festival occasions, still occur in the Little Italys of American cities as links with a potent past.

Saint Valentine's Day

Saint Valentine, who in medieval times became the patron of lovers and the protector of those who suffer lovesickness, was a Roman who had been imprisoned for succoring persecuted Christians. He became a convert, then was beheaded outside Rome on the Flaminian Way. A cult attached to this saint has been attested to by inscriptions with his name that have been unearthed at the site on the Via Flaminia where a church was raised over his sepulcher. An early Christian cemetery also existed here. During Constantine's reign, *martyria*, or shrines of witness, were built on the sites where martyrs had died, in order to celebrate what became, through death, their heavenly birthday or feast day. Thus began the historical commemoration of saints, the focus on shrines as places of pilgrimage, and the importance of the relics of saints in such shrines.

Valentine's Day, February 14, is said, by ancient tradition, to be when birds choose their mates—whence, it surely follows, Valentine greetings to a loved one came into being. As Marianne Moore's poem to Saint Valentine declares, "Verse—unabashedly bold—is appropriate."

Saint Valentine's Day and its observances conveniently replace the old pagan festival of the Lupercalia, which fell on February 15 and entailed in its purification rites the striking of married women with a goat-hide thong called *februa* (from which we get the month's name) to make them fertile—a rather loose association with love but enough, perhaps, to have been transmuted into Saint Valentine's patronage of lovers.

The origin of many festivals has to be sought in far-off rites. The Carnival custom of masquerading and reveling derives from the Roman era, when people dressed in frightening disguises to "drive the wintery demons away" from their homes and fields in anticipation of spring. The Lupercalia was a rite of cleansing and expiation in preparation for spring, which has been subsumed into the service of Lent. And the word *Lent* itself comes from the Anglo-Saxon *lencten*, meaning "spring." (In Italy the period is known as *Quaresima*, which signifies forty days, the time span of the Lenten observance.)

Analogous to the purification of self, which is the basis for Lenten fasting as one approaches the rebirth of land and life in spring, is the peasants' February ritual of cleaning up the fields in preparation for the new growing season. As I observed it during my own Italian country life, first comes the very orderly chopping of trees during the winter months, when whole poplar groves and stands of other trees seem to disappear. All the brush of hillsides is tidied; branches and limbs are faggoted and bundled for selling or burning. The entire countryside is alive with work: new groves and avenues are planted with seedlings for the rewooding. Fields are given a going-over—all the old corn shocks are burned and the land plowed over and left fallow; in adjacent fields the hand sowing of crops begins. It's a most orderly and satisfying procedure to observe; it's like spring housecleaning and the spiritual cleansing of Lent. Everything in home and field and self is done for renewal, which is the promise of spring.

And in this observed natural order, which was the great gift of my rural life, I learned the natural rhythm of foods so that the seasons and their bounty were anticipated, and anything eaten out of season seemed wrong—out of place and time. After a winter of spinach and cabbage, we craved the artichokes of Carnival season; then spring lamb, fresh peas, asparagus, and strawberries. The summer brought its bounty of incredible fresh fruits and vegetables; in fall there were woods' mushrooms, truffles, chestnuts, and squash. Winter meant sausages and pork products, radicchio, Sorrento walnuts, Christmas breads, blood oranges, and sweet ricotta. Each new fruit or vegetable was a prize, eagerly awaited, not just frozen lumps from a freezer compartment. Over the winter the tangerines got drier and drier and then disappeared from the market. Suddenly the first tiny strawberries again appeared. The slow, natural maturing of things in their season is, like the holidays, what we waited for.

Carnival in Ivrea

Every locality in Italy holds some form of carnival merrymaking in the last days before Ash Wednesday, but the most unusual and interesting from a historical point of view took place in Ivrea, where Antonio worked for Adriano Olivetti's Communità project during 1954 and 1955. Ivrea is a picturesque town in the Canavese valley of the Piedmont, located strategically on the River Dora Baltea at the entrance to the autonomous region of Valle d'Aosta. This route through the valley, following the river course, was the ancient way to Gaul. Valle d'Aosta is ringed by the Alps and has Europe's highest mountains, including Mont Blanc, Monte Rosa, Gran Paradiso, and the Cervino.

Founded a century before Christ as Eporedia, Ivrea is known as "the beautiful," and "*Ivrea la bella*" is still spelled out in a flower bed at the train station. The town is the headquarters of the international Olivetti business machine firm, and yet has retained all its flavor of the past. From Ivrea we often explored the surrounding country, with its enticing and strategically placed feudal castles like Fenis and Issogne, or the Bard fortress that once defended the mountain passes (at least until Napoleon's descent into Italy). We visited remote Aosta, which still conserves the great arch of Augustus and parts of a Roman theater; we skied at Gressoney La Trinité in view of the Alps; and at the watering resort of Saint Vincent, Antonio received one of his literary prizes. Every scrap of this hard-won land of northern Italy is put to use; the south sides of difficult hills and mountains are terraced frugally and expertly with the vines that produce the excellent wines of the Canavese region, like the superb but rare Caluso.

Ivrea's Carnival, in contrast with the carefree pre-Lenten celebrations that take place elsewhere, is laden with symbolism to commemorate the town's liberation from feudal tyranny and glorifies the legendary figure of the miller's daughter, "La Mugnaia," as heroine of the insurrection. It's a mix of Mardi Gras, Fourth of July patriotism and rhetoric, and the suspense of a Miss America pageant as to who will be chosen La Mugnaia.

The story of Violetta, the miller's daughter, goes back to medieval times and has to do with popular uprisings against two tyrants and the hated taxes they imposed on milling as well as on marriage— the latter tax extended into the hated *jus primae noctis*, or "right of the first night." In the popular imagination, all despots were merged into one who, desirous of Violetta, tried to impose his "right" over her. Still dressed in her wedding white, she stabbed him to death and severed his head to display to the people thronging beneath the castle. This was the signal for revolt and the final destruction of that stronghold, which was the symbol of oppression. Today an orange, carried on swordpoint, symbolizes the severed head of tyranny.

Down through the centuries, the popular uprising has been remembered and exalted. Once each parish of Ivrea used to celebrate its own carnival version of the *mugnaia* story. Under Napoleon, at the time of his Italian campaign, the festivities were united into one celebration for the whole town under the command of a "general" who appeared in Napoleonic uniform. Actually, as Antonio noted in an article he wrote on Ivrea's Carnival, it was a parody of liberty—and an astute move by the occupying Napoleonic government, who thus curried favor with the populace.

Thus, each year during the last days of Carnival, the townspeople (plus any tourists or visitors to Ivrea) are commanded to appear in the red cap of revolution, under penalty of being pelted with oranges if found without it. This liberty cap is the same one familiar to us from the French Revolution: conical with the peak turned down in front. It originated in the cap of red felt placed on the head of a Roman slave when he was freed; such caps, raised atop spears, became symbols of liberty, and when Caesar was murdered, the conspirators marched forth in a body with such a cap elevated as a token of liberty. So from the ancient world to France and back, the red liberty cap endures in the ceremonies of Carnival.

Early in the morning on January 6, the feast of Epiphany, a colorful band of pipers and drummers appears in the streets of Ivrea to play the march that announces the opening of Carnival. Between then and the last Sunday of Carnival, the people nominate the general who will be hailed by all the authorities—civil, religious, and military—as the head of the Carnival festivities. The general in turn nominates his own retinue of officers, all of whom will be garbed as Napoleonic troops, an incongruity that Antonio scoffed at as a travesty of the lightheartedness that's supposed to prevail in Carnival. With his Veneto upbringing, he found Ivrea's customs too solemn, too musty with age, and too comically formal to be relevant to the festival. What was really missing, he noted in his account, was the spontaneity and irreverence that's supposed to prevail at this time of year, linking itself to the ancient customs of driving out bleak, wintery spirits and making way for the gracious rebirth of spring.

One year the honor of portraying La Mugnaia was given to our friend Anna Bonfanti, the wife of artist Egidio Bonfanti. Her selection was kept a guarded secret until she appeared on the balcony of the Municipal Building, just before dusk on the Saturday before Fat

Tuesday (*martedì grasso*), wearing the traditional red liberty cap with her white gown and ermine wrap. She was escorted by the general and his officers and five specially selected boys to represent the town's five parishes. With her appearance before the crowd in the square below, Carnival reigned over the town.

Actually, to follow all the events of the February Carnival in its culminating week would be exhausting. But I did take three-year-old Linda to the Fat Tuesday children's parade, enjoying, as she did, the hordes of becapped, beplumed and trinket-decked students who marched abreast through the streets of Ivrea to the municipal square. The streets were filled with sellers of colored hats, horns, paper streamers, violets (in memory of Violetta), masks, and costumes.

In the square the town hall was adorned in its official banners, and martial music filtered out from somewhere inside. Lining the way to the building were horses festooned in tapestry and bearing baskets of mimosa. When the marching pipers and drummers arrived in the piazza, a great storm of cheers, whistles, and horns was let loose. Then the resplendent general of Carnival, on foot this time, arrived in the square with all his attendants and the keeper of the Great Book of Carnival, to the unfurling of more banners from the town hall and an intensifying of the music. High up in the tower, the great bell began clanging, and the whole procession disappeared inside then appeared on the tricolor-draped balcony with the mayor of Ivrea and the city notary, who read out the rules of Carnival concerning the obligatory wearing of the red cap, the zones declared free from the war of the oranges, etc.

Next came a procession through town of beautifully costumed children on horseback; the horses were also gorgeously garbed in plumes, drapes, and cockades. It was quite an amazing sight—all those children followed by their mothers, cousins, and aunts by the dozen up and down the town.

The following day, in the square usually given over to the cheese market, came the *Fagiolata Benefica*, or Beans with Sausage Give-away, a way of distributing some of the abundance of Carnival to those without means. That was followed by the whole pageant of Carnival characters clambering down to the ancient Roman bridge, where La Mugnaia threw a stone into the Dora to represent the storming of the old castle.

The afternoon parade (including floats and farmers on tractors) was the occasion where La Mugnaia would be judged for the accuracy of her aim as she responded to the cheers of the crowd along the walks and in overlooking balconies by tossing them chocolates, candies, sprigs of mimosa, and hand-blown kisses.

On Monday and Tuesday, there were more processions, and this time with more frenzy—the hurling of oranges had begun. Storefronts were boarded up, and pedestrians had taken shelter in the free zone, where orange throwing was supposedly forbidden. Each evening had been scheduled for gala dinners, opera and plays, balls for the celebrities and more popular dancing for the people of each parish. Finally, late Tuesday evening, the burning of the liberty pole took place, followed by the funeral march in which Carnival was declared dead; after yet another midnight supper to honor La Mugnaia, closure was declared. Church bells tolled in Ash Wednesday, the beginning of forty days of penitence before Easter.

I especially enjoyed all the extravagance and tradition of Italian Carnivals, whether in Ivrea or Rome, because they provided a rich contrast to the family observance in Syracuse, New York, which was much simpler.

For Fat Tuesday, Grace Fahey has told me, her grandmother (my grandfather's sister) made homemade macaroni on her *chitarra*, a wire-strung machine on which the dough was rolled between the fine strings of the "guitar." The sauce for the pasta was made special with cinnamon, nutmeg, and cloves and was cooked with a large, stuffed *braciola* of beef that was then taken from the sauce and cut into slices. When the portions were served, whoever

113

got the string that had been hidden in the pasta became the clown of the evening. According to Grace, my grandfather, who spent holidays at his sister's house and was known to Grace as zio Peppino, always seemed to receive this booby prize. He then responded by toasting each person at the table in a rhyme made up on the spur of the moment. The dessert *sfingi* were doused with sweet wine and followed by other Carnival sweets—the fritters known by the name for firecrackers, *castagnole*, because they sometimes pop while frying, and the cookies with such colorful names as *cenci* (rags), *nodi* (knots), *chiacchere* (chatter), or *bugie* (lies)—this last because it's said that as with lies, you cannot stop after the first.

Pancakes, known in Italy as *crespelle*, are always eaten on Shrove Tuesday (the English term for Fat Tuesday) because they are rich, using up the last eggs, butter, and cream before Lent. My version is from I Tre Galletti restaurant at Pontecchio, Marconi's birthplace near Bologna, Italy's "fat city" par excellence. In the English of Chaucer's day, the word for pancake was "crisp" or "cresp," which plainly establishes a kinship with the Italian *crespa*. The pancake tradition is still very much a part of the English observance of Shrove Tuesday, the name of which offers an interesting insight into national character; whereas in most European countries with their Fat Tuesday (*martedì grasso, or mardi gras*) the emphasis is on indulgence that last day before Lent, in England the term *Shrove* derives from *shrive*, which means to hear confession and grant absolution. In England it was customary for confession to be heard on the Tuesday before Ash Wednesday, thus to be "shriven" of sin in preparation for Lent. More curious to me is the fact that *shrive* ultimately comes from the Latin *scribere* and Italian *scrivere*, meaning "to write." Either one can write one's way to absolution, or writers live a penitential life as it is!

During the years when Antonio worked in Ivrea for Olivetti, we resided in the nearby village of Strambino. There I lived, for the first time, a life of seasonal changes in rhythm with an era and custom now gone even from that rural part of Italy.

Gone into the past is my weekly excursion to Friday market in Ivrea, on the little local train with the peasant women from the countryside. Market day was as good, in its elemental way, as its opposite extreme—sophisticated dining and theater in Turin. The market stands started on the Lungadora, the promenade along the River Dora, and went up into town, spilling over into each square with the impressive black-cloaked animal brokers always gathered in the main square. It ended in a riot of color of flowers, plants, cheeses, fruits, sacks of beans and seeds, and vegetables along the tree-lined avenue near the park.

Week after week, the goods followed an orderly pattern. Fabrics, notions, felt flowers, and yarns nearest the old bridge; next, cutlery, baskets, copper basins, and polenta kettles; toward the park where the children played were the enticements: biscuits, candies, toys, and pinafore aprons; then came basic items like shoes, underwear, corduroy pants, flannel nightgowns, and thick wool sweaters. One particular square specialized in *zoccoli*, the wooden shoes of the peasants, and there were heaps of them in all sizes from baby to gigantic. I bought Linda a pair of gay red ones with a flower cut in the tip of each, and she loved to wear them as much as I loved her to, for they kept her feet dry in the dishwater- and dung-filled streets of Strambino. When we returned to the States to live, she still had her *zoccoli*, and they became the rage of her country day school when she wore them at her Christmas performance to recite how Befana would leave lumps of coal in them instead of chocolates if she weren't good.

There was always something new at market day: a vendor leading a small donkey with a saddle pack of bottled lavender water on one side and a pack of loose lavender on the other; the linoleum seller, whose acrobatic act was complete with microphone and shouts to pity him: "*o poveri noi, o poveri noi*"; the traveling purveyor of fine arts—the man on a bicycle who wore a wide-pocketed smock stuffed with pictures to sell, and more "art" in a knapsack on his back and in his basket on his handlebars. I asked him where he sold his wares, and he said proudly he covered the whole Masino-Strambino territory, an area not much larger than Central Park.

Market sounds included the constant calls of the vendors in their French-influenced dialect—"*Madamina, qua . . . Madamina*"—and the market itself produced a heightened state of alertness and exhilaration in the great game of getting a bargain, or at least trying not to get cheated or played for a fool by the wily tradespeople. Once a knife and scissor sharpener man stopped by in Strambino, and after a lot of demonstrating and dickering, Rosetta, our housekeeper, refused his price of 350 lire for sharpening three scissors; he went away, angry and muttering, only to come back and demand 400 lire for having had his time wasted.

Living in Strambino occasioned my interest in Italian food. Planning two meals a day Italian style, I wrote in my diary, "will either kill me or teach me to cook." I learned to cook. I suppose it was because I was confined to home and to small village life, where each day centered around marketing and eating. And in this period of my life, when I had two small children who needed my time and attention, there wasn't much else I could do. My Italian improved as I began to read *Cucina Italiana*, a luscious monthly food magazine, and to dip more and more into my *Cucchiaio d'Argento*. I kept a housebook of accounts and meals. I learned about the nineteenth-century culinary master, Pellegrino Artusi.

Indeed, I rather fancied myself, as an American emigré and would-be writer, a female Artusi myself, who temporarily was putting aside story writing for culinary lore. Just as Artusi did a century earlier, I was living in a small rural Italian community. He, too, had taken time from his literary interests to write his famous recipe book while he lived in Forlimpopoli. And what a book—as only a literary scholar could do: recipes interspersed with charming anecdotes, stories, bits of history, ironic asides on the Italian character, and a robust humanist's love for all aspects of life, with a major concern for good food and drink. I could dare to think of myself putting together a compendium of recipes because I was trying them out each day with Rosetta, who lived in as mother's helper and taught me a lot about life in the Italian boondocks.

When, after more than thirty years, I went back to Strambino to see Rosetta again, she was a real signora who had made good. She and her husband, Marcello, had worked hard in the years since their marriage and had prospered. She invited me for dinner at their home, and after we dined on her inimitable chicken with rosemary and white wine, we walked in her garden and saw the dovecote, the peacock run, the fountain Marcello had made, the roosts where their chickens and rabbits came from, the fruit trees and vegetable patch, the vines of grapes. And adjacent to Marcello's aviary of tropical birds and his generously stocked wine cellar was the larger freezer that held what Rosetta called *la bontà di Dio*— God's bounty—her winter supply of garden produce and enough dressed chickens for one or two a week, plus all the feast days.

Rosetta drove me through the environs of Strambino, where once, perched on the back of Marcello's motorcycle with her arms around Linda, they had gone to Scarmogna to get fresh milk from the model dairy of a Turin noble known as the farmer-count. With the opening of an Olivetti plant between Strambino and Conte Roberto's farm, my old country village has taken on a prosperous and modern look with dozens of new, well-to-do homes along the main route. Now there is even an *autostrada* to Turin. The palazzo on the road to the station where we had lived and which had once seemed the grandest place in the village now looked shabby and decrepit. Someone had scrawled on the side wall in large letters, *"Dove tramontono i ricordi"*—where memories wane. Was it a song title, or the truth? Everything had changed in the years since I lived there.

"We don't lack for anything," Rosetta told me proudly on that visit, and Marcello reinforced her words: *"L'America è qui adesso, signora"*—America is here now. And it was true. But before I left, in the old way, they loaded me with honey, fresh figs, hazelnuts, their photos, and a lucky chestnut to ward off colds.

So much of our concern in the former days, I remembered, was food. Antonio came home for the dinner at noon each day, and each evening there was another meal. I recall Rosetta once rushing out of the kitchen to run to the upper village for a branch of rosemary because the roast wouldn't be right without it, and therefore she couldn't continue cooking. I think of my perusing and learning the foods at market; the occasional shopping and eating-out expeditions in the fine restaurants of nearby Turin, which was part of my education; my introduction to the incredibly perfect *agnolotti* of Strambino's local inn, Il Cappello Verde; the wine tastings of the region and the journeys to remote towns in search of a certain cheese, a famed sweet, a rare wine.

It occurred to me then as I began a collection of artisan-made kitchen implements that much of American cooking might have seemed tasteless to me because not only the right ingredients weren't used, but not even the right tools. Stirring spoons had to be wood, for instance, so as not to impart a metallic taste to sauces and such. Choppers must chop finely and easily, as the *mezzaluna* does; without the right tools, American cooks could be tempted into bad substitutes—insipid dry parsley leaves, too-strong garlic powder or celery salt, the abomination known as cooking wine. I began to appreciate fresh herbs, olive oil, freshly ground pepper from the mill, freshly grated cheese from the hunk, a light grating of nutmeg over spinach or as a piquant difference in mashed potatoes.

In my Italian kitchen my wooden tools were made by an artisan in Rivarolo—scoops, ladles, spoons, mortar and pestle, bowls. All elegant, ingenious, pleasing to look at and to handle. The food mill through which I passed tomatoes or other things to purée was like a moon-landing craft on its tripod feet and with its interchangeable disks. I called it, in fact, *il lunare*, regardless of whatever its real name was in Italian. I remember wonderfully shaped jugs, brown earthenware baking dishes and stewing pots bought at market, hand-woven baskets, wood-banded sieves, coffee grinders, pepper mills, molds and flasks and oil cans, and the great copper kettle for the polenta. Even the corkscrew for the wine bottle, with its wings that raised and lowered, was an ingenious work of art. Nonetheless, my Italian kitchen in Strambino was nothing compared to the old-fashioned kitchens in the great houses of Antonio's ancestors, about whom he wrote in a great profusion of memory and nostalgia once we were living in the States and Italy was far away. From those old family kitchens, I still have cruets, pewter bowls, and a gigantic domed copper bread box, which accompany me wherever I go.

But I can't wax romantic about my Italian kitchen without admitting that it had its drawbacks, too. Our Strambino apartment was in a modern building that was still incomplete when we moved in. We got some very special terms because the landlord, a former mayor of Strambino in the Fascist regime, who liked to be called by his honorary title of *cavaliere*, was eager to have a noted Italian journalist and his American wife as tenants. He let himself be persuaded to give me the two modern notions I wanted—a closet in the bedroom and hot water in the kitchen. Though he himself lived in a pink palazzo and had servants, a prospering wool mill, three cars, and a television (in those days!), still he thought my requests quite capricious.

"Signora," I can still hear him saying, with a sweep of his hat and a courteous half-bow, "no one in Strambino has running hot water in the kitchen. Dishes can be washed satisfactorally with sand, soda, and cold water."

"And laundry, *Cavaliere?*" I asked.

"Well, you must have noticed by now!" he answered with just a trace of impatience tempered by another little bow. "There's a stream just behind this very building, where all the washing is done. It was during my administration that it was roofed over and permanent rock slabs provided—there's even a light bulb for washing at night!"

But I got my hot water heater in the kitchen, plus a closet that proved a disaster since it had an outside wall, making everything in it so damp that in order to stop the mold, we had to put in an electric heater, the result being a tremendous electric bill. Coming from the States, I never realized hot water was such a convenience—it had always been there, something that seemed part of things from the first day of creation. In Strambino I lived in a world of constant plugging and unplugging of the boilers in kitchen and bathroom, trying to curtail the exorbitantly high-cost of electric current. The extent of our profligate baths and daily washings (measured by the number of diapers hung out to dry on the back balcony) was always a topic of village gossip.

All Strambino talked of my follies. I was *l'Americana*, the eccentric of the place. I think it was only because of Rosetta, who (though bemused herself) good-naturedly interpreted my ways to the villagers, that I was given a tinge of credibility in that place at that time.

Saint Blaise's Day
Agnolotti di Strambino
Veal Marengo
Italian Carrot Cake

Saint Agatha's Day
Artichoke Pie with Pastry Crust
Cremini

Saint Valentine's Day
Rice Timbale with Saffron
Ossobuco Milanese
Broccoli Rabe
Cannoli with Mascarpone
    Filling

Fat Tuesday
Crespelle
Veal Roast with Mustard Sauce
Sautéed Savoy Cabbage
Baked Pears and Ginger Cream
Carnival Fritters

Saint Blaise's Day

AGNOLOTTI DI STRAMBINO
6 SERVINGS

> *2 to 3 slices pork loin, beef, or veal, cooked or*
>   *uncooked (about 1 pound)*
> *4 to 5 leaves Savoy cabbage, parboiled*
> *2 large eggs, beaten*
> *1 teaspoon freshly grated nutmeg*
> *3 tablespoons grated Parmesan cheese*
> *Freshly ground black pepper, 2 to 3 twists of the mill*
> *2 big sheets of fresh pasta (or 6 to 8 strips from a pasta*
>   *machine) kept moist between damp towels*
> *4 tablespoons unsalted butter*
> *Grated Parmesan cheese to pass at the table*

1. If the meat is uncooked cut off any extra fat, melt a tablespoon of butter in a small skillet, and cook it quickly over medium heat until done on both sides. Do not overcook.

2. Put the meat through a grinder on the finest setting.

3. Put the cooked, drained cabbage through the grinder.

4. Put the meat and cabbage in a bowl. Add the eggs, and stir to mix well. Add the nutmeg, Parmesan cheese, and pepper. Set aside.

5. Keep the pasta covered with a damp cloth until ready for use. Put a sheet of pasta on a floured work surface. Drop little dabs of filling in even rows on the pasta sheet, positioning the filling so that each dab is at the center of a 2-inch square. Cover this piece of pasta with another and, with your fingers, press the two together around each bit of filling. (The edges must be well pressed together, or cooking water can seep in.) If the pasta does not stick together, wet your fingers, and moisten the edges.

6. Cut between the 2-inch squares with a sharp knife or pastry cutter so that the mounds of filling are in the center of each square. Put the *agnolotti* on a flour-dusted baking sheet. They can stand an hour or so before cooking.

7. Bring a large pot of water to a boil; add salt and the *agnolotti*, a few at a time. Keep the water boiling; cover the pot. Cook about 5 minutes or until the edges are tender. Remove with a slotted spoon, and drain.

8. Serve with butter and Parmesan cheese.

VEAL MARENGO
6 TO 8 SERVINGS

> *¼ cup olive oil*
> *4 pounds tender stewing veal, cut into 2-inch cubes*

4 tablespoons unsalted butter
4 medium onions, coarsely chopped
4 tablespoons all-purpose flour
6 ripe tomatoes, peeled, seeded, and chopped
1 cup dry white wine
2½ cups chicken stock or canned broth
2 cloves garlic, chopped
Salt and freshly ground black pepper, to taste
2 dozen mushroom caps
2 tablespoons chopped fresh parsley

1. Put the olive oil in a heavy casserole, over medium-high heat. When the oil is sizzling, add the veal and brown, turning often.

2. In a medium skillet melt 2 tablespoons of the butter over moderate heat, and brown the onions, stirring often.

3. Add the onions to the veal. Reduce the heat, and cook 4 to 5 minutes. Sprinkle with flour and blend it in thoroughly. Add the tomatoes, wine, chicken stock, garlic, salt, and pepper.

4. Cover the casserole and simmer 1 hour.

5. Melt the remaining 2 tablespoons of butter in a skillet, and sauté the mushrooms 3 to 4 minutes over moderate heat.

6. Add the mushrooms to the casserole. Simmer over low heat for another 30 minutes, or until the veal is tender.

7. Sprinkle with the parsley, and serve.

ITALIAN CARROT CAKE
8 SERVINGS

4 eggs, separated
¾ cup sugar
Freshly grated rind of 1 lemon
3 cups finely grated young, tender carrots

>2 cups (half pound) finely ground blanched
>   almonds
>1 heaping tablespoon self-rising flour
>½ teaspoon ground ginger
>Confectioners' sugar or whipped cream

Preheat the oven to 325° F.

1. Liberally grease and flour a 9-inch cake pan.

2. In a medium bowl beat the egg yolks, sugar, and lemon rind together thoroughly until the mixture thickens. Mix in the carrots, almonds, flour, and nutmeg.

3. In a separate bowl beat the egg whites until they form stiff peaks. Gently fold them into the carrot mixture, and turn the batter into the prepared pan.

4. Bake on the middle rack of the oven for about 50 minutes or until the top is firm and golden brown. Cool on a rack before removing from the pan.

5. Serve with a dusting of confectioners' sugar or whipped cream.

Saint Agatha's Day

ARTICHOKE PIE WITH PASTRY CRUST
8 SERVINGS

>2 cups sliced artichoke hearts (or two 9-ounce
>   packages frozen artichoke hearts, thawed)
>Pie Crust (see recipe below)
>½ cup ricotta cheese
>2 eggs, beaten
>2 slices white bread

½ cup milk
2 tablespoons unsalted butter
1 large onion, chopped
1 finely chopped shallot
½ pound ham, diced
2 tablespoons chopped parsley
Salt and freshly ground black pepper, to taste
Dried oregano, to taste

Preheat the oven to 450° F.

1. Cook fresh artichoke hearts in lightly salted boiling water over moderate heat for 35 to 40 minutes or until tender. (To cook packaged hearts, follow package directions.) Drain and cool.

2. Roll out half the Pie Crust dough onto a lightly floured work surface. Fit it into a 9-inch pie plate, letting 1 inch of dough hang over the edge. Roll out the remaining dough for the top crust. Put it between 2 pieces of wax paper, and refrigerate it while you prepare the filling.

3. Put the cooked artichoke hearts in a bowl. Stir in the ricotta cheese and eggs. Tear the bread into pieces, and in a small bowl soak it in the milk. When all the milk is absorbed, add the bread to the artichoke mixture, and combine lightly.

4. Melt the butter in a good-sized skillet over moderate heat. Sauté the onion and shallot until soft, stirring often. Add ham. Reduce the heat to low and cover; cook 5 minutes.

5. Add the contents of the skillet to the artichoke mixture. Stir in the parsley and mix well. Add salt, pepper, and oregano to taste. Spoon the mixture into the pie crust, and cover with the top pastry. Pinch the bottom and top crusts together.

6. Bake the pie 35 to 40 minutes on the middle rack of the oven, until the pastry is golden.

7. Let the pie cool 10 minutes on a rack before serving.

PIE CRUST DOUGH
YIELD: 2 9-INCH CRUSTS

1½ cups whole wheat flour
½ cup all-purpose flour
Pinch salt
½ cup olive oil
½ cup very cold water

1. Put both flours in a bowl with the salt.

2. Mix the olive oil and water. Add to the flour mixture and, using a fork, mix it until a ball can be formed.

CREMINI (*Santina's Little Fried Creams*)
YIELD: 20 BITE-SIZE PIECES

2 eggs
2 tablespoons sugar
2½ tablespoons all-purpose flour
Pinch salt
Freshly grated rind of 1 lemon
1 cup milk
1 tablespoon Mistra (or other anise liqueur)
¼ cup all-purpose flour for coating
1 cup fine breadcrumbs
1 egg, beaten
Peanut oil for deep frying

1. Beat the eggs and sugar together in a small saucepan until well blended.

2. Place the saucepan over low heat. Gradually add the flour and salt, beating well after each addition.

3. Stir in the lemon rind. Gradually add the milk in a slow stream. Stir constantly over low heat until the mixture thickens.

4. Beat in the Mistra.

5. Turn the mixture out onto a marble slab or baking sheet, and chill until set.

6. Heat the oil in a deep skillet to 375°.

7. Cut the chilled mixture into diamond shapes, and lightly coat with flour, dip into beaten egg, then coat with breadcrumbs.

8. Drop the pieces into the hot oil, and cook until golden. Drain on paper towels. Serve hot.

Saint Valentine's Day

RICE TIMBALE WITH SAFFRON
8 SERVINGS

> ³/₄ cup unseasoned breadcrumbs
> 4 tablespoons unsalted butter
> 2 cups Arborio rice (Italian long-grain rice)
> ¹/₄ teaspoon saffron
> 4 cups hot chicken broth
> 6 tablespoons grated Parmesan cheese

Preheat the oven to 350° F.

1. Butter a 7-inch, deep angel food cake pan or a ring form, and coat with breadcrumbs.

2. Heat 2 tablespoons of the butter in a deep saucepan over medium-low heat; when it is golden, stir in the rice. Keep stirring until each grain is coated, about 3 minutes.

3. Dissolve the saffron in 2 tablespoons of the broth.

4. Add ½ cup of hot broth to the rice, stirring. Cook over medium-low heat until the broth is absorbed. Repeat, adding broth ½ cup at a time and stirring until the broth is used up.

5. Add the saffron mixture after the rice has absorbed all the broth, about 20 minutes. The rice should be tender but still somewhat firm, or al dente. Add the Parmesan cheese. Let stand until cool.

6. Fill the ring form with the cooled rice. Dot with the remaining butter. Put the ring in a larger pan, and fill it with boiling water to come halfway up the sides of the ring.

7. Bake 30 to 40 minutes on the middle rack of the oven.

8. Let stand a few minutes on a cooling rack, then carefully unmold onto a serving plate. Fill the center of the ring wih mushroom sauce, fresh spring peas, or asparagus tips.

OSSOBUCO MILANESE
6 SERVINGS

> 2 tablespoons unsalted butter
> 2 tablespoons olive oil
> 1 small onion
> ¼ cup all-purpose flour
> Salt and freshly ground black pepper, to taste
> Six 2-inch-thick veal shanks, cut across the bone
> 1 cup dry white wine
> 1½ cups chicken broth
> 2 cloves garlic
> 1 cup parsley sprigs

1. Heat the butter and olive oil in a heavy, flameproof casserole large enough to hold the veal shanks comfortably. Over moderate heat brown the whole onion, turning it; then discard it.

2. Spread the flour on a sheet of wax paper, and add the salt and pepper. Lightly flour each *ossobuco*.

3. Over medium-high heat, brown the *ossibuchi* in the casserole, turning them to brown evenly. If they start to curl, cut through the skin with a sharp knife.

4. Raise the heat to high and pour in the wine; cook briskly until the wine evaporates. Add enough broth to cover. Bring to a boil, reduce the heat to low, cover, and simmer for 1 hour.

5. Chop the garlic and parsley together until very fine. Ten minutes before serving, add to the *ossibuchi*, and mix well.

BROCCOLI RABE
6 TO 8 SERVINGS

> *3 pounds fresh broccoli rabe*
> *½ cup olive oil*
> *2 cloves garlic, minced*
> *Salt and freshly ground black pepper, to taste*
> *1 teaspoon fresh lemon juice*

1. Rinse the *rabe*. Cut off the tough stalks and remove the large, tough leaves. Drop into boiling salted water and cook 5 minutes. Drain thoroughly. (Save some of this water to use in the skillet for a more liquid version.) Chop the *rabe*.

2. Put the olive oil in a large skillet over moderate heat and add the garlic, salt, pepper, lemon juice, and chopped *rabe*. Cook, turning frequently, until tender.

CANNOLI WITH MASCARPONE FILLING
YIELD: 12 CANNOLI

> *¾ pound cream cheese*
> *¾ pound ricotta cheese*
> *2 tablespoons heavy cream*
> *Juice of ½ lemon*
> *1 tablespoon sugar*
> *⅓ cup Candied Orange Peel (see recipe, page 000)*
> *¼ cup chopped pistachio nuts*
> *¼ cup chocolate chips*
> *12* cannoli *shells*

1. To make the *mascarpone* filling, mix the cream cheese, ricotta cheese, cream, lemon juice, and sugar in a blender until smooth and creamy.

2. Add the orange peel, nuts, and chocolate chips. Refrigerate until ready to serve.

3. Just before serving, fill the *cannoli* shells from one end and then the other, pressing in gently with a spatula to fill the center.

Fat Tuesday

CRESPELLE (*Italian Crêpes*)
YIELD: 18 CRÊPES

BATTER

> *1¼ cups milk*
> *1¼ cups all-purpose flour*
> *3 tablespoons olive oil*
> *3 eggs*
> *⅛ teaspoon salt*
> *1 to 2 tablespoons unsalted butter*

FILLING

2 tablespoons unsalted butter
½ pound mushrooms, stems trimmed and sliced
Salt and freshly ground black pepper, to taste
⅔ cup milk
10 ounces fontina cheese, cut in small pieces
1 ounce gorgonzola cheese, crumbled
2 egg yolks
¼ cup milk
¼ cup grated Parmesan cheese

1. To make the batter, put the milk in a medium bowl, and gradually sift in the flour. Beat with a fork or whisk until all the flour is blended in. Add the olive oil, eggs, and salt, beating until thoroughly mixed. Let stand 2 to 3 hours at room temperature or overnight in the refrigerator.

2. Put ½ teaspoon of the butter in a heavy 8-inch skillet, and melt it over moderate heat. Tilt and rotate the pan so that the bottom is evenly coated with butter.

3. Stir the batter. Pour 2 tablespoons, all at once, into the center of the pan. Quickly lift the pan from the heat and tip it in several directions with a circular motion, so that the batter covers the bottom completely.

4. Return the skillet to the heat. Cook until the pancake has set and turned a pale brown on the bottom side. Turn it with a spatula and brown it very lightly on the other side. Transfer to a platter.

5. Coat the bottom of the skillet with ¼ teaspoon of melted butter and proceed as in step 3 until all the batter is used up. Preheat the oven to 425° F.

6. To make the filling, put the butter in a skillet over moderate heat. Cook the mushrooms, seasoned with salt and pepper, 2 to 3 minutes. Set aside.

7. Heat the milk in the top of a double boiler over simmering water.

Blend in the fontina and gorgonzola cheeses, stirring until they melt. Beat the egg yolks in a bowl, and add ¼ cup of the cheese mixture; beat vigorously. Pour back into the cheese mixture and cook, stirring constantly, 3 to 4 minutes. Remove from the heat.

8. Take ½ cup of the cheese mixture, and combine it with the mushrooms. Add the milk to the remaining cheese mixture, and mix well.

9. Spread 1 tablespoonful of the mushroom-cheese mixture on each pancake. Roll up and place, seam side down, in a 9 × 12-inch baking dish.

10. Spoon on the cheese sauce and sprinkle with the Parmesan cheese.

11. Bake 15 minutes, or until the top is browned.

VEAL ROAST WITH MUSTARD SAUCE
6 TO 8 SERVINGS

> 2 pounds top round or boned rolled shoulder of
>   veal
> 3 cloves garlic, minced
> 1 teaspoon minced rosemary leaves
> ¼ teaspoon crushed black peppercorns
> 2 tablespoons olive oil
> 2 tablespoons unsalted butter

MUSTARD SAUCE
> 2 tablespoons chopped onion
> 6 tablespoons chopped parsley
> 6 tablespoons unsalted butter, softened
> 4 tablespoons Dijon mustard
> 1 cup dry white wine
> Pan drippings

1. With a small, sharp knife, cut 1-inch slits in the veal.

2. Mix together the garlic, rosemary, and peppercorns. Insert a little of the mixture into the slits cut in the meat.

3. Put the olive oil and butter in a heavy, flameproof casserole over medium-high heat. Brown the veal, turning it with wooden spoons so that it browns evenly. Reduce the heat to low and cook, partially covered, for 2 hours or until the meat registers 160° F on a meat thermometer. Turn the veal occasionally. If it seems to be sticking, add 1 tablespoon water.

4. To make the mustard sauce, blend the onion, parsley, butter, and mustard. Set aside.

5. When the roast has finished cooking, remove it to a warmed platter. Pour the wine into the casserole over high heat and deglaze, scraping up the browned bits with a wooden spoon. Stir frequently, and continue cooking until the liquid has reduced to a rich sauce.

6. Stir in the onion mixture, and cook 2 minutes.

7. To serve, slice the meat, and arrange it on a serving board or platter. Pour the mustard sauce over the sliced veal.

SAUTÉED SAVOY CABBAGE
6 SERVINGS

3 to 4 tablespoons olive oil
4 cloves garlic
1 medium head Savoy cabbage, shredded and core
    discarded
2 tablespoons light soy sauce
Freshly ground black pepper, to taste

1. Heat the oil in a large skillet. Cook the garlic, stirring, over moderate heat until soft and golden, then discard it.

2. Stir in the cabbage and sauté quickly, tossing, until it wilts and

133

reduces in volume. Add the soy sauce. Cover and cook over medium-low heat until tender, about 15 minutes. If the cabbage starts to stick to the pan, add 1 to 2 tablespoons water.

3. Add a few grindings of pepper to the cooked cabbage, and serve immediately.

BAKED PEARS AND GINGER CREAM
8 SERVINGS

> *8 firm Bosc pears*
> *1⅛ cups sugar*
> *One 3-inch stick cinnamon*
> *3 cloves*
> *2 cups dry red wine*

GINGER CREAM
> *½ pint heavy cream, whipped*
> *1 teaspoon sugar*
> *1 tablespoon grated fresh ginger or 1 teaspoon dried*
> *ginger*

Preheat the oven to 350° F.

1. Peel the pears with a vegetable peeler, leaving the stems on.

2. Mix the sugar, cinnamon, cloves, and wine in a shallow baking dish. Place the pears in the baking dish, turning to coat them evenly with the mixture.

3. Bake on the middle rack of the oven until tender, about 50 minutes. Baste and turn the pears frequently.

4. Mix the sugar and ginger into the whipped cream.

5. Serve the pears warm or chilled, topped with the flavored whipped cream.

CARNIVAL FRITTERS (*Castagnole*)
YIELD: 18 FRITTERS

> *1 cup hot water*
> *8 tablespoons unsalted butter*
> *1 tablespoon sugar*
> *½ teaspoon salt*
> *1 cup sifted all-purpose flour*
> *4 eggs*
> *1 teaspoon freshly grated orange rind*
> *1 teaspoon freshly grated lemon rind*
> *4 cups peanut oil*
> *Confectioners' sugar*

1. Combine the water, butter, sugar, and salt in a small saucepan. Bring to a boil. When the butter is melted, add the flour. Stir vigorously with a whisk until the mixture leaves the sides of the pan, a matter of seconds. Remove from the heat and cool slightly.

2. Add the eggs, 1 at a time, beating vigorously with a spoon after each addition. Add the grated orange and lemon rinds. Mix thoroughly until smooth.

3. In a deep skillet heat the peanut oil to 300° F (the temperature is important because if the oil is too hot, the fritters will cook too fast on the outside and not puff up.)

4. Drop the batter by the tablespoonful into the hot oil, no more than 4 or 5 at a time. When the fritters are browned and puffed, remove them with a slotted spoon, drain on paper towels, and sprinkle with confectioners' sugar.

Four

MARCH

Ash Wednesday

Ash Wednesday is the first day of Lent, and its name reflects the ancient ceremony, introduced around 600 by Pope Gregory I, of tracing a sign of the cross with blessed ashes on the foreheads of the faithful. The sign was a token of contrition and penance, and a reminder of death, which comes to all as the natural end of life. The Christians of the so-called Dark Ages were mindful of death and tried to live so as to guarantee a holy one. The ashes used in the ceremony come from burning the palms that were consecrated on Palm Sunday of the previous year.

Pope Gregory I, called Gregory the Great, was a former Benedictine monk who during his reign (590 to 604) consolidated the supremacy of the Roman patriarchate into the still enduring papal system. He also instituted monastic orders and dispatched Saint Augustine on his mission to convert England to Christianity. Gregory was great, too, in the legends he bequeathed. The first year of his reign, when plague broke out in Rome, Pope Gregory ordered processions through the streets of the stricken city to plead for God's intercession. Returning to Saint Peter's, Gregory saw a vision of the Archangel Michael on the summit of what was left of Hadrian's tomb. The angel was brandishing his unsheathed sword, which the pope took as a sign that the plague would cease. When it did, Gregory had a chapel built on the spot where the archangel had appeared and gave the site the name by which it has been known ever since, Castel Sant'Angelo. It was the military stronghold of Rome for almost a thousand years.

It was first decreed at the Council of Nicaea, in 325, that Easter should be observed on the first Sunday following the first full moon after the vernal equinox. This makes Easter a moveable feast rather than a fixed one as Christmas is, and it can occur between March 22 and April 25. The date of Easter then determines the other moveable feasts: Ash Wednesday, Ascension Sunday, and Pentecost. Ash Wednesday opens the penitential season of Lent, signifying the end of Carnival revels, and can fall between February 4 and March 11. Fasting and abstinence are the new order; meals become simple if not meager.

"Ash Wednesday" is the title T. S. Eliot gave to the first poem of his to celebrate the peace to be found in orthodox religion. It has been called a poetic liturgy, a meditation on the storing-up of grace for the life to come, and an approach to mystical communion with God. A medieval meditation recorded by scholar Giovanni

Papini, sums up the fleetingness of human life in six words, the last of which is ashes:

HOMO? HUMUS
FAMA? FUMUS
FINIS? CINIS

Man's life is a brief transformation of the earth of which he's composed into the final ashes he becomes, and between the beginning and the end is only the brief moment of ephemeral spiraling smoke, which for some is called fame.

Lent

There were no Carnivals in my life when I was growing up in Syracuse, but I certainly remember Lent. It was a period for "giving up" a particular pleasure as a sign of penitence and sticking to that renunciation for the forty days preceding Easter. It could be abstaining from desserts or from eating snacks between meals, or, hardest of all for me, giving up going to the movies on Saturday afternoon. This giving up of what was so pleasurable was the whole point of the spiritual exercise, and the harder it was, the more grace one accumulated. Lent toughened the spirit, made one reflect on values, and symbolized a retreat from things of the world. It had its own rigorous appeal. Lent was a time for taking stock of oneself, and when I was a student at The Convent School, we had special spiritual retreats for this time of year.

Historically, fasting was more grueling than it is now, when there is only a minimal reduction in food, with, at most, abstinence from meat on Wednesdays and Fridays. The Lenten period was begun in imitation of Jesus' fast in the desert, which lasted forty days. Early Christian observance was very strict, a deliberate test of commitment and self-renunciation.

The early observance was for the faithful to abstain from "flesh meat and from all things that come from flesh, such as milk, eggs, cheese, and butter." Again, it was Pope Gregory the Great who formulated the rule. These early Christians restricted themselves to only one meal per day, which they took in the evening. Gradually, the severity of fasting diminished, and now it is mostly symbolic, although some voluntarily retain the old, strict ways.

Is it perhaps a relic of old sexist attitudes that in Italy *Carnevale* is represented as an indulgent fat man, and *Quaresima*, or Lent, as a scraggly old woman? In some parts of the Abruzzi, her straw figure, pierced with feathers to represent the weeks of Lent, is strung up in town, and on each Saturday a feather is plucked out until she's denuded and cut in two. For mid-Lent the Venetians cremate a big rag doll that symbolizes Lent and dance around it, shouting, *"Bruciano la vecchia"*—"Let the old hag burn!" To symbolize the meager pickings of the period, an effigy in the form of a herring was burned toward the end of Lent. A Lenten vegetable dish is ironically called *cappon magro*, "lean capon," and is meant to pass for the missing meat.

Though Lenten rules are no longer strict (except that no solemn celebration of marriages can take place during this period), it is a good time to cut down on eating after the winter's bounteous feasts, and all folk cultures seem to practice a period of purifying the body as well as the spirit, as witness "spring tonics" and "blood purifiers." Hard biscuits are called *quaresimali* and perhaps meant to signify the austerity of the season, but then, on the other hand, Rome bake shops are also filled with the delicious cream-filled buns called *maritozzi quaresimali*, again named after Lent but not in the least penitential.

Still, an effort is made to cut down on rich foods during the season before Easter; ingenuity is shown in devising egg and pasta dishes; fewer sweets and more fruits are eaten. After all, in the times before canned and frozen foods, it was the period when winter food stores were lowest, so abstinence came naturally. I remember

140

my mother's "goody-good" egg dish at this time of year, and the story of "Stone Soup," that ingenious account of how a delicious soup could be made from a stone and water . . . with, a little help from a touch of this, a pinch of that.

Particularly suitable for Lent are pretzels—the name derives from the Latin word *bracellae*, meaning little arms, and their shape is meant to simulate arms crossed over the chest in prayer. The basic dough of pretzels is flour, water, and salt only, without any shortening, thus highlighting the abstinence of the season. Early Christians used to make small breads during Lent, and then, from Ash Wednesday to Easter, these breads were shaped into crossed arms to remind the fasters that Lent was a time of prayer. It's strange that such a penitential food has become bar food and a universal snack and that the prayerful origins of the item are all but lost to memory.

Instead of making pretzels, my mother used a similar basic dough recipe to make *pizza fritta*, which was a wonderful and simple Lenten treat for my brothers and me. The dough (a basic bread dough, which could also be purchased in a 1-pound lump from the Italian bakery) was torn into pieces and dropped in a kettle of hot oil. The dough swelled up and turned into odd, ragged, golden brown shapes, which were then popped into a brown bag filled with sugar and shaken until they were coated. Eaten fresh and warm like that, they were delectable, and as a sweet, they claim origin in the frugality and imagination of the Italian immigrant.

Over the centuries the rigors of Lent became progressively mitigated: first Sundays became exempt from fasting, then mid-Lent Sunday became a kind of minifestival in itself. Now Saint Joseph's feast day, which has its own delectable specialties and falls about halfway through Lent, has taken over as the midway reprieve until Easter arrives.

My grandfather's name was Giuseppe. He was an old man when I remember him, and someone I couldn't know because he spoke only a few words of English, and I didn't know Italian then; I thought of him as a foreigner, not a grandparent, and I was shy with him the few times, at Christmas, I ever saw him. He would say, "You-a gooda gal?" I'd mumble, "Yes, Grandpa." And he would hand me a nickel. He seemed old, worn-out, poor, betrayed by the vision that had brought him to America and had never given him the elusive prize it seemed to have promised his questing youth. He and all his brothers and sisters, save one, had left their birthplace, the fishing village of Spadafora near Messina, and emigrated to America in the late nineteenth century. Only one brother, Filippo, took a different route when he left Sicily. He went to Rome and got a government job in the Marine Ministry. I met zio Filippo when I first got to Italy, and he was a dignified old man, retired and living on a modest pension, but obviously better off than my grandfather in America had been.

A few years ago, I met the granddaughter of my grandfather's sister, who is, thereby, my father's second cousin, and one of those missing relatives from my father's family whom I never knew. Grace Pizzuto Fahey's recollections of her great-uncle, my grandfather, are more plentiful than mine, for he used to eat often at her grandmother's home, and always on holidays. When his wife died, he lived in a long and affable relationship with a woman whom no one in my family would receive or name because of the stigma attached to such relationships. But Grace's mother was evidently a sensible woman not given to social pressures, and willing to receive her brother and "his woman." Grace even remembers a Lenten dish my grandfather was famous for—*stoccofisso*, a dried cod marinated, then stewed with olives and potatoes, and served with plenty of crusty bread to sop it up.

In my grandfather Grace knew a much different person from the one I remember, and she describes zio Peppino (as she called him) as a handsome, good-time man who dressed well, used snuff, and had an eye for the ladies. He was a romantic who, in reality, held a humble job and made little money, but who saw himself in a different light. Grace said he felt that life and responsibilities kept holding him down. But he loved celebrations, and most of all his name day on March 19, when the Saint Joseph dinner was always in his honor. It seems well suited to his character—that break in the middle of the austerity and penance of Lent, the respite from strict fasting when the joys and good times of Carnival return for one brief day. Pasta with a sardine and fennel sauce was always served. This colorful and abundant Sicilian pasta dish (which in addition to the sardines and fennel includes pine nuts, raisins, and tomato sauce over thick *perciatelli*) is always served with a bread-crumb topping rather than grated cheese. This use may have originated as an economy measure among a poor people but is now ingrained in tradition and is culinarily very sound, since the texture and taste of the roasted crumbs blend extraordinarily well with the sardines. The pasta dish is followed by other fish courses, fresh greens, and egg dishes of all kinds. Italians of other regions mark the break in fasting with their own local specialties, including meat dishes.

Saint Joseph, called in the Gospels "a just man" and honored as the patron of the universal Church, is also the protector of homes and families, so his feast day is a very special holiday and, in the old times in Italy, was a day of "open house," when people came and went, eating from a laden buffet table called the Saint Joseph's table. This is a custom especially dear to Sicilians, for whom the traditional observance of the saint's day is prolonged into a real pageant. In the old days in Sicily, where Saint Joseph is greatly revered as the patron saint of the whole island, there were large public feasts as well as the private open house. Religious tableaux representing the Holy Family were presented in the major squares, and buffet tables were set up for the poor, under the auspices of the rich.

Recently some American churches have begun reviving the Sicilian custom of the Saint Joseph's table on the saint's feast day. Such tables, sponsored by parishioners and the social clubs of descendants from particular Sicilian towns, are open to public viewing and feature spectacular arrays of traditional feast-day specialties. Noted in a newspaper account of a New Jersey church that featured a Saint Joseph's table were these dishes, just a sampling of the whole table: pizza *piena*, pizza *rustica*, *pasticcio* of spinach and meat, *baccalà*, finocchio, onion torta, *ceci* beans, *cuccidate*, oranges, marmalades, *zeppole*, *biscotti*, *cannoli*, rice fritters, ricotta and wheat pie, and, of course, the finest of wines and the traditional blessed breads of Saint Joseph. After the viewing everything is auctioned off, with the proceeds going for charitable activities—and then the feasting begins!

One food especially beloved of Sicilians is *ceci*, or chickpeas, and with this unlikely ingredient they show all the expertise and imagination of a poor people creating miracles out of what is at hand. For Santa Lucia's Day they make a porridge of wheat kernels and chickpeas, known as *cuccia*. For Saint Joseph's Day there is a pastry known as *cuccidate*, with a filling of chickpeas mixed with ground almonds, spices, and orange. The chickpea is so ancient a food, it has been found in neolithic sites. Waverly Root has said that chickpeas and fat put up in amphorae in Pompeii, and then exported throughout the Roman territories, were the pork and beans staple of the ancient world. It was certainly true of my grandfather's Sicilian world.

Saint Joseph's Day is a disarming, Boccaccian paradox: it is a feast of the family but also of that dark underside of the family, unwed mothers; cuckolded husbands; orphans; and the elderly, homeless, and needy. Saint Joseph is also the patron of the poor, and in Italy his feast day is a time to take notice of those who have no family or people to take care of them, much as Christmas or Thanksgiving are here. When we lived in Italy, I always made sure I included anyone far from home or without a place to be for the holiday.

Saint Joseph's feast is both deeply reverent and irreverent; it commemorates the Holy Family through Joseph, the spouse of the Virgin Mary, and stepfather of Jesus, but it also recognizes in a human and tolerant way the deviants from normal home life. In Italy *la sacra famiglia*, "the holy family," has become a term of irony, referring to the once fortresslike Italian family unit. Times have changed, and modernity has enlarged the old family circle; to be focused exclusively on one's immediate family is now considered antiquated and antisocial. Saint Joseph's most recent updating was instituted in 1955 under Pius XII, who termed May 1 the Feast of Saint Joseph the Worker in order to counteract the communist takeover of that laborers' holiday in Europe. Italians integrate everything: communist workers can readily accept Saint Joseph, the carpenter and patron of craftsmen, as their own.

A charming legend about Saint Joseph as the divinely destined spouse of Mary is re-created in the custom of serving a loaf of braided bread with the meal. This loaf is meant to symbolize the omnipresent staff of Saint Joseph, which, according to legend, bloomed with entwined blossoms to single him out from among all her suitors as Mary's spouse-to-be.

My family's other Giuseppes were from the Veneto region: Giuseppe Barolini, Antonio's father, who died when his son was a boy of nine, was a naval officer from a Venetian family of sea captains; Antonio's zio Giuseppe, a Vicenza lawyer who married Antonio's zia Giulia, became his second father, for he and zia Giulia remained childless. Our Saint Joseph's menu always combined something of both Italys, north and south. What could not be left out in some shape or form, however, were the Saint Joseph's pastries.

These puffs or fritters, in fact, begin to appear in Rome long before March 19; they seemed to appear right on the heels of Carnival and Ash Wednesday! Romans easily succumb to indulgence and good times, and postwar affluence has extended the presence of the special Saint Joseph's Day treats into weeks of displays in the windows of bars, *pasticcerie*, and bakeries. There were *sfinge* filled with ricotta and chopped, glazed fruit; *zeppole* (from the verb *zeppare*, "to cram full") filled with huge mounds of whipped cream; sugar-dusted fried *frappé*, and the pastry-cream-filled *bigné*. I well remember their omnipresence in earliest spring as I walked Niki home from her convent school at Trinità dei Monti, and it was impossible for her to get down Via Sistina and across Piazza Barberini without "something for San Giuseppe."

Yes, I always agreed, one must keep up traditions, and so in gratitude for the lightening of the Lenten obligations, and for the beginning of spring, we honored Saint Joseph by eating the treats associated with him.

In contrast with treats and sweets is the other saint I always think of in March: Saint Benedict of the monastic rule. His practice was nettle soup, a speciality, also, of my daughter Susanna, who lives in the Marche region of Italy, outside the beautiful walled town of Urbino. When Susi first wrote to say she had made a soup of *ortiche* (burdocks, or stinging nettles), I thought she was mistaken in what she called them. But then I found that the master, Artusi, also mentions them and that, indeed, it was an ancient monastic practice to make nettle soup, since the picking of the prickly nettles is a penance in itself. Susi had a different view: "Pick the small top leaves of the nettle with gloves on," she wrote me, "or else your appetite to eat anything will be completely gone." Wild spring greens, nettles included, are of course known as a tonic, purifying the blood. Less known, perhaps, is the European saying that you will become beautiful by eating nettles in the spring.

I have not yet picked nettles or thistles for eating, but I did pick wildflowers in the mid-March fields near Strambino when we lived there. On one Saint Joseph's Day, a holiday from work for Antonio, we went to a popular trattoria in Castellamonte. Whole families on holiday were there, sitting at bottle- and food-filled tables for hours, breaking the Lenten fast on this special day of dispensation. I was pregnant at the time, and I remember getting queasy just looking at the plates and mounds of food at all the tables, viewing the eating that went on and on and on until well into the afternoon.

Long before the others, I had finished. I took Linda for a walk down a country path outside of town, where we found a stream and picked wildflowers—yellow primula, violets, snowdrops, wild cyclamen, and a blue flower called Madonna's eyes. Later we gathered some pussywillows and came across a whole meadow of wild croci. I still have those flowers, pressed and framed, a memento of a long-ago Saint Joseph's Day.

Holy Week

Holy Week is a time of sadness and mourning but begins triumphantly on the Sunday before Easter, recalling Christ's entry into Jerusalem accompanied by people bearing palms and crying, "Blessed is He that cometh in the Name of the Lord." Once called Palm Sunday, it is now known as Passion Sunday, and the gospel Passion by Matthew, Mark, or Luke is read during the mass.

In Italy baskets of olive branches as well as palms fill the churches, and the scene of their blessing inside Saint Peter's is truly dazzling: a cardinal arch-priest celebrates mass moving about the magnificent high altar, wearing a purple robe with a long train, surrounded by acolytes in rich gold-embroidered vestments. On one side sit the canons in crimson silk and white ermine capes; opposite them, the monsignori in black tunics, fine white lace, and gray fur capes. The air is filled with incense and music. After the service, golden palms are distributed among the clergy, olive branches to the congregation. Then the cardinal, canons, monsignori, and all the rest go in procession into the piazza, leaving by one door and reentering through another to symbolize the entry of Christ into Jerusalem. There is no doubt about it—it is a grand show. All of Holy Week, as celebrated in Rome, is filled with splendid pageantry. Elsewhere—in Taormina, for instance, where I have also observed it—Holy Week is a folk occasion, simple and moving and filled with the emotion and poetry of the humble. However different, each observance has its place.

Holy Thursday is known as the Mass of the Lord's Supper, and commemorates the Last Supper of Jesus with his disciples. It is also called "Maundy" Thursday from *mandatus*, recalling Christ's great mandate, when, after washing his disciples' feet, he said, "A new commandment give I unto you, that ye love one another." In the Cathedral at Taormina, this ceremony of the washing of the feet took place with the bishop washing the feet of twelve poor men as a sign of humility. In some parts of Europe, it is called Green Thursday, deriving from the green vestments used in the day's liturgy and giving rise to the eating of green vegetables and salads or other green dishes on that day. Another custom, much observed in Rome where the profusion of beautiful churches makes it especially appealing, is the visit to seven different churches (again the magic number, analogous to the seven fish of Christmas Eve).

Good Friday, with *good* meaning "holy," is the commemoration of Christ's crucifixion, and thus the most solemn and reverent day of Holy Week, especially in the hours from noon to three o'clock, which was the time Christ hung on the cross. When I was a child, this was a time when my brothers and I kept silence. And even now it is a time when Italian cities become quiet, when no church bells ring, and traffic seems to disappear. It is, of course, a strict fast day, but it is also a day for hot cross buns, which with their cross of icing recall the crucifixion. A peculiarly Italian bun is one baked with rosemary, a much-used herb from ancient times. The powerful aroma of rosemary was not only a food preservative, but was thought to preserve memory as well: soldiers going to war gave their wives a pouch of the dried herb to remember them by, and Shakespeare gave us Ophelia's words, "There's rosemary, that's for remembrance."

On Good Friday the Stations of the Cross are said in all the churches, but the most spectacular observance is the Via Crucis, staged on the Palatine Hill at night in a procession led by the pope, lighted by a huge flaming cross, and alive with the swaying and dipping of lights from hundreds of candles carried by the multitude of participants. At the basilica of Saint John in Lateran, the devout stand in line all day to ascend on their knees the twenty-eight steps of the Holy Stairway, which is said to be the one Jesus climbed to present himself before Pontius Pilate.

The Good Friday I recall most vividly is the one we spent in Taormina, when we were in Sicily during the children's Easter vacation. The business of that town came to a halt during the evening Good Friday procession down the Corso, the main street in the precipitous, terraced setting overlooking the sea. This was the procession of the *Addolorata*, the anguished Mother of Jesus seeking her crucified son. All the shops and homes were darkened, and on both sides of the Corso, lines of black-robed women held candle-lit lanterns that threw out a wavering red light into the dusk.

Is this searching madonna a reevocation of the grieving Greek goddess Demeter, who sought her abducted daughter, Persephone, throughout the land? It is altogether plausible that the classical myth has melded with the Catholic beliefs in Sicily, for the island was a center of Demeter worship. The historian Lucia Chiavola Birnbaum finds the pre-Easter search of the mother for her son a folk expression of the peasants' reverence for the mother image more than a religious observance. In fact, she notes, the peasants who carry the searching madonna "cause it to waver before entering the Church because the peasant men and women are not certain the Madonna will find her son inside."

In the street below our *pensione* windows, a crowd thickened behind the procession. Between the formation of black-garbed women were little girls in white communion dresses and veils, who bore on silver plates the instruments of Christ's passion—the nails, the whip, the bag of silver pieces for which he was betrayed by Judas. Then came the figures. Christ lay in a glass coffin carried on the shoulders of six young men of Taormina whose heads were ringed with thorns. A band followed, playing Chopin's "Funeral March." Then came the figure of the sorrowing Mary, Mother of God, banked by hundreds of white Easter lilies, a cloth handkerchief in her plaster hands.

It was very touching, and for an hour each year, during this procession to the cathedral, the people of Taormina seemed to reclaim their town from the tourists; Taormina lived in the Good Friday pageant of death.

Holy Saturday eve is called the Easter Vigil, and Saint Augustine called it the "Mother of all Vigils," with ceremonies held after sundown and including blessing of the new fire, procession with the paschal candle, and blessing of holy water, which is called Easter water. In Rome and elsewhere, Holy Saturday is the day for the priest to bless homes and shops with holy water. And in our family it was the day to prepare the Easter eggs for the hunt on Easter morning. In pre-Christian times, eggs were a symbol of spring and fertility. An egg seems lifeless, but it contains life, just as the earth stores life through the winter. In the Christian era, the egg became

150

also the symbol for the rock tomb out of which Christ emerged to make manifest the resurrection to life everlasting. Easter eggs are said to be painted and decorated so colorfully to remind us of the joyousness of this great promise.

Lent
Stracciatella Soup
Juanita Piccoli's Pasta Twists
  with Cauliflower
Syracuse Fish Stew
Green Gnocchi with Sage
  Butter
Baked Zucchini Frittata
Winter Fruit Compote
Pretzel Cookies

Saint Joseph's Day
Pinzimonio Dip
Perciatelli with Sardine and
  Fennel Sauce
Broiled Veal Rolls
Celery Leaf Fritters
Asparagus Parmigiana
Ricotta Puffs

Holy Week—Holy Thursday
Herb Buns
Linda's Lavish Lenten Lasagne

Holy Week—Good Friday
Donna's Grandpa's Best Fish
Sautéed Escarole

Holy Week—Holy Saturday
Ricotta Dip
Pizza Fritta
Aunt Josephine's Easter Egg
  Baskets

Lent

STRACCIATELLA SOUP
6 SERVINGS

6 cups chicken broth
3 eggs
½ cup grated Parmesan cheese
2 tablespoons minced parsley
1 cup cooked rice (optional)
Freshly ground black pepper, to taste

1. In a medium saucepan, bring 5 cups of the chicken broth to a boil.

2. Meanwhile, beat the eggs in a bowl until just blended; add the cheese, parsley, and the remaining cup of broth. Beat well.

3. When the broth is boiling, pour in the egg mixture, stirring constantly with a wire whisk for 1½ minutes. The mixture will form little flakes in the broth. Add rice if desired.

4. Remove the soup from the heat, add a few grindings of pepper, and serve with the remaining grated cheese to pass at the table.

JUANITA PICCOLI'S PASTA TWISTS WITH CAULIFLOWER
6 SERVINGS

> ¼ cup currants
> 1 small cauliflower, broken into florets
> 1 medium onion, chopped
> ½ cup plus 1 tablespoon olive oil
> ¼ cup pine nuts (pignoli)
> 1 pound fusilli (pasta twists)
> 2½ cups Basic Tomato Sauce (see recipe, page 55)
> 1 cup breadcrumbs
> Pinch dried oregano (optional)

1. Soak the currants in warm water to cover for 20 minutes, then drain.

2. Cook the cauliflower until tender but still firm, about 10 minutes; drain.

3. Over moderate heat sauté the onion in ½ cup of the olive oil until soft. Add the cooked cauliflower and coat lightly with the oil. Add the pine nuts and currants. Remove from heat.

4. In boiling, salted water cook the pasta al dente. Drain.

5. Heat the Basic Tomato Sauce; add the sautéed mixture.

6. Heat the remaining tablespoon of oil in a small skillet, add the breadcrumbs, and cook over very low heat, stirring constantly, until golden brown. If desired, add oregano.

7. Drain the pasta and toss with the sauce mixture. Sprinkle the breadcrumb mixture over the pasta.

SYRACUSE FISH STEW
4 TO 6 SERVINGS

1/4 cup olive oil
1 medium onion, minced
2 cloves garlic, crushed
2 stalks celery, chopped
5 to 6 fresh plum tomatoes, chopped, or one 16-
ounce can of tomatoes
1/2 cup dry white wine
1/2 cup water
3 large fresh basil leaves, chopped
4 sprigs parsley, chopped
1 teaspoon salt
1/4 teaspoon freshly ground black pepper
2 pounds squid, cleaned and cut into 1-inch rings
1 dozen mussels, scrubbed, beards removed
1 pound boneless bass, cut into 3-inch pieces
1 pound boneless codfish, cut into 3-inch pieces

1. Place the olive oil in a large skillet over moderate heat. Cook the onion, garlic, and celery until brown, stirring frequently. Stir in the tomatoes, wine, basil, parsley, salt, and pepper. Reduce the heat to medium-low, and simmer for 10 minutes. Add the water.

2. Add the squid to the stew, and simmer for 30 minutes.

3. Add the mussels, bass, and codfish, and simmer until the fish flakes easily at the touch of a fork and has turned opaque; about 15 minutes.

4. Discard any unopened mussels.

5. Serve, accompanied by crusty bread.

GREEN GNOCCHI WITH SAGE BUTTER
4 SERVINGS

1½ pounds fresh spinach or one 10-ounce package
    frozen spinach, thawed
1 cup ricotta cheese, placed in a fine sieve to drain
2 tablespoons unsalted butter, softened
⅔ cup flour
1 egg plus 1 egg yolk, beaten
¾ cup freshly grated Parmesan cheese
Salt and freshly ground black pepper, to taste
Pinch freshly grated nutmeg

SAGE-BUTTER SAUCE

3 tablespoons unsalted butter
6 fresh sage leaves, chopped
¼ cup freshly grated Parmesan cheese

1. If you are using fresh spinach, wash it thoroughly. Cook the spinach about 5 minutes in a pan over moderate heat with only the water clinging to the leaves. Drain the spinach, and squeeze it dry. Chop and set aside.

2. Combine the ricotta cheese, the butter, flour, eggs, Parmesan cheese, salt, pepper, and nutmeg in a medium saucepan. Add the spinach, mix thoroughly, and cook 3 minutes over moderate heat, stirring constantly. Remove from the heat and cool.

3. Pinch off one piece of the spinach-ricotta mixture at a time and shape quickly into a small ball. Dip your fingers in the flour to keep from sticking. Set gnocchi on a sheet of wax paper, and continue until all the mixture has been used.

4. Bring 4 quarts of salted water to a boil, then reduce to a simmer. Put the gnocchi in the water a few at a time, and cook until they surface, about 3 minutes. Remove with a slotted spoon, and place in a warmed serving dish.

5. To make the Sage-Butter Sauce, melt the butter over moderate heat in a small saucepan. Add the sage leaves, and cook 1 minute. Pour over the gnocchi, and sprinkle with the Parmesan cheese.

BAKED ZUCCHINI FRITTATA
4 TO 6 SERVINGS

1 pound zucchini
1 medium onion, chopped
2 tablespoons olive oil
½ teaspoon dried oregano
4 ounces salted dry ricotta cheese
3 eggs, beaten
¼ cup grated Parmesan cheese

Preheat the oven to 375° F.

1. Grease an 8-inch pie plate.

2. Dice the zucchini into ¼-inch pieces, and put in a colander to drain.

3. Place the olive oil in a medium-heavy skillet over moderate heat. When the oil is hot, sauté the onion until soft, stirring often. Add the zucchini and oregano, and cook a few minutes, stirring.

4. Put the mixture in the prepared pie plate. Crumble the ricotta

156

cheese over the mixture. Pour the beaten eggs evenly over the top, then sprinkle with the Parmesan cheese.

5. Bake 45 minutes on the middle rack of the oven, or until the eggs are set.

WINTER FRUIT COMPOTE
4 TO 6 SERVINGS

> 2 Golden Delicious apples
> 1 Anjou pear
> 3 tablespoons fresh lemon juice
> 3 tablespoons unsalted butter
> ¼ cup bitter orange marmalade
> 3 navel oranges

1. Peel the apples and the pear, and cut them into eighths. Toss the slices in a bowl with the lemon juice.

2. Melt 2 tablespoons of the butter in a large skillet over moderate heat. Sauté the apple and pear slices until tender, turning gently. Transfer them to a bowl with a slotted spoon.

3. Add the remaining tablespoon of butter and the marmalade to the skillet. Cook, stirring constantly, until the marmalade melts. Pour mixture over the fruit slices.

4. Peel the oranges, removing all pith and membranes. Separate into segments.

5. Add the orange segments to the bowl and toss gently. Serve immediately.

PRETZEL COOKIES
YIELD: 4 DOZEN

½ pound unsalted butter, softened
2 cups sugar
1 teaspoon anise extract
3 tablespoons whiskey
6 eggs
5½ cups sifted all-purpose flour
1 tablespoon baking powder

1. In a large bowl cream the butter with the sugar until light and fluffy. Stir in the anise extract and whiskey, and beat in the eggs.

2. Sift the flour with the baking powder and stir into the mixture. Blend thoroughly.

3. Shape the dough into 2 logs measuring 2 inches in diameter. Wrap tightly in plastic wrap, and chill overnight.

4. Preheat the oven to 375° F. Grease a baking sheet.

5. Cut the dough logs into ⅜-inch-thick slices. On a lightly floured work surface, roll each slice into a rope about 14 inches long. Bring the ends together and twist them around each other once. Bring the ends back toward the loop and press to seal on both sides of the loop, making a 3-loop pretzel. Repeat with the remaining dough.

6. Place the cookies on the baking sheet 1 inch apart.

7. Bake 15 to 18 minutes, until the bottoms are browned and the tops white and firm to the touch.

8. Cool on a rack.

PINZIMONIO DIP
4 TO 6 SERVINGS

Celery
Fennel
Peppers
Scallions
Cucumber, cut in lengths
Broccoli florets
Rutabaga, sliced thinly in rounds
Artichokes, steamed
½ cup olive oil
Pinch coarse salt (sea or kosher)
Freshly ground black pepper, to taste

1. Clean and prepare the vegetables, cutting them into serving pieces. Put on ice or in ice water to keep crisp.

2. Make the dip by mixing the olive oil, salt, and pepper in a bowl.

PERCIATELLI WITH SARDINE AND FENNEL SAUCE
6 SERVINGS

5 tablespoons olive oil
1 pound fresh sardines
1 clove garlic, minced
2 cups fresh tomatoes or canned Italian plum
    tomatoes, drained, with juice reserved
2 tablespoons tomato paste
1 tablespoon chopped fresh basil leaves, or ½
    teaspoon dried basil

2 cups chopped fresh fennel greens (the feathery tops)
Dash red pepper flakes
Salt and freshly ground black pepper, to taste
1 pound perciatelli *(a thicker, tubelike spaghetti)*
1 tablespoon pine nuts (pignoli*)*
1 cup fine breadcrumbs

1. Heat 2 tablespoons of the oil in a skillet over medium-low heat, and cook the sardines gently, 5 minutes on each side. When they are done, remove them from the pan, split them in half, and remove the bones.

2. Add 2 more tablespoons of the oil to the skillet and return the cooked, boned sardine fillets, along with the garlic. Stir, and cook about 3 minutes over moderate heat.

3. Add the tomatoes and the tomato paste, which has been mixed with the drained juice (if canned tomatoes are used). Season with the basil, fennel greens, red pepper flakes, salt, pepper, and nuts. Cover the skillet, and simmer 30 to 40 minutes.

4. For the topping, heat the remaining tablespoon of oil, add the breadcrumbs, and cook over very low heat until golden brown.

5. Cook the pasta al dente, and drain.

6. To serve, toss the sauce with the pasta, then top with the breadcrumb mixture.

BROILED VEAL ROLLS (*Saltimbocca alla romana*)
6 SERVINGS

1½ pounds veal rump, thinly sliced and cut into
    3-inch squares
¼ pound prosciutto, chopped
1 clove garlic, minced
3 tablespoons grated Parmesan cheese

1 tablespoon minced parsley
Salt and freshly ground black pepper, to taste
3 tablespoons olive oil
1 cup fine breadcrumbs
Pinch fresh rosemary leaves

Preheat the broiler to its highest setting.

1. Spread the squares of veal on a flat work surface.

2. Mix together the prosciutto, garlic, Parmesan cheese, parsley, salt, and pepper.

3. Place 1 teaspoon of the mixture in the center of each square. Roll up the veal, and secure it with a metal skewer.

4. Dip each roll in the olive oil, then in the breadcrumbs.

5. Broil 5 inches from the heat source for 5 minutes. Turn and broil another 5 minutes. Sprinkle with rosemary. Serve immediately.

CELERY LEAF FRITTERS
6 SERVINGS

½ cup water
Pinch salt
⅓ cup all-purpose flour
2 cups chopped celery leaves
Peanut oil for deep frying

1. Put the water in a shallow bowl. Add the salt to the flour, and gradually sift the mixture into the water, beating constantly with a whisk.

2. Add the celery leaves to the batter, and mix well.

3. Heat the oil. (For deep-frying instructions, see Apple Fritters recipe, page 327.) Drop the batter mixture into the oil 1 tablespoon at a time, and cook until brown. Drain on paper towels. Serve hot.

> *3 tablespoons olive oil*
> *1/2 cup sifted all-purpose flour*
> *Pinch salt*
> *12 tablespoons tepid water*
> *1 egg white*
> *2 cups chopped celery leaves*

1. Stir the olive oil into the flour, then add the salt and water and stir until it is the consistency of a smooth cream. Let the mixture stand 2 hours.

2. Just before using the batter, beat the egg white until stiff. Stir it into the batter.

3. Add celery leaves and cook as described in the basic recipe above.

ASPARAGUS PARMIGIANA
6 SERVINGS

> *Salt*
> *2 pounds fresh asparagus*
> *1/2 pound unsalted butter, melted*
> *1/2 cup grated Parmesan cheese*

1. In a pot wide enough to hold the asparagus flat, bring 1 inch of lightly salted water to a boil.

2. Break off the tough ends of the asparagus. Scrape off the scales, and wash the asparagus carefully. Place the spears in the boiling water, partially cover the pot, and cook until tender, about 10 minutes.

3. Preheat the oven to 450° F. Drain the asparagus and put it in a baking dish. Cover with the melted butter, and sprinkle with the cheese.

4. Bake, uncovered, 5 to 10 minutes.

RICOTTA PUFFS
YIELD: 1½ DOZEN

PUFFS

>1 cup hot water
>8 tablespoons unsalted butter
>1 tablespoon sugar
>½ teaspoon salt
>1 cup sifted all-purpose flour
>4 eggs
>1 teaspoon freshly grated orange rind
>1 teaspoon freshly grated lemon rind

FILLING

>1 pound fresh ricotta cheese
>½ cup sugar
>4 ounces unsweetened baking chocolate, grated
>2 tablespoons orange-flavored liqueur, such as Grand
>   Marnier
>¼ cup (1 ounce) Candied Orange Peel, chopped (see
>   recipe, page 48)

1. To make the puffs, preheat the oven to 450° F, and grease a baking sheet.

2. Combine the water, butter, sugar, and salt in a saucepan. Bring to a boil. When the butter melts, add the flour. Stir vigorously with a whisk until the mixture leaves the sides of the pan—a matter of seconds. Remove from the heat and cool slightly.

3. Add the eggs, one at a time, and beat vigorously with a spoon after each addition. Add the grated rinds. Mix thoroughly until the mixture is smooth. Drop by tablespoonfuls 2 inches apart on the prepared baking sheet.

4. Bake for 15 minutes. Lower the heat to 350° F, and bake for 15 to 20 minutes. Cool.

5. To make the filling, beat the ricotta cheese until light and fluffy. Drain it if necessary to remove excess liquid.

6. Add the sugar, chocolate, and liqueur. Beat until the mixture is creamy.

7. Stir in the Candied Orange Peel.

8. To assemble the Ricotta Puffs, split the puffs open and fill them.

Holy Week—Holy Thursday

HERB BUNS
YIELD: 2 DOZEN

> 1 1/4 cups lukewarm water
> 1 package active dry yeast
> 8 teaspoons sugar
> 1 teaspoon salt
> 3/4 cup olive oil
> 4 to 4 1/2 cups all-purpose flour
> 3/4 cup golden raisins
> 6 minced fresh sage leaves, or 3 tablespoons minced
>   fresh rosemary leaves

1. Pour the water into a large bowl, and sprinkle the yeast into the water. Stir in 2 teaspoons of the sugar, and let stand until frothy.

2. Add the salt and ¼ cup of the oil. Gradually mix in 3½ cups of the flour.

3. Toss the raisins with ½ cup of the flour, and add them to the dough.

4. Turn the dough out onto a lightly floured work surface, and knead it until smooth and elastic, about 10 minutes. Add more flour as necessary to make a fairly stiff dough.

5. Place the dough in a greased bowl, turning to coat it well. Cover it with a damp towel, and let the dough rise in a draft-free spot until doubled in bulk, about 1½ hours.

6. Return the risen dough to the lightly floured surface. Poke a hole in the dough, and pour the remaining oil into it; sprinkle in the sage or rosemary. Knead gently to disperse the oil, then knead for about 5 minutes to work the oil and sage thoroughly into the dough.

7. Form 24 buns, and place them about 1½ inches apart on un-greased baking sheets. Cover lightly with plastic wrap and let rise until almost doubled in bulk, about 1 hour.

8. Preheat the oven to 425° F. With a sharp knife gently cut a cross into the top of each bun. Sprinkle with the remaining sugar.

9. Bake for 10 minutes, then reduce the heat to 375° F and continue baking until the buns are golden brown, about 10 minutes.

LINDA'S LAVISH LENTEN LASAGNE
6 SERVINGS

1½ pounds fresh pasta sheets

SPINACH FILLING

2 pounds fresh spinach, cooked, or two 10-ounce
packages frozen spinach, thawed
2 cloves garlic
2 tablespoons pine nuts (pignoli)
¼ cup olive oil
½ teaspoon salt
¼ teaspoon freshly ground black pepper

BALSAMELLA SAUCE

4 cups milk
8 tablespoons unsalted butter

½ cup all-purpose flour
½ teaspoon freshly grated nutmeg
½ teaspoon salt
Freshly ground black pepper, to taste

CHEESE MIXTURE

1½ pounds ricotta cheese
½ pound mozzarella, shredded
⅔ cup plus 3 tablespoons grated Parmesan cheese

1. Fresh pasta can be used without previous cooking.

2. To make the spinach filling, drain the spinach, and squeeze or press out as much water as you can. In a blender or food processor purée the spinach, garlic, pine nuts, and olive oil. Add the salt and pepper; mix well. Set aside.

3. To make the *balsamella*, or white, sauce, scald the milk in a small saucepan; do not let it boil. In a larger saucepan melt the butter over moderate heat, add the flour, and whisk together 1 minute. Reduce the heat to medium-low. Stir in the nutmeg, salt, and pepper, then add the milk, a little at a time. Cook, stirring constantly, until the mixture thickens. Set aside.

4. To make the cheese mixture, combine the ricotta cheese, mozzarella, and ⅔ cup of the Parmesan cheese in a medium bowl.

5. Preheat the oven to 350° F. Cover the bottom of a large baking pan evenly with a thin layer of white sauce. Cover with a layer of pasta.

6. Follow with thin layers of spinach filling, white sauce, and the cheese mixture. Repeat, making 3 to 4 layers and finishing with a pasta layer. Spread the last of the white sauce on the pasta.

7. Sprinkle the remaining 3 tablespoons of Parmesan cheese evenly on the lasagne.

8. Bake 30 minutes on the middle rack of the oven, or until the top is a golden brown. Let the lasagne rest 5 to 10 minutes before serving.

Holy Week—Good Friday

DONNA'S GRANDPA'S BEST FISH
4 SERVINGS

> *¼ cup all-purpose flour*
> *Pinch salt*
> *Freshly ground black pepper, few twists of the mill*
> *4 fillets of sole (about 1 pound)*
> *¼ cup olive oil*
> *2 tablespoons unsalted butter*
> *1 clove garlic, minced*
> *Juice of 1 lemon*
> *¼ cup chopped parsley*

1. Mix the flour, salt, and pepper on a sheet of wax paper. Lightly dust the fillets with the seasoned flour on both sides.

2. Pour the olive oil into a large skillet over medium-high heat. When it is hot, fry the fillets, turning once. Remove to a warmed platter.

3. Add the butter to the skillet, and fry the garlic until golden.

4. Add the lemon juice and parsley. Pour the sauce over the fish, and serve immediately.

SAUTÉED ESCAROLE
6 SERVINGS

2 pounds escarole
¼ cup olive oil
1 large clove garlic, cut in slivers
Salt and freshly ground black pepper, to taste

1. Wash the escarole, removing any old and bruised leaves. Drain it, and tear leaves in pieces. Put the escarole in a steamer and steam, covered for 10 minutes.

2. Heat the oil in a large skillet over moderate heat; sauté the garlic until limp, then discard it. Add the drained escarole, salt, and pepper and cook, covered, 10 minutes.

Holy Week—Holy Saturday

RICOTTA DIP
YIELD: 2 CUPS

1 pound ricotta cheese
2 tablespoons red wine vinegar
Salt and freshly ground black pepper, to taste
2 tablespoons fresh basil leaves
3 tablespoons parsley
2 scallions
Carrots
Celery
Fennel
Radishes

1. Purée the ricotta cheese, vinegar, salt, and pepper in a blender or food processor.

2. Remove the purée to a serving bowl. Put the basil, parsley, and scallions in the blender or food processor, and chop.

3. Mix with the ricotta purée.

4. Serve with fresh raw vegetables, such as carrots, celery, fennel, and radishes.

PIZZA FRITTA
8 TO 10 SERVINGS

1 pound bread dough, purchased at an Italian
*   bakery*
1 quart peanut oil for frying
¼ cup sugar

1. Pour oil to a depth of 1 inch in a deep skillet over medium-high heat. Pinch off a small piece of dough, and immerse it in the oil to test the temperature—the dough should float to the surface in less than a minute and take on a golden color.

2. Break off pieces of dough, and immerse several at a time in the hot oil. When they rise to the surface, turn over with vegetable tongs, and let brown all over.

3. Drain on paper towels. Toss in a bag with the sugar. Eat warm.

AUNT JOSEPHINE'S EASTER EGG BASKETS
YIELD: 1 DOZEN

5 cups sifted all-purpose flour
1 cup sugar
5 teaspoons baking powder
½ teaspoon salt
1 cup vegetable shortening

4 eggs, beaten
1 teaspoon vanilla extract
12 eggs, hard-cooked and colored

FROSTING

1 pound confectioners' sugar
¼ cup vegetable shortening
1 teaspoon almond extract
Water or milk for binding
Multicolored sprinkles
Vegetable food coloring

Preheat the oven to 375° F.

1. Grease a 12-cup muffin tin or two 6-cup tins.

2. Sift together the flour, sugar, baking powder, and salt into a large bowl. Cut in the shortening with a pastry blender or 2 knives until the mixture resembles coarse cornmeal. Make a well in the center; drop in the beaten eggs and vanilla. Mix with a fork until the dough is smooth and pulls away from the sides of the bowl.

3. With floured hands gather up the dough and form it into a ball.

4. On a lightly floured work surface, roll the dough out to ½-inch thickness. Cut the dough into 3-inch rounds to fit into the muffin cups. Line the cups with the rounds, pressing gently to make them fit. Place 1 colored egg in the center of each cup.

5. Cut twenty-four 3-inch strips from the leftover dough. (You may have to gather up the pieces and roll them out again.) Form handles by placing 2 strips, crisscross fashion, over each egg. Press the ends of the strips into the lining pastry to seal the edges.

6. Bake in the center of the oven until lightly browned, 15 to 20 minutes. Cool 5 to 10 minutes on a rack before removing the baskets from the muffin tin, then cool thoroughly.

7. To make the frosting, combine the confectioners' sugar with the shortening, the almond extract, and enough water or milk to

make a smooth paste. Divide into several cups and add a few drops of food coloring for several colored frostings. Frost the baskets, and decorate the sides and handles with colored sprinkles. With the remaining frosting, pipe the names of family and friends on the baskets, using a pastry tube.

Five

APRIL

April Fools' Day

April—the word deriving from the Latin verb *aperire* and the Italian *aprire*, "to open"—signifies the opening to spring. It refers both to the earth, which in this month is opened to receive seed, and to the opening of buds into flowers. Yet as T. S. Eliot said in his familiar line, "April is the cruellest month." Cyril Connolly's explanation is that spring is a call to action, hence to disillusion. But what it starts with is tomfoolery.

173

April 1 is known as a day when practical jokes are in order, and the butt of the joke is an April fool—except in Italy or in France, where the "fool" is a "fish." It's said that the term "April fish" was jokingly applied to the recalcitrants who stuck to the old ways and dates rather than accept the calendar reform that replaced March 25 as New Year's Day and eliminated April 1 as the culmination of New Year's festivities, when one played the last jokes of the season. In general, anyone easily fooled was an April fish. Irreverently, Napoleon's subjects called him *poisson d'Avril* when he married his second wife, Marie-Louise of Austria, on April 1, 1810—and perhaps history has borne this out. Still, it is curious that the image of the fish has been reversed, as it were, to connote a fool. Earlier, the fish was associated with monks, the educated and thinking class of medieval times, for they ate great quantities of it, and thus it was thought of as "brain food."

April fish, the Italian *pesce d'aprile*, begin to appear in March in all the sweet shops as chocolate fish. In their glittery colored wrappings alongside the spectacular Easter eggs of the season, they made tempting displays. On one April 1, I prepared an all-sweet dinner for Niki, who was the pickiest of eaters at the dinner table but the most gluttonous of chocolate in the entire family. At her place an edible confectionary frying pan held chocolate fish, marzipan sugar peas and carrots, a candy egg, and even bread that was chocolate-coated nougat. "I'm glad I'm the April fool!" she said.

Even in the austere days of postwar Italy in the late forties, when sheep could still be seen pasturing in Rome's empty lots on the upper Via Nomentana (where I had a room in the apartment of an impoverished duchess); when the streets of downtown were full of gypsies asking for ten lire; when we riders hung precariously on the overloaded steps of jammed buses—even then the store windows were full of chocolate fish and eggs for the Easter season.

On April 1, 1949, I was sitting in the sun at an outdoor café on the Via della Conciliazone. It is the wide, modern avenue leading to Saint Peter's, which the Fascist government bulldozed through a very old and distinctive section known as the Borgo in order to commemorate their concordat with the Vatican. Formerly, twisting, picturesque streets and exquisite Renaissance façades had surrounded Saint Peter's, and I was trying to imagine the emotion and stunned surprise one would feel emerging from the warren of Borgo alleyways right into the splendor of Bernini's colonnade, fronted by the majesty of the great church and the mysteriousness of the Vatican.

Intruding into my thoughts came the real-life spectacle of a self-proclaimed new messiah, who was walking barefoot away from Saint Peter's to a waiting limousine in front of one of the many souvenir shops that line the street. The woman accompanying him (described by the newspaper I was even then reading as the virgin mother of four children) was swathed in blue material and walked with a lowered gaze and studied reverent air at his 6-foot, 3-inch side. He had come to Saint Peter's for an interview with the current pope, since three other popes in this messiah's alleged 2,000-year life span had granted such. He was quoted as being much sorrowed at the change in the Colosseum, which had been all marble and thronged with people the last time he saw it. He was staying on Via Veneto, at the Grand Hotel, and was supported by the 80,000 Americans at home who believed in him. A cartoon in the Rome paper showed him with the caption, "Is *He* part of the Marshall Plan?" The people in Saint Peter's Square that April 1 were having great fun with the messiah, running from cafés and shops to stare at him and calling out *pesce d'aprile*—April fish—to him. All this before the days of gurus and maharishis: *plus ça change, plus c'est la même chose*.

When we lived in Strambino, near Ivrea, I remember remarking on the flood of chocolate fish, roosters, and eggs that stuffed the *tabacchi* and stationers' windows, the bars, the newspaper stands, and the groceries. When I asked Antonio how the store owners managed to sell it all, he replied ironically that they melted down the unsold Christmas chocolates right after Befana to use for Easter sweets. Thus I learned the expression, *cioccolato d'uova*, or egg-chocolate, to pertain to anything that is not choice grade.

The fish graffiti that appeared on town walls reminded me of the secret signs early Christians in Cecil B. De Mille's biblical films used to scratch on catacomb walls for clandestine meetings. The fish was used as a symbol of Christ because the same five Greek letters forming the word fish (*icthus*) are the initial letters in the phrase, Jesus Christ, Son of God, Savior. Thus the fish symbol alone could be used to summarize the faith of the early Christians. Again, one of Christ's miracles was the multiplying of the fish and loaves, and he exhorted his disciples, many of them fishermen, to be "fishers of men."

Also chalked on walls in a more direct message was the scrawl *"Chi legge questo è scemmo"*—"whoever reads this is a fool." And at home Rosetta would tell of extravagant orders for chamomile tea or yogurt being telephoned into bars for delivery to addresses that then turned out to be nonexistent—the typical fool's errand of the day.

Curiously, the "fool's errand" may be a relic of the Roman festa, Cerealia, held in mid-April. The legend of Proserpina is embodied, of course, in the whole springtime ritual of rebirth and reflowering. The legend goes that Proserpina was sporting in the flowering meadows of springtime Sicily when Pluto saw her and carried her off to the lower world as his bride. Her mother, Ceres (originally the ancient Italic Mother Earth, the personification of the fruits of the harvest, and the protectress of agriculture, and then later identified with the Greek Demeter, goddess of grain and abundance), heard the screams and went in search of the voice, but in vain. From this, it's said, comes the common April Fools' Day prank of sending someone on a fool's errand.

In the Olympian myth Persephone (of whom the Roman counterpart is Proserpina) was the wife of Hades (Pluto) and queen of the infernal regions. As the personification of seasonal changes, she passed six months of the year on Olympus and six in Hades; while on Olympus she was beneficent, but in Hades she was stern and terrible.

In pre-Hellenic mythology, however, there is another, earlier, more positive version. In *Lost Goddesses of Early Greece*, Charlene Spretnak addresses the whole question of female deities in the ancient world and their transformation by a patriarchal society into a lot of vain, envious, complaining and quarreling female shrews or victims who always seem to be seeking revenge on the male gods or mortals. Paleolithic documentation shows the oldest god-head in "the cult of the Mother Goddess," that is, women as "the spring and harbor of life." The Demeter-Persephone sacred story of mother and daughter is extremely ancient, certainly pre-Olympian, and long predates the Judeo-Christian deification of father and son.

Rather than the violent abduction and rape perpetrated on Persephone by Hades, who forcibly made her his queen in the underworld, the more ancient account has Persephone going into the underworld to be queen of the dead of her own volition in order to initiate the drifting and purposeless dead souls into tranquillity and wisdom. Just as death is part of living, so the dark world is the other side of the bright world of flowering plants and sun and life. Demeter and Persephone complement each other, and each spring Persephone returns to her mother, who expresses her joy through the earth's flowering. And when Persephone returns to the realm of the dead, so Demeter mourns, and the earth stops bearing its fruits.

It is a beautiful tale of sacrifice and redemption. Festivals in pre-Homeric Greece, a time that precedes the supremacy of warrior gods like Zeus and Apollo and the reduction in the power of the great goddess, were celebrated in memory of the sorrows and joys of Demeter and Persephone. Secret women-only rites were practiced to celebrate the mysteries of Demeter-Persephone, and the culminating episode of the holy pageant was the showing of an ear of grain: "that great and marvelous mystery of perfect revelation, a cut stalk of grain," according to mythologist Joseph Campbell, who likens it to the raising of the wafer-host at mass, the wafer being made of flour from grain. Again is revealed the sacredness of grain, which was the gift of the great goddess to humankind.

Spring, when Persephone returns and flowers the land, always reminds me of the time we lived in Strambino, in the country, before we lived in Rome. There was something very sweet about the simplicity of life in Strambino; its very lack of excitation meant that life was orderly and predictable. The view from our windows was to the eternal Alps, majestic and not about to be replaced with condominium towers. There was a sequence and inevitability to works and days; one looked about and saw the past, and everything seemed to flow from it. It was not displaced in the rush and the rash of tearing down and replacing that seems endemic in an impatient, forward-facing America.

On my last Sunday in Strambino, I looked from the terrace to the Campo Sportivo below, and it was like a Seurat painting—all pointillism of delicate spring colors. The great plane trees that lined the walkway were not yet in full leaf but only a cloud of tender chartreuse buds; near the pine trees, children were scampering about, gathering bouquets of violets, daisies, buttercups, forget-me-nots. The Strambinese were strolling in their one-day-a-week outfits, their Sunday promenade taking them to signora Maria's kiosk in the far corner for an ice, a juice, an espresso, a chance to see and be seen.

We were returning to the States, where Antonio's post as U.S. correspondent for *La Stampa* called us, and I knew there would be other beautiful springs in other places. Nothing, however, would be like the bucolic view of life that was Strambino, as has proved true.

178

Easter Sunday

Once the word *Easter* was thought to have come from the name of the Anglo-Saxon goddess of spring, Eastre. Now the thinking is that it derives from the Old High German *eostarun*, or dawn, which comes from the East, as the word suggests. Either derivation, I think, fits the season, for it is both spring and, after the darkness of winter, it is dawn. The Italian word for Easter, however, is *Pasqua*, which retains a connection to *pasch*, the word for the Jewish Passover deriving from *pesach*, a Hebrew verb meaning to jump or pass over, thus emphasizing the Judeo-Christian tradition.

In my Catholic childhood, an important observation of the Easter season was fulfilling one's Easter duty—that is, the obligation to confess one's sins and to receive Holy Communion at least this one time during the year. By ancient custom it is also a day for making peace. People who have been on the outs during the year try to make up at this time. In this spirit one Easter we had our five-year-old daughter Niki baptized into the Christian community at the Anglo-American church of Saint George in Taormina when we were on holiday there.

The symbol of peace, the dove, gives form to the traditional sweet bread, the *colomba pasquale*, which is to Easter what panettone is to Christmas. And as with the panettone, the *colomba* is something we go out to buy—for the fun of visiting the confectioners' shops, where all manner of sweets can be found, including sugar lambs, couchant, bearing Christ's flag of victory between their forelegs; or the extremely decorative, murderously sweet Sicilian cream cakes.

Easter is so triumphal! It is the single most important festal day of the Christian calendar, marking the beginning of Christianity as a religious faith. But it is also important as a human manifestation of faith in renewal and the perennial potency of change through growth. Spring rites can be shown to be carefully observed in all cultures. It is, after all, such a fundamental tenet of human belief—that darkness can be overcome, that life is resurgent, that through penitence and atonement we live again. It is hopeful and beautiful, and it falls at the time of year when we can believe that "the winter is past /. . . the time of the singing of birds is come. . . . "

Lent culminates in Holy Week, and by the time of Holy Saturday, when we start coloring and decorating all those hard-boiled eggs, the joy has returned. When I was a child, in my family we had Aunt Josephine's Easter Egg Baskets, with colored eggs tucked inside, to look forward to. The same bread dough that made the baskets could also be shaped into animals, dolls, or even into a circular form encasing an odd number (and always odd—for good luck) of colored eggs. In earlier times these confections, shaped like the donor, and with a hard-boiled egg set in each, were used as ex-voto offerings—the egg, of course, being the traditional reference to life.

Easter in my American childhood also meant a new outfit for going to church on Easter Sunday, the exciting hunt with my brothers for the hidden Easter eggs to stuff into our baskets along with the chocolate eggs and marshmallow bunnies and jelly beans, and Virginia baked ham for dinner. Living in Italy and experiencing the superb Roman roast called *abbacchio*, which is either young lamb or kid, made me change the menu to spring lamb—the veritable paschal lamb with its long tradition to the Jewish Passover, at which a lamb was sacrificed and eaten.

The entry of another food onto my Easter menu was quite recent. A reader of my novel *Umbertina*, writing from New Mexico to say how moved she was by that story of the old-world immigrants and their traditions, sent me a recipe for ricotta-wheat pie that is wonderful to eat and rich in symbolism. Such pastries are almost sacramental in significance, for the wheat grain symbolizes not only food, but also the mystery of resurrection as well. In some parts of Italy, farmers still bring wheat to church on Good Friday to be blessed. Wheat is a part of the Easter ritual of rebirth as is the egg, the lamb, and the dove of the *colomba* sweet bread.

Easter Monday, or Pasquetta

One entirely new Easter custom that I acquired in Italy is *Pasquetta*, or little Easter, which is Easter Monday. This is always a holiday in Italy, and it is just as adamantly always a day for either picnicking or eating at a trattoria in the country. It is a secular holiday, a welcome to spring, and reflects a pleasure as old as the world— eating outdoors.

Years ago when I was in Paris on an Easter Monday, the streets were deserted—everyone seemed to have headed for the Bois de Boulogne, where every scrap of ground was taken over by picnickers. I can remember seeing a policeman pick branches from the lilac bushes and give them out to all the women. There were balloons, *glace* wagons, and loads of children.

In Rome we have observed *Pasquetta* on the terrace of a popular trattoria, just outside the walls on the Via Appia Antica, which was known as I Trenini, from the trains that passed in the distance. Other wonderful sites we visited outside Rome were the excavations at Ostia Antica, towns like Frascati or Marino or Tuscolo in the Alban hills, and, in other directions, Hadrian's Villa on the road toward Tivoli, or the Etruscan site at Veio. Another super place for a picnic was in the meadows off the Via Flaminia, around the twentieth kilometer outside Rome, where sheep still grazed in the distance. And we have spent *Pasquetta* on the shores of Lake Garda, at the so-called grottos of Catullus in Sirmione.

The year we were in Sicily, on Easter Monday we went to Isola Bella, a point of high land joined to the beach at Capo Sant'Andrea by a sandy causeway just below Taormina and as beautiful a place as its name promised. The traffic was utterly maddening—the procession of Easter Monday cars and buses bearing people out of the towns was endless; people swarmed everywhere, in every bit of green and shade, picnicking on every patch of ground. Isola Bella was an ideal picnic setting, with its green cover and rocky promontories and little coves and cypress-covered hills.

It was also thronged with Sicilians still in their Sunday best— mothers in wool skirts and sweaters, the men in long pants with white shirts and ties, the children swathed in pinafores and kerchiefs under the hot sun. We and the few other foreigners were dressed in beach clothes, sitting on the sand near the water under umbrellas while the overdressed Sicilian children were anxiously watched over by their parents in between the elaborate laying out and consuming of food, including monumental *pizze rustiche* and *torte pasqualine* of sausage or spinach. I still remember the distress with which I watched growing fleets of bright orange skins begin to fill the blue, blue waters off the Beautiful Island.

For *Pasquetta* I once devised not a hero, but a bread boat from a loaf of Italian bread. I filled it with leftover lamb, chopped vegetables, tomato, and other seasonings and I thought of my father's favorite saying, which has to do with boats:

> Questo è il mondo
> chi sa navigare
> e chi va a fondo.
> Chi navigare non sa
> Presto a fondo va.

Loosely, it means that in the world there are those who know how to sail their boat and those who don't; the latter sink. It is a harsh saying, leaving no room for the less able to ask for help. It is pitiless, realistic—the wisdom of hard-won self-reliance, which taught a man to pull himself up by his bootstraps and the devil take the hindmost. And yet, having won the ease of American well-being, in his ninth decade my father still declaims that old Sicilian saw.

Rome's Birthday

The saints were certainly close to us in Rome—their churches at every corner, their visages and stories familiar to us from famous paintings. And they did seem to predominate in feast days. The charm of their legends lent a richness and reference to everyday life, and even today Italian newspapers record the saint of the day along with other vital notices such as the weather and which pharmacies are open. One did not have to be a believer to be close to the saints, as Montale captured so perfectly in one of the *Zenia* poems in memory of his deceased wife, which I translated for him:

> "Did she pray?"   "Yes, she
> prayed to St. Anthony to
> help her find
> lost umbrellas and other things
> left in theatre cloakrooms."
> "Is that all?"   "Also for her
> dead ones and for me."
>   "It's sufficient," said the priest.

Along with religious festas, we also had secular occasions of remembrance, and one of the best for us when we lived in Rome was the Eternal City's anniversary each April 21 in observance of Rome's founding in 753 B.C. What better occasion for eating out than when the fuchsias, pinks, and purples of the budding trees are in evidence, along with the flamboyant flowering Judas tree—when wisteria hangs in heavy globules along the walls of old Rome? When better to savor the real Roman dishes like the veal rolls with prosciutto known as *saltimbocca alla romana*, artichokes in the Roman or Judaic style, or the fried ricotta dessert known not too delicately as *pali del nonno*—grandfather's balls? Entrance to all the Rome museums was gratis during the anniversary week and all the more reason to have an outing.

It's also nice to know that a shop called Di Giorgio at #85 Via San Francesco di Sales (alongside Rome's Regina Coeli prison), which supplies the Vatican with candles, has among its wares a special wedge-shaped candle with which to celebrate Rome's birthday. Once on the night of Rome's birthday, we were going to a literary party for visiting author Georges Simenon, when we caught sight of flaming torches all along the wall at Porta Pinciana in celebration. "For Rome, I think," said Antonio, "not Simenon."

All my favorite Roman dishes are a speciality of Piperno's, one of my favorite eating places, both for the quality of the food and its superb location for viewing one of the most awesome old palaces in Rome, Palazzo Cenci. The restaurant is in a little square not many yards removed from the busy traffic of Via Arenula, but in atmosphere and adjacent architecture, it's centuries away from the modern day. Sitting at an outside table and looking up the sinister conglomeration that "still seems to reek of ancient evil and nameless crimes," the tragedy of the ill-fated Beatrice Cenci is brought vividly to mind. It is a still-trafficless part of Rome, filled with a brooding quiet that evokes properly sinister associations of past times. There is a famous Guido Reni portrait, said to be of Beatrice, in the Barberini Palace, whose gardens our Rome apartment overlooked. She is known as the "Beautiful Parricide" for having helped plot the death of her cruel and vicious father, a Roman nobleman of dissolute ways, who had removed her and her stepmother to virtual imprisonment in a desolate castle in the Sabine hills after he was fined 100,000 scudi for alleged sodomy. She was executed in her twenty-second year. When I was a schoolgirl growing up far away from Rome and never anticipating living there, I first read of her in Shelley's drama *The Cenci*, and her story haunted me. Every year, on the anniversary of her public decapitation, which took place September 11, 1599 in the square in front of Castel Sant'Angelo, the Society of Cab Drivers (or, formerly, Coachmen) have a mass said for her in the twelfth-century Cenci chapel fronting the Palazzo Cenci.

April 25 is not only the feast day of Saint Mark the Evangelist, the patron saint of the Venetian republic (and of lawyers and glaziers) and greatly revered by all Veneto families, including the Barolinis, but it's also Liberation Day, marking the Allied victory in Europe in 1945. We have a beautiful antique soup tureen, which, surprisingly, I found at a roadside flea market on a long-ago trip to Calabria. It has, for undivined reasons, "Roma" writ large on one side and "Venezia" on the other. So on Rome's birthday we turn it to commemorate that city, and on Saint Mark's Day we turn it to Venice and serve from it the very traditional rice and pea soup called, in Venetian dialect, *risi e bisi*. It is said that each year on Saint Mark's Day this soup was ceremoniously offered to the doge of Venice. The peas represent the arrival of spring and the rice abundance, which in a supremely mercantile city like Venice was always a good augury. The dish is said to have been served at all official banquets in the republic of Venice as well.

Saint Mark is the author of the second book of the New Testament, which is held to be the earliest written account of Jesus' life. Mark was with Peter in Rome as disciple and secretary, writing from material given to him by Peter. According to legend, Mark then went on a preaching voyage along the shores of the Adriatic. When the vessel in which he was traveling was caught in a great storm and driven into some coastal islands and lagoons, an angel appeared to Mark, saying, "On this site, a great city will arise to your honor." Four hundred years later, the people of the mainland, fleeing before Attila the Hun, sought refuge among those islands, where they established the city of Venice.

Saint Mark later founded the Christian church in Alexandria, which was the place of his martyrdom. In the ninth century, purveyors of holy relics brought his body to Venice, giving the city its patron saint and, it is said, its preeminence over rivals. The Serene Republic adopted as its own the saint's emblem of the winged lion.

That Saint Mark's Day and the liberation of Italy in World War II coincide was noteworthy in our family. Antonio, editor of the Vicenza paper and author of anti-Fascist editorials, was sentenced by the occupying Germans but managed to flee Vicenza by bicycle to escape being taken. He first took refuge in the medieval Benedictine abbey of Praglia 12 kilometers from Padua. There the monks hid him in an underground vault, where he was amazed to find himself in the company of the precious lion of San Marco, which had been secreted there for safekeeping at the beginning of the war. The great emblem of the evangelist is known to every tourist in Venice from its proud perch atop the column in Saint Mark's Square. It is Saint Mark who is invoked against sudden and unexpected death. Antonio loved to recount that story, and how, the moment he looked into the jade eyes of the stone lion, he knew he would be protected and would come out safely.

April Fools' Day
Seafood Risotto
Broiled Trout Clitunno Style
Sautéed Green Beans
Strawberries with Orange Juice

Easter
Asparagus Wrapped in
   Prosciutto
Capellini with Peas and Ham
Roast Lamb
Sage Potatoes
Stewed Fava Beans
Dandelion Greens Salad
Easter Pie

Pasquetta
Eggplant Dip
White Bean Salad
Cold Stuffed Artichokes
Barbara's Sausage Bread
Stuffed Capon

Rome's Birthday
Green Pasta with Four Cheeses
Saltimbocca alla Romana
Braised Spring Peas
Horace's Torte

Saint Mark's Day
Risi e Bisi
Pork Loin Vicenza Style
Lemon Herb Asparagus
Spumetti

April Fools' Day

SEAFOOD RISOTTO
6 SERVINGS

> *12 cherrystone clams*
> *12 mussels*
> *3 tablespoons butter*
> *2 tablespoon olive oil*
> *1 clove garlic*

1 small onion, chopped
1 small stalk celery, chopped
1½ cups Arborio rice (Italian long-grain rice)
½ cup dry white wine
2 cups seafood stock (strained juices of clams and
mussels, plus bottled clam juice to make 2 cups)
8 to 10 peeled medium shrimp
2 tablespoons finely minced parsley

1. Steam the clams and mussels in a small amount of water over moderate heat, covered, just until they open. Remove the clams and mussels from the shells, and set the seafood aside. Strain the broth, and add bottled clam juice to make 2 cups.

2. Heat 2 tablespoons of the butter and the olive oil in a large saucepan. Add the garlic clove, cook until golden, then discard. Add the onion and celery and cook, stirring, until soft.

3. Stir in the rice, wine, and seafood stock. Cook slowly, stirring occasionally, about 10 to 15 minutes.

4. Separately, heat the clams, mussels and shrimp in the remaining tablespoon of butter for about 2 minutes.

5. When the rice is cooked and the liquid absorbed, stir in the seafood.

6. Sprinkle with minced parsley, and serve.

BROILED TROUT CLITUNNO STYLE
6 SERVINGS

4 slices bacon, chopped fine
2 cloves garlic, chopped fine
6 sprigs parsley, chopped fine
6 small trout, cleaned and washed
Kosher salt and freshly ground black pepper, to taste

6 large sprigs fresh rosemary
½ cup olive oil, for basting
3 lemons, cut into wedges, for garnish

Preheat the broiler.

1. Combine the bacon, garlic, and parsley.

2. Sprinkle the insides of the trout with salt and pepper. Divide the bacon mixture evenly, and fill the trout. Lay a sprig of rosemary inside each trout.

3. Brush the trout with some of the olive oil. Lay them on an oiled broiler pan.

4. Broil the trout 5 minutes. Turn, brush with oil, and broil an additional 5 minutes.

5. Serve at once, garnished with lemon wedges.

SAUTÉED GREEN BEANS
6 SERVINGS

1½ pounds fresh green beans, washed, trimmed, and
snapped in half
2 to 3 tablespoons olive oil
1 clove garlic
Salt and freshly ground black pepper, to taste
1 squeeze lemon juice

1. In a covered saucepan over moderately high heat, steam the beans in a steamer over ½ cup of water until cooked but still firm. Drain.

2. Heat the olive oil in a large skillet. Cook the garlic clove over moderate heat until golden, then discard it.

3. Stir in the beans, and cook until coated with the garlic-flavored oil and heated through.

4. Add the salt, pepper, and squeeze of lemon juice. Mix well, and serve at once.

STRAWBERRIES WITH ORANGE JUICE
6 SERVINGS

> *1 quart fresh strawberries*
> *Superfine sugar, to taste*
> *1 cup fresh orange juice, strained (2 to 3 oranges)*

1. Wash and hull the berries. Place them in a bowl.

2. Sprinkle with the sugar; add the orange juice, and mix gently.

3. Chill the berries for about 1 hour before serving.

Easter

ASPARAGUS WRAPPED IN PROSCIUTTO
6 SERVINGS

> *24 medium-thin fresh asparagus spears*
> *24 thin slices prosciutto*

1. Trim asparagus so they are of equal length, and rinse. Have ready a pan of lightly salted boiling water. Immerse the spears and blanch them, about 6 minutes, until they are tender but somewhat firm.

2. Gently lift them out and plunge them immediately into cold water.

3. Drain the spears; refrigerate until ready to serve.

4. To serve, wrap each spear in a slice of prosciutto. Arrange on a platter or on individual plates.

CAPELLINI WITH PEAS AND HAM

2 tablespoons unsalted butter

2 tablespoons olive oil

3 tablespoons chopped shallots or onion

¼ pound cooked ham, diced in ¼-inch pieces

3 tablespoons minced parsley

Salt and freshly ground black pepper, to taste

½ cup chicken broth or water

1 pound fresh green peas, shelled, or one 10-ounce
  package frozen peas, thawed

1 pound capellini *(very fine pasta)*

½ cup whipping cream

½ cup grated Parmesan cheese

1. Heat the butter and olive oil in a skillet over moderate heat. Add the shallots or onion, and cook until soft, stirring occasionally, 3 to 4 minutes.

2. Add the ham, 2 tablespoons of the parsley, salt, and pepper to the skillet. Cook, stirring, for 2 minutes. Add ¼ cup of the broth and then the peas; simmer 2 minutes.

3. Have ready a large pot of salted boiling water. Cook the *capellini* al dente.

4. Just before the *capellini* have finished cooking, add the cream to the skillet, and stir until heated through and well blended.

5. Drain the *capellini*, put them on a long, shallow platter, and pour on the ham-pea sauce. Sprinkle with grated Parmesan cheese and the remaining parsley. Toss, and serve immediately.

ROAST LAMB
6 SERVINGS

> *6 sprigs fresh parsley*
> *2 large sprigs fresh rosemary or 1 teaspoon dried*
> *rosemary*
> *1 to 2 tablespoons fresh marjoram or ½ teaspoon*
> *dried marjoram*
> *2 to 3 cloves garlic*
> *⅓ cup olive oil*
> *4 pound boneless leg of lamb*
> *Salt and freshly ground black pepper, to taste*
> *1 cup dry white wine*

Preheat the oven to 500° F.

1. Chop the herbs and garlic together very fine; mix with 2 teaspoons of the olive oil to make a paste. If necessary, add more oil.

2. Make a number of slits in the lamb, and insert some of the paste.

3. Pour 3 tablespoons of the oil into a roasting pan large enough to hold the lamb. Dip a pastry brush in oil, and brush the meat thoroughly with it. Sprinkle with salt and pepper.

4. Roast the lamb 15 minutes on the middle rack of the oven. Baste with the wine. Cover the pan, and reduce the heat to 350° F. Cook 1¾ hours. Lamb will be well done.

5. Remove the roast from the oven and allow to rest 15 minutes before carving. Serve with pan juices.

SAGE POTATOES
4 TO 6 SERVINGS

> *4 to 6 medium russet potatoes, peeled*
> *¼ cup olive oil*

192

1 clove garlic
3 to 4 fresh sage leaves, minced
Kosher salt and freshly ground black pepper, to taste

1. Cut the potatoes in half lengthwise, then across, into 1-inch-wide pieces. Cover with acidulated cold water until ready to use. Pat the pieces dry just before cooking them.

2. Heat the olive oil in a skillet over moderate heat. When it is sizzling, add the garlic, and cook, stirring, 1 minute. Remove the garlic and add the drained, dried potato pieces, shaking the skillet to coat them with oil. Stir in the sage, salt, and pepper. Cover, and reduce the heat to low.

3. Cook the potatoes 10 to 15 minutes, tossing occasionally, until tender. Remove the cover, increase the heat to high, and cook, tossing, until the potatoes are crisp. Drain the potatoes, and serve immediately.

STEWED FAVA BEANS
4-6 SERVINGS

3 pounds fava beans in pod
juice of ½ lemon
2 tablespoon olive oil
2 cloves garlic, minced
2 tablespoon minced parsley
salt and pepper to taste

1. Bring to boil salted water in a medium saucepan. Shell fava beans from their pods.

2. Add beans to boiling water and cook briefly, 1-2 minutes. Drain beans in a sieve under running cold water.

3. Slip off skins and put beans in a bowl. Add olive oil, lemon juice, garlic, and parsley with salt and pepper to taste.

DANDELION GREENS SALAD
4 SERVINGS

> *1½ pounds (1 large bunch) tender young*
> *dandelion greens*
> *4 slices bacon, chopped*
> *2 teaspoons sugar*
> *¼ teaspoon dry mustard*
> *2 tablespoons red wine vinegar*
> *Salt and freshly ground black pepper, to taste*

1. Wash the dandelions very well, in several changes of water. Drain them in a colander, pat dry, and shred the leaves into a large bowl.

2. In a large, heavy skillet over moderate heat, cook the bacon until crisp. Remove the crisp bacon bits with a slotted spoon, and add them to the greens.

3. Add the sugar, dry mustard, and vinegar to the bacon fat remaining in the skillet. Stir until the sugar has dissolved.

4. Pour the sauce over the greens. Add salt and pepper, toss, and serve immediately.

EASTER PIE
8 SERVINGS

Prepare ¼ pound wheat grains (available in Italian groceries, or use 1 can Asti cooked wheat). If using the uncooked wheat, soak it overnight, drain, and boil 1 hour in salted water, then rinse it in a sieve with cold running water. Add prepared wheat or canned wheat to scalded ¼ cup milk, ¼ teaspoon salt, and ¼ teaspoon sugar and boil for 5 minutes. Remove from heat.

Preheat oven to 350°.

Dough:

> *2 cups flour*
> *4 tablespoons butter*
> *½ cup sugar*
> *2 egg yolks*
> *pinch salt*
> *¼ cup milk*
> *1 teaspoon lemon juice*

Filling:

> *2 cups sugar*
> *1½ pound (3 cups) ricotta cheese*
> *6 egg yolks, beaten*
> *½ cup diced candied citron, orange peel*
> *1 teaspoon vanilla*
> *2 tablespoon slivered toasted almonds*
> *4 egg whites, beaten stiff*

1. In large bowl mix together the flour and sugar. Make a well in center and drop in the egg yolks, lemon juice, and butter cut in pieces. Combine until well blended. Add the milk and mix until dough holds together, adding a bit more milk if needed.

2. On a lightly floured work surface, roll the dough to an ⅛ inch thickness, large enough to line a deep 10 inch pie dish. Trim off excess dough and reserve.

3. In a large bowl beat ricotta with sugar. Add egg yolks, vanilla, candied fruit, and almonds. Blend well.

4. Stir in cooked wheat mixture. Fold in beaten egg whites. Pour filling into pastry lined pie tin. Roll out reserved dough into long strips with pastry cutter and arrange lattice style over the filling. Press ends into edge of dough lining pie tin and flute at edge.

5. Bake one hour, or until firm in center. Remove to rack and let cool.

EGGPLANT DIP (Signora Vita Parrino's *Caponata*)

1 medium eggplant
3-4 plum tomatoes
2 stalks celery, diced
6 tablespoon oil
1 red onion, sliced
20 pitted green olives
1 tablespoon capers
2 tablespoon wine vinegar
1 tablespoon sugar
salt and pepper to taste

1. Cut eggplant lengthwise and sprinkle with salt; leave until moisture forms.

2. Plunge tomatoes in boiling water briefly, remove skins, cut in pieces, and put aside.

3. Rinse eggplant, cut in small pieces, and sauté in 4 tablespoons of oil until soft, then remove from pan to plate and put aside.

4. Add remaining oil to pan and sauté the sliced onion, then add diced celery and cook until soft; finally add tomato, olives, and capers and let blend together a few minutes.

5. Add eggplant, vinegar, and sugar. Stir well together and let simmer 10-15 minutes.

6. Serve warm or cold, with crusty bread as antipasto or as an accompaniment to roasted meat.

WHITE BEAN SALAD
6 TO 8 SERVINGS

> *4 cups cooked white beans (1 pound dried white kidney beans, prepared according to package directions) or two 16-ounce cans* cannellini *beans*
> *½ cup olive oil*
> *¼ cup fresh lemon juice*
> *1 teaspoon dry mustard*
> *1 clove garlic, crushed*
> *Salt and freshly ground black pepper, to taste*
> *3 tablespoons minced parsley*

1. Put the drained beans in a large bowl.

2. To make the dressing, combine the olive oil, lemon juice, mustard, garlic, salt, and pepper in a jar with a lid. Close the jar and shake vigorously.

3. Measure ¼ cup dressing, and pour it over the beans. Toss lightly, and sprinkle the salad with parsley. Serve at room temperature.

COLD STUFFED ARTICHOKES
6 SERVINGS

> *6 medium artichokes*
> *Juice of 1 lemon*
> *2 tablespoons olive oil*
> *½ cup minced onion*
> *1 minced clove garlic*
> *1 cup coarse dry breadcrumbs*
> *3 tablespoons grated Parmesan cheese*
> *1 tablespoon minced parsley*
> *Salt and freshly ground black pepper, to taste*
> *6 tablespoons olive oil*

1. Wash the artichokes well, and trim off the stems and large leaves at the base. Slice 1 inch off the tops, and trim the points of any leaves with spiky tips. Spread out the artichokes to expose the center. With a serrated grapefruit spoon, scrape out the prickly pale inner leaves and the choke.

2. Put the artichokes in a large bowl. Add the lemon juice and enough water to cover them.

3. Put the oil in a small heavy skillet over moderate heat. When it is sizzling, add the onion and garlic. Cook, stirring constantly, until the onion is soft. Set aside.

4. Mix together the breadcrumbs, cheese, parsley, salt, and pepper. Add the onion-garlic mixture, and mix well.

5. Drain the artichokes. Stuff them with equal amounts of the mixture. In a heavy pot just large enough to hold them, place the artichokes upright. Pour in 2 cups of water, and drizzle the olive oil over the artichokes. Cover and cook over low heat, so that the water just simmers, for 45 minutes or until the artichokes are tender but still firm. Cool. Serve at room temperature.

BARBARA'S SAUSAGE BREAD
6 SERVINGS

> 1 pound sweet Italian sausages
> 1 clove garlic, crushed
> 1 egg, separated
> 8 ounces mozzarella cheese, shredded
> ½ cup grated Parmesan cheese
> ⅛ teaspoon salt
> Freshly ground black pepper, to taste
> 1 pound pizza dough (can be purchased at an
>   Italian bakery)

Preheat the oven to 350° F.

1. Remove the casings, and break up the sausage meat. Put the sausage meat and the garlic clove in a medium heavy skillet. Cook over moderate heat, until the meat is cooked through and lightly browned. Discard the garlic. Drain the meat on paper towels.

2. In a large bowl beat the egg white lightly. Add the sausage, cheeses, salt, and pepper. Mix thoroughly.

3. On a floured work surface, stretch the pizza dough into a rectangle to fit a cookie sheet. Spread the sausage mixture evenly on the dough, leaving 1 inch of uncovered dough all around. Roll up, jelly roll style. Seal well by pinching shut along the length and at the ends. Beat the egg yolk lightly, and brush the roll with it.

4. Place the sausage bread on a baking sheet. Bake 1 hour on the middle rack of the oven. Cool somewhat before slicing.

STUFFED CAPON
6 SERVINGS

> *One 5- to 6-pound capon*
> *4 tablespoons oil*
> *Salt and freshly ground black pepper, to taste*
> *1 cup chopped onion*
> *1 small clove garlic, minced*
> *½ cup chopped green bell pepper*
> *½ cup chopped celery, with some of the leaves*
> *½ cup sliced mushrooms*
> *2 cups cooked wild rice*
> *½ cup chopped toasted almonds*
> *¼ teaspoon dried ground sage*
> *¼ teaspoon dried thyme leaves, crumbled*

Preheat the oven to 450° F.

1. Wash the capon, and pat it dry with paper towels. Rub it inside and out with 2 tablespoons of the oil, and sprinkle it inside and out with salt and pepper.

2. Put 1 tablespoon of the oil in a skillet over moderate heat. When it is sizzling, add the onion, garlic, bell pepper, and celery. Cook until the onion is translucent, stirring often.

3. In a separate skillet, over moderate heat, cook the sliced mushrooms in the remaining oil, until just wilted.

4. In a medium bowl, combine the onion mixture, mushrooms, wild rice, almonds, sage, and thyme. Add salt and pepper, and mix well.

5. Stuff the capon with the mixture. Fasten the openings together with stuffing pins. Put the bird on a rack in a roasting pan, breast side up, and slide it onto the middle rack of the oven. Immediately reduce the temperature to 350° F.

6. Roast the capon 20 to 25 minutes to the pound, basting frequently with pan juices. When the bird is cooked, remove it to a warmed platter. Let it sit 10 to 15 minutes before serving; carving will be easier.

Rome's Birthday

GREEN PASTA WITH FOUR CHEESES
6 SERVINGS

> *¼ pound fontina cheese, cubed*
> *¼ pound imported gorgonzola cheese, crumbled*
> *¼ pound Bel Paese, cubed*
> *1 pound spinach pasta*
> *Sprinkle of cayenne (red) pepper*

½ cup grated Parmesan cheese, plus more to pass at
   table
1 cup heavy cream
2 tablespoons minced parsley or chives

1.   In the top of a double boiler, over simmering water, melt together the fontina, gorgonzola, and Bel Paese cheeses with 2 tablespoons of heavy cream. Stir until well blended.

2. Cook the spaghetti in a large pot of boiling, salted water.

3. While the spaghetti cooks, add the red pepper to the cheese mixture, stir in the ½ cup Parmesan cheese and the remaining heavy cream. Cook 5 minutes, stirring occasionally.

4. Drain the spaghetti, and put it in a serving bowl. Add the cheese mixture and stir. Sprinkle with the parsley or chives. Serve immediately, with additional Parmesan cheese.

SALTIMBOCCA ALLA ROMANA
6 SERVINGS

12 veal scallops
Salt and freshly ground black pepper, to taste
12 fresh sage leaves
12 very thin slices prosciutto
6 tablespoons unsalted butter
¼ cup dry marsala wine
Wooden toothpicks

1. Place each scallop between 2 sheets of wax paper and pound it as thin as you can with a wooden mallet.

2. Season the veal scallops with salt and pepper. Place a sage leaf on each and top with a slice of prosciutto. Roll up, then fasten each roll with a toothpick.

3. Over moderate heat, put the butter in a large skillet. When sizzling, add the veal rolls and cook until they are evenly browned.

4. Add the wine and then lower the heat and cook 5 minutes, turning the rolls.

5. Arrange the veal rolls on a serving dish, remove the toothpicks, and pour on the pan juices. Serve at once.

BRAISED SPRING PEAS
6 SERVINGS

> 2 tablespoons unsalted butter
> ½ cup chopped onion
> 1 teaspoon all-purpose flour
> 1 cup broth or water
> Heart of iceberg or Boston lettuce
> 1 tablespoon chopped parsley
> 1 tablespoon chopped fresh mint
> 3 pounds fresh green peas, shelled
> Salt and freshly ground black pepper, to taste

1. Put the butter in a large saucepan over moderate heat. When it is sizzling, add the onion, and cook until soft. Add the flour and cook about 1 minute, stirring.

2. Add the broth or water, stirring, to make a thin sauce.

3. Add the lettuce heart, parsley, mint, and peas. Cook covered over moderately low heat until the peas are tender and the liquid is reduced, about 15 minutes.

4. Remove the lettuce heart. Season the peas with salt and pepper, and serve immediately.

HORACE'S TORTE (*Sbrisolona*)
8 SERVINGS

1 cup almonds, blanched and skins removed
1½ cups unbleached flour
1½ cups fine cornmeal
¾ cup sugar
grated rind of one lemon
pinch salt
1 egg plus 1 egg yolk, beaten together
8 tablespoons unsalted butter

The Italian word for this cake derives from *briciola*, crumb, and refers to its crumbly texture.

1. Reserve ½ cup almonds and put remainder on lightly greased baking sheet to toast 3-7 minutes in 350° oven.

2. Grind toasted almonds fine in blender or food processor, then put in large bowl with flour, cornmeal, sugar, lemon rind, and salt.

3. Add eggs to dry mixture and work in by hand. Using pastry blender, add butter and work it quickly into mix.

4. Handling dough as little as possible, knead it on floured surface until it holds together. Wrap dough in waxed paper and chill in the refrigerator for 20 minutes.

5. Preheat oven to 400°. Grease and flour lightly a 12 inch round cake pan. Place dough in pan and spread it evenly with fingertips; dough will be crumbly. With reserved almonds, arrange in a pattern on the dough.

6. Bake 40-45 minutes until golden, the torte will remain flat.

7. Remove from oven to rack to cool. Before serving, sprinkle with confectioner's sugar.

RISI E BISI
6 SERVINGS

> 1½ cups Arborio long-grain rice
> 2½ tablespoons butter
> 2 tablespoons olive oil
> 1 teaspoon crushed fennel seeds, or 2 tablespoons
>   chopped parsley
> 1 small onion, finely chopped
> 1 ½ pounds fresh peas, shelled or 1 package frozen
>   small peas
> 2-3 cups chicken broth, kept hot in a separate pan
> ¼ cups grated parmesan cheese

1. Put half the butter and all the olive oil in a large saucepan add onion and sauté until it is soft and golden.

2. Add rice and stir until the grains are becoming translucent.

3. Add wine and cook quickly until it is evaporated.

4. Add peas and some of the broth, cooking until liquid is absorbed, then adding more broth until it is all used and rice is cooked al dente, about 15 minutes.

5. Add fennel or parsley, cheese, and remaining butter. Stir thoroughly to incorporate.

6. Serve immediately with additional grated cheese in a separate bowl to be passed around and added to taste.

PORK LOIN VICENZA STYLE
6 TO 8 SERVINGS

¼ cup plus 1 tablespoon all-purpose flour
½ teaspoon salt
¼ teaspoon freshly ground black pepper
2½ pounds boneless pork loin with some fat
    removed
4 slices bacon, chopped
2 to 2½ cups milk
2 tablespoons unsalted butter

1. Mix ¼ cup of the flour with the salt and pepper; coat the roast with the mixture, and shake off any excess.

2. In a heavy Dutch oven or oval cast-iron or enamel casserole just large enough to hold the roast comfortably, render the bacon fat over moderate heat. Remove the bacon bits. Add the roast, and brown on all sides.

3. Add 1 cup of the milk. Cover tightly, reduce the heat to very low, and simmer 2 to 2½ hours, until the roast is tender. Baste often with the remaining milk.

4. Transfer the roast to a warmed platter. Scrape the browned bits adhering to the pan; add the butter and 1 tablespoon of flour; stir until the sauce thickens. Serve the sauce over the sliced roast.

LEMON HERB ASPARAGUS
6 SERVINGS

2 pounds uniform-size asparagus spears, washed
4 thinly sliced scallions
3 tablespoons chopped parsley
Salt and freshly ground black pepper, to taste
1 tablespoon fresh lemon juice
¼ cup olive oil
1 tablespoon freshly grated lemon rind

1. Snap off the ends of the asparagus spears; they should be of equal length. Tie them in a bundle with kitchen string. Stand the bundle upright in a deep, narrow pot filled with lightly salted boiling water, with the tips out of the water. Cover and cook 15 minutes over moderate heat, until just tender.

2. Drain the asparagus in a colander. Remove the string, and arrange the spears on a round serving plate, with the tips pointing toward the center.

3. Put the scallions, parsley, salt, and pepper in a blender container, and mix together. Add the lemon juice, then, with the blender on low speed, trickle in the olive oil. Blend for a minute into a liquid dressing.

4. Pour the dressing over the asparagus. Garnish with the lemon rind. Serve at room temperature.

SPUMETTI *(Meringues)*
YIELD: 4 TO 5 DOZEN

⅔ cup egg whites
1 pound confectioners' sugar
2 tablespoons unsweetened cocoa

2 teaspoons cinnamon

1 pound coarsely chopped hazelnuts or cashew nuts

Preheat the oven to 325° F.

1. Cut brown paper to fit 2 baking sheets. Grease the paper lightly.

2. In a large bowl beat the egg whites until stiff.

3. Combine the sugar, cocoa, and cinnamon in a small bowl. Slowly, in several stages, add the mixture to the beaten egg whites, beating well after each addition.

4. Fold in the chopped nuts.

5. Drop the mixture by teaspoonfuls onto the prepared baking sheets, leaving space between them.

6. Bake 15 minutes; cool on baking sheets. The *spumetti* can be stored for several weeks in a tin.

Six

MAY

May Day

In *The Merry Wives of Windsor*, Shakespeare beautifully and precisely captures the lovesickness of May in describing young Master Fenton: "he capers, he dances, he has eyes of youth, he writes verses, he speaks holiday, he smells April and May. . . ."

This is what Salvatore Salomone-Marino, physician by profession and folklorist of Sicilian customs by passion, observed a century ago on the intricate overlay of rituals that celebrate May:

209

May is the month of flowers and love, the fecundator par excellence. . . . In the course of time and events it has been impossible for this more or less reasonable animal called man to abandon his nature and change completely. . . . Even when he turned his faith to Christ and threw down his idols and cursed heathenism, he still kept a great heritage of customs, habits, and beliefs while giving them new names and investing them with new fashions. . . . Thus the Feasts of Flora, so much celebrated by the ancient Romans, survive today and are celebrated annually by our peasants on the first day of the fifth month. . . .

May, the month of love, was prefaced in Italy by *calendimaggio*, the eve of May Day and the time in some towns for young men to serenade their sweethearts with original love songs. In Assisi, for instance, the upper and lower town vie with each other in a competition of medieval love songs set against a backdrop of torchlight, and authentic costumes and instruments of the thirteenth century. Before his mystical conversion, Saint Francis of Assisi was himself one of the liveliest participants in this secular folk festival.

The gathering of flowers for May baskets or for adorning the home is a very old ritual. Traceable to the daisy-filled fields of Sicily is the old, old rite of young girls plucking off daisy petals to ask whether or not they are loved, whether or not they will marry.

> I see May, and I gather May
> I wish luck from God;
> Flowers of May I pick in the fields,
> Lord, look to my good fortune!

And the good fortune invoked by the girls is, of course, a good marriage. Even the daisy chain, thought to be the hallmark of the Vassar girl, goes back to the customs of Salaparuta in Sicily, where the girls customarily weave garlands of flowers and carry them in procession. In Paris, where I once found myself on the first of May, people exchange little bouquets of lilies of the valley and, caught by the occasion, a struggling American artist friend, Hugh Weiss, even splurged on one for me.

In Syracuse, Sicily, on May 1, another festa for Santa Lucia takes place to commemorate the miracle she wrought when the city was suffering from famine and all resources had been exhausted. Just when hope had given out, a ship sailed into port laden with wheat. Its arrival was announced by a dove flying into the duomo, where the people of the city were praying to Santa Lucia. As on her December feast day, the May Day festa for the saint again sees her *bara* (coffin) moved in procession under a shower of flowers. And before the Society for the Prevention of Cruelty to Animals intervened, there used to be a ceremony during which the youngest nuns of the convent of Santa Lucia, which adjoins the cathedral, dressed all in white, came out on their balcony to launch doves, turtledoves, and other small birds into the crowds below. The people, using nets or hats to catch them, often wounded or killed many and, of course, the ones that were captured came to no good end either.

Easter season is fifty days long and ends on Pentecost (from the Greek word meaning "fiftieth"), which usually falls in May. The other moveable feasts, fixed by the date of Easter and also usually in May, are Ascension Day, which comes ten days before Pentecost, and Corpus Christi (in honor of the Holy Eucharist), eleven days after Pentecost.

Pentecost, adapted from the Jewish festival following Passover, is also called Whitsunday and commemorates the descent of the Holy Spirit upon the Apostles, the preaching of Peter and the other apostles in Jerusalem, and the baptism of some 3,000 Jews into the Christian community. As such, it is regarded as the beginning of the Catholic Church. The Easter bread called *colomba*, for its dove shape, is especially appropriate at this time since the dove is the sign of the Holy Spirit.

In the village of Monterubbiano in the Marche region, where

we once had a *rustica*—a vacation farmhouse—a unique pentecostal observance is celebrated. It's based on the legend that the forebears of the marchigiani people, the ancient race of Piceni, held a spring festival to honor the sacred bird which was said to have guided the first inhabitants to that spot. The mingling of pre-Christian legend with devotion to the pentecostal Holy Spirit is quite striking in this case. Each year it's renewed with a parade in medieval costume through the brick-paved streets of Monterubbiano, culminating in games in the municipal square. When we took part, it was a day for feasting at the very rustic inn of Giovanni and Santina Pazzi, enjoying her specialties—the renowned stuffed olives, fried creams, and mixed grill accompanied by the slightly tart San Giovese wine of the region. How well I remember the florid, smiling face of Santina and her hearty manner! She loved the way we relished her food and gave us recipes for everything, plus bottles of her private stock of San Giovese wine for, in those days, fifty cents the bottle. It is sad now to think of the Pazzis gone and the inn closed.

In Orvieto the flight of the dove (*la festa della palombella*) is re-created each year at Pentecost. A portable Gothic-style tabernacle containing the Madonna and Apostles at the Last Supper is situated on the monumental steps of the glorious cathedral. The cupola on the facing church across the piazza from the duomo houses a structure suggesting the heavens and containing a dove within a candlelit ring. At high noon, to the sound of firecrackers, the dove will be shot out like a rocket to run along a cord toward the tabernacle, where it will set off a halo of fireworks around it and light up red flames above the heads of the Apostles and the Madonna. This popular show not only represents the descent of the Holy Spirit, but if the dove hits its mark squarely, it means a good crop year for the onlookers.

Ascension Day, as one of the "dated" events of Jesus' life, has been observed since the early days of Christianity. At the end of the fourth century, it was already universally celebrated in the entire Christian world of the time and has remained a holy day of obligation. In most parts of Europe during the Middle Ages, some sort of bird—chicken, pigeon, pheasant, duck, goose, or the special delicacy of guinea hen—was eaten on Ascension Day to recall Christ's "flight" to heaven. If not partaking of an actual bird, then people baked pastries in bird shapes to mark the event and also as the sign of the Holy Spirit. Whitsunday, which is the English designation for the feast of Pentecost, refers both to White Sunday, for the newly baptized who wore white, and to the wit and wisdom with which the apostles were said to be filled by the Holy Spirit on that day.

In Rome a superstition has it that if a fresh egg is placed in a basket with a lit candle and put on a windowsill on the eve of Ascension Day, the Madonna, who passes over the whole world that night, will bless it. A year later, if the egg is opened, a pure wax will be found within, which is said to keep misfortune and sickness away.

Belief needn't be literal: in eggs turning to wax, or in sacred guide birds, or whatever. But beliefs and mythologies are the expression of archetypal images and symbols. Belief in the inexplicable, in the mysterious succession of seasons, and in the miraculous bounty of nature connects us to the collective unconscious and to the long line of humanity before us who observed rites and festas.

In Florence, where I once spent a spring semester following the university program in Italian language and literature, May is *Maggio Musicale*, the musical month, and Ascension Day means the *festa del grillo*, cricket day. For the Italians, as for the Etruscans, Romans, and Greeks, the cricket is a harbinger of spring, whose chirping was connected to the muses and music. Tiny reed cages with crickets were painted on the walls of Pompeiian houses, and the pastoral poet Theocritus wrote of them. It was thought that the longer the cricket lived after being caged, the longer the life of its owner. In Florence crowds of families go to the Cascina public gardens to buy *grilli* in tiny, prettily painted cages rather than, as formerly, catching them themselves. It's a colorful and merry occasion (except for the crickets), and the Florentines say that if the cricket you are taking home sings, it means good luck, although freeing the *grillo* means the same thing as well.

Corpus Christi has always seemed a strange feast to me, since I could connect it with nothing that had been celebrated at home in the States. Yet in England it was a regular time for the performance of religious dramas by the trade guilds, and many of the Corpus Christi plays are still extant there. Our Puritan heritage must have seen to it that they were not imported here. In Italy it remains an elaborate festival, and in all the towns and cities, streets are decorated with banners and hangings. In Rome, where I first observed the feast, I was awed and amazed at the great number of decorative tapestries and carpets that were hung out of windows and over balconies to honor the Eucharistic procession proceeding through the streets from each parish church, escorted by lines of little girls scattering flowers in the path of the Holy Host.

Genzano, above the lake of Nemi in the hills outside Rome, is a lovely town famed for carpeting its entire main street with an intricate floral mosaic (called *infiorata*) created by many artisans from the blossoms of white acacia, golden broom, red roses, orange poppies, violets, and blue cornflowers, and following a chalked outline done on the pavement by the premier artist. Over this mass of blooms, with patterns including the angel of peace, the town arms, and geometric elaborations, goes the annual procession of clergy and worshipers from the principal square to the church. The concept of floral mosaics is said to have been invented by Benedetto Drei, head gardener at the Vatican more than three hundred years ago, for Rome's observance of the feast of Saint Peter. But Genzano's

214

first floral tribute was in homage to Pope Pius VI (1775–1800), who happened to pass through the town on one Corpus Christi day of his reign.

Far removed from Genzano but similar as a floral tribute was the chair lavishly garlanded in flowers that Marion Ascoli once prepared to celebrate her husband Max's birthday at Cliffdale Farm, their country home, not far from where we lived at Shady Lane Farm. Max and Antonio, both Italian born and great talkers, met often, and I always thought that that birthday tribute, created out of blooms from both her gardens and her greenhouse, was a beautiful and original gesture to an Italian gentleman from his American wife.

That was also the period when our eldest daughters were attending Scarborough Country Day School, where May Day festivities were held on the great lawn of Beechhurst, the Vanderlip home. The Vanderlips had founded the school, and each May Day they invited the children and their parents to picnic on the grounds among the magnificent plantings, looking out over the Hudson River and across to the palisades. The setting and the occasion gave rise to one of my own early but favorite stories, "Opera Libretti and a Mayday Carol," a story of time's passing and actions left undone. Now the May Days on the great lawn are no more, nor the school, and the Beechhurst mansion has been turned into condominiums.

Whether on the shores of the Hudson or in the Umbrian hill towns, May evokes beautiful scenes in my memory. The May following Antonio's death, Robert and Sally Fitzgerald, through my friend Maggie Haferd, who administered the USIS in Rome, invited us to spend the weekend with them at their country place in San Fortunato delle Colline, a locality just outside Perugia.

Robert Fitzgerald, who died in 1985, was then at the height of his fame as poet, translator of the classics, and Boylston Professor of Literature at Harvard. Sally is also multitalented—she paints, translates, studies languages, and knew everything about her surroundings and how to live in Italy and raise children there. Robert and

215

Sally and their six children had settled in Italy as the most agreeable and least expensive place in which to raise such a large family. And they did it with both economy and great style. The country place they bought in 1961 was a classic main house with two attached farmers' houses in another wing, all facing onto a great paved court-yard. It was a beautiful sight when we drove up—the whole façade covered with climbing roses and ivy. Toward the back, where the golden wheat fields shimmered and dipped in the breeze, a big, thick, gnarled wisteria shaded the patio and made a cool pergola.

Inside was a long, cool entry hall paved in classic country fashion with shiny brick *cotta* tiles. Off this lay the original chapel, with white walls setting off the old beams, and masses of brilliant flowers and leaves in the chapel, the corridors, and the rooms opening off them. Downstairs was the large reception-living room, a ping-pong and game room, a television room, a guest suite, a small formal dining room, and a good-sized kitchen with a large hearth. Upstairs, off another corridor, was an upstairs sitting room, a small studio for painting, the master bedroom suite, and four other bedrooms with bathrooms. The entire third floor was where Robert worked.

The effect was serene and in simple good taste. Books were everywhere—antique furniture, few but fine paintings on the walls. *"Che bella!"* I breathed. It was my own idea of what a family, a home, a way of life should be. Sally and only two of the children, Benedict and Barnaby, were there that weekend.

We dined in the country kitchen, where a Latin blessing was said before eating. With amazing easy manners and good humor, the two boys got up from the table to serve and clear. Aside from the beauty of the place, what I remember best was the beatific platter of pasta that Sally served the evening of our arrival: it was, of course, *pasta fatta in casa*, homemade with the wheat from their fields and eggs from an adjoining peasant family. And the wild asparagus from the countryside, which was sprinkled over the pile of golden noodles, was like a tribute to spring and Flora herself. This had to be the prototype of all *pasta primavera!*

Concurrent with church celebrations are the festivals that take place in various parts of Italy in various seasons to highlight the arrival and abundance of a special local food product. There are festivals of fish, grapes, truffles, cheese, peaches, chestnuts—anything can be a cause for a festa. One of our favorites was May's strawberry festival at Nemi in the Alban hills outside Rome, an area known from antiquity for its sacred groves.

In antiquity the first day of May was the occasion for the youths of Rome to go into the fields, singing and dancing in honor of the good goddess, *Bona Dea,* who gave rich wombs to women and rich fields to men. The phallus, as symbol of fertility, was openly honored by men and women alike. In England the people added their own local hero, Robin Hood, to the feast and honored the maid Marian with the election of a May queen.

All the feasts, pagan and Jewish and Christian, seem involved in a ritual celebration of the revitalization and flowering of the earth and, by extension, of humankind. Salvatore Salomone-Marino thus describes Ascension Day in Sicily:

> It is a day of universal purification, both for man and for beast useful to man, for plants and for earth and water, for air, since through divine power all disease-carrying germs that threaten the life and health of man and our beasts and things useful to us are destroyed.
>
> The benediction of Heaven comes down to earth at exactly midnight: salt water becomes sweet, and the sweet, pure; both, of course, are blessed; as is blessed the dew covering things, bringing within its molecules the most exquisite essences to flowers, glucose to fruits, seeds to ears of grain empty until then. The peasant, carefully watching, is assured by the limpid

sky, recognizing in the sparkle and imperceptible movements of the myriad stars what makes possible the delivery of the beneficent dew, the essence, the glucose, the grains. That is poetry, that is myth, that is faith!

In my Convent School days, I recall the solemn and very moving procession through the grounds to the grotto shrine of the Blessed Virgin Mary, who was crowned with a wreath of flowers. It was always a gorgeous pageant, with the honor of the crowning going to the top girl of the senior class, and all classes, from the kindergarten babes on up, participating. "Fill we today/our hearts with love and flowers. . . ." we sang as we proceeded in our uniforms and veils through grounds abloom with azaleas and rhododendrons, daffodils and tulips, and dozens of other flowering shrubs and trees.

By college the queen had become another. At Wells College, May Day was a grand occasion, and the queen, the most beautiful of the junior class, and her attendants rode to the festivities in Henry Wells's old stagecoach. In my freshman year I was one of the Maypole dancers and can still recall the beauty of the setting in the natural amphitheater behind Macmillan Hall. We honored May Day with dancing, singing, and a performance of *As You Like It* on the green. It is said that all the characters in May Day rites embodied the power to endow crops and women with fertility and good luck, and that the Maypole itself was a huge phallic symbol of fertility. At the time in the forties when I was attending a women's college, none of us, I'm sure, was knowingly celebrating our fertility. But we were certainly drawn to some powerful remembrance of spring, to the blossoming of the land and the nearness of summer as people always have been.

May Day celebrations, like many Christmas customs, were suppressed during Puritan dominance in England and America, and although they reemerged somewhat in the eighteenth and nineteenth centuries, the triumph of industrialism transformed the erstwhile fertility celebrations into the festival of international labor, the color and pageantry of former May Days being replaced by processions of trade unionists filing behind banners. *O tempora! O mores!* In southern Italy, as Lucia Chiavola Birnbaum has pointed out in her book on feminism in Italy, *Liberazione della donna*, a contemporary celebration of May Day features the Madonna and her Son, the Red Christ (*cristo rosso*). The Madonna of these rituals is a mother figure of peasant memory, closer to the pagan archetype, perhaps, than to the Virgin of Church doctrine.

In most of the world, May Day now is a purely secular occasion. With the notable exceptions of the United States and Canada, May 1 is observed as Labor Day and celebrates the alliance of workers all over the world. The consolation, while living in Rome, was that since no one (except the restaurateurs) worked on May Day, it was a good day for eating out in one of the city's many beautiful squares. That is one of Rome's great pleasures.

I remember the pang of indignation and nostalgia I felt once I was back in the States and read about Rome in an article on the "lifestyles" page of my local paper—a restaurant report by someone who had just come back from Rome. She had, she wrote, treated herself to eating in the best spots. A fig she had! Her list stressed all the tourist standbys, where Romans themselves would never think of dining. She raved about the 3-foot-high menu of Da Meo Patacca, a restaurant in Trastevere owned by an American with a pronounced sense of show biz, where bands parade through the thronged outdoor tables while costumed singers in the windows in the adjacent buildings belt out operatic arias or "When Irish Eyes Are Smiling." Waiters bring balloons, and it truly is a Disneyland-type spectacle. For rarefied and refined dining, the reviewer suggested the restaurant of the Hilton Hotel, with its views of the lighted city and orchestra playing romantic songs. Those are places for people who could be in Los Angeles, not Rome.

The real Roman dining experience is neither in a circus ring nor a colorless hotel ballroom. The writer missed the whole meaning of eating out in Rome, which is not for the view or elaborate decor or touristy tricks, but to enjoy good food and wine and conversation in authentic Roman eating places, where service is pleasant but not fawning, where tourists are not in evidence, and where special dishes not mentioned on the menu can be discussed and made up for one's pleasure. What Roman would go all the way to Monte Mario just to look at the lights of the city! Who would think of going to eat in a place echoing with popular music and making conversation impossible?

Romans love comfort and like to go to places where they can stay put and chat for hours; they like the small, friendly places burrowed into the narrow streets and exquisite squares of center Rome (*centro*). They make a great thing out of choosing their meals, discussing the courses, the appropriate wines, the seasonal firsts, considering alternatives, thinking of their livers or their mothers, and finally deciding. One writer friend once decided that his meal, spare but elegant, would be a perfectly ripened pear and a piece of perfectly aged Parmesan cheese. What is never spare is the wit and the verbal exchanges of Italians at table—something that would never tolerate the distraction of singing waiters or worse.

And our dining out could be at the Archimede, just up the street from where we used to live near the Pantheon in the heart of Rome; or Tullio's, for outstanding Tuscan steak; or Otello's; Piperno's; Angelino's at Tormargana; Toto's; or L'Antiquario on Via dei Coronari for wonderful *pasta alla puttanesca*; or the reliable Bolognese place at Piazza del Popolo, with its magnificent serving wagon of boiled meats. When we finally left wherever we were, there'd be the slow amble through nighttime Rome, which, with the cessation of the day's turmoil and traffic, can still be a joy. I remember very well coming from Romolo's garden in Trastevere one evening and happening on Federico Fellini and his movie crew as they were shooting a film; he and an assorted group of character actors—the freaks he so loves—were seated at café tables between takes, and it all seemed perfectly natural in the city.

Romans don't often invite people to dinner at home, perhaps because eating out in that city is so enjoyable. But some home dinners have been memorable: the receptions of literary critic Maria Luisa Astaldi in her private townhouse, which was filled with modern masters like De Chirico, Morandi, and Guttuso, were Roman high style at its best, as were the elegant supper parties of Luigi and Paola Barzini in their villa outside Rome at Tomba di Nerone. When he was with Dacia Maraini, Alberto Moravia invited us for a memorable lunch: four courses in twenty minutes! I had always given little credence to Antonio's contention that the little king, Vittorio Emanuele III, wanted to spend no longer than twenty minutes eating, from start to finish, when he sat to dinner. But such was Moravia's tour de force: from *pasta all'acciughe*, through beefsteak and potatoes, salad, and fruit, he ate voraciously, conversing without stop, and carried us along with him.

Vicenza author Goffredo Parise, whose story "The Wife Who Rode Horseback" I was then translating because Richard Burton was interested in it as a film project for himself and Elizabeth Taylor, had us as a whole family to a homey Sunday dinner in his new place on the Via Camilluccia and entertained us with accounts of his trip to China, part of it the pure fantasy he used so well in his surrealistic novels. Then there was the dinner that Giorgio Bassani, author of *The Garden of the Finzi-Continis*, challenged me to put on, to see, I suppose, whether an American could do so creditably. I did—with a baked Alaska finale that was a novelty and triumph. I mentioned to him that evening that I had looked for the Finzi-Contini house and garden in Ferrara when we were recently there; he answered that at one time along the Corso Ercole I, there had

221

been a piece of land where such a walled villa and park *might* have been. I was somehow more pleased that there was no such landmark, that all had been invented.

Lastly, but not least in any sense, was Antonio's birthday, which became a summation in itself of everything about May. The very special *Pasticcio di Macaroni* included here was something Antonio taught me, first performing it himself and calling on me for utensils and bowls and ingredients like a surgeon in action. Antonio's favorite bird was the *faraona*, or guinea hen, which Artusi has said was the symbol of brotherly love to the ancients. It is a fowl that is delicate in taste—sweet, pink-fleshed, moist, and tender—and with a beautiful plumage that in Italian poultry shops is still left as a ruff around it in order to distinguish it from other birds. A touch of wild fennel in the stuffed bird provides a wonderful whiff of spring. And then, of course, to end the meal are the delectable strawberries of the season. Such a meal is rather time-consuming, but as our venerable and wise old friend, the critic and author Giuseppe Prezzolini, knew and wrote, the supreme gift Italy gives its visitors is lessons in the art of living—and living well means taking the time.

May Day
Pasticcio di Macaroni
Roast Guinea Hen with Black Olives
Green Bean and Fennel Salad
Maddalena Cake with Strawberries

May Day

PASTICCIO DI MACARONI
6 SERVINGS

> *1½ ounces dried mushrooms*
> *1 pound macaroni (elbow or small penne)*
> *3 tablespoons olive oil*
> *3 tablespoons unsalted butter*
> *¾ cup chopped onion*
> *½ cup chopped celery*
> *½ cup chopped carrot*
> *½ pound ham, cubed*
> *1 cup cooked chicken, cubed*
> *Salt and finely ground black pepper, to taste*
> *1⅔ cups White Sauce (see recipe below)*
> *2 pastry crusts (see recipe below)*
> *1 egg beaten with 2 tablespoons water*

1. Soak the mushrooms for 20 minutes in tepid water to cover.

2. Meanwhile, cook the macaroni al dente. Drain, put into a large bowl, and set aside.

3. Preheat the oven to 350° F. Put the oil and butter in a skillet over moderate heat. When sizzling, stir in the onion, celery, and carrot, and cook, stirring often, until soft. Remove the skillet from the heat.

4. Add the ham and chicken, salt and pepper to the mixture. Drain the mushrooms, chop them, and add them to the mixture.

5. Combine the mixture with the macaroni, blending well. Stir in the White Sauce.

6. Butter a 10-inch springform pan. Roll out 2 pastry crusts. Line the pan with one of the pastry crusts.

7. Put the macaroni mixture in the crust. Top with the second crust, and pinch the edges together to seal them.

8. Brush the top with the egg and water mixture. Cut a 3-inch slit in the crust.

9. Bake 40 to 45 minutes on the middle rack of the oven, until the crust is golden. Let the *pasticcio* stand 5 to 10 minutes before serving.

WHITE SAUCE

> 2 cups milk
> 4 tablespoons unsalted butter
> 1/4 cup all-purpose flour
> 2 tablespoons Parmesan cheese

1. Scald the milk in a small saucepan over low heat; do not let it boil.

2. In a larger saucepan over moderate heat, melt the butter. Add the flour and cook, whisking constantly, for 1 minute.

3. Reduce the heat, and stir in the milk, a little at a time. Continue cooking, stirring constantly until the sauce has thickened.

4. Remove the pan from the heat, and stir in the cheese.

> 2 cups all-purpose flour
> Pinch salt
> ½ cup olive oil
> ½ cup very cold water

1. Place the flour and salt in a medium bowl.

2. Put the olive oil and water in a 2-cup measure. Slowly add to the flour and salt, mixing with a fork until a ball has formed. Chill until ready to use.

ROAST GUINEA HEN WITH BLACK OLIVES
4 TO 6 SERVINGS

> 2 guinea hens (2 to 3 pounds each, thawed if
>   frozen) or 2 Cornish game hens (Note: A
>   specialty butcher can supply fresh dressed guinea
>   hens during the fall months, or frozen hens at
>   other times.)
> Salt and freshly ground black pepper, to taste
> ¾ cup pitted black olives
> 2 sprigs fresh marjoram, or ½ teaspoon dried
>   marjoram
> 8 slices pancetta (unsmoked Italian bacon) or
>   standard bacon
> ¾ cup chicken broth, heated
> ¼ cup dry white wine

Preheat the oven to 375° F.

1. Wipe the birds inside and out with paper towels.

2. Salt and pepper the hens' cavities, then fill with the equally divided olives and marjoram.

3. Wrap the breasts with the slices of *pancetta* or bacon, attaching with toothpicks.

4. Place the hens on their sides in an oiled roasting pan. Roast 10 minutes. Baste with pan juices and broth, turn them to the opposite side, and cook another 10 minutes. Baste, remove the *pancetta*, and turn the hens breast up. Cook 10 minutes more. Baste again, and test for doneness; if necessary, roast a little longer. Remove the hens to a warmed platter.

5. Skim the fat from the pan juices. Pour the juices into a small saucepan, and add the wine. Over high heat, reduce the sauce by ⅓.

6. Cut the hens into serving pieces, and pour the sauce over them. Serve at once.

GREEN BEAN AND FENNEL SALAD
6 SERVINGS

> *1 pound fresh green beans*
> *1 large head fennel*
> *¼ cup olive oil*
> *2 tablespoons red wine vinegar*
> *1 clove garlic, crushed*
> *Salt and freshly ground black pepper, to taste*

1. Wash the beans, and cook them in a steamer over ½ cup of water until just tender. Remove to a salad bowl.

2. Remove the feathery leaves from the fennel, and wash and trim the head; cut it crosswise in thick slices into the salad bowl.

3. In a jar mix together the olive oil, vinegar, garlic, salt, and pepper. Cap the jar and shake vigorously. Dress the salad and serve.

MADDALENA CAKE WITH STRAWBERRIES
6 TO 8 SERVINGS

> *1 quart strawberries*
> *Superfine sugar, to taste*
> *3 eggs plus 2 yolks, at room temperature*
> *1½ cups sugar*
> *1¼ cups cake flour*
> *¼ teaspoon salt*
> *8 tablespoons unsalted butter, melted and cooled*
> *Freshly grated rind of 1 lemon*

1. Wash, hull, and slice the berries. Put them in a bowl and sprinkle with superfine sugar.

2. Preheat the oven to 375° F. Butter and flour a 12-inch round cake pan, and set it aside.

3. In the top of a double boiler, combine the eggs and yolks and sugar. In the lower part of the double boiler, heat the water to a simmer; do not let it boil. Beat the egg mixture over the hot water with an electric beater until it turns very pale yellow and thick, about 2 minutes.

4. Remove the pan from the water, and continue beating until the mixture is completely cool and very thick, about 3 minutes. Scoop into a large bowl.

5. Sift the flour and salt together 3 times. Gently fold it into the egg mixture with a rubber spatula. Fold in the cooled butter. When thoroughly blended, fold in the grated lemon rind.

6. Pour the batter into the prepared cake pan. Bake about 30 minutes on the middle rack of the oven.

7. Cool the cake in its pan on a rack. Serve it sliced, covered with strawberries.

Seven

JUNE

In Rome, when summer arrived our life centered on the terrace, bright with blooms and overlooking the grounds and gardens of Palazzo Barberini. We lived in the very heart of the city, and it was glorious. On a clear morning, when I flung open the *persiane*, which shuttered the long windows by night, I could see all the way across Rome to the dome of the Pantheon—like the shell of an immense basking turtle in the near distance—and then, beyond, to the hills of Janiculum, where an equestrian statue of Garibaldi stands guard. At dusk there was the swoop of swallows over the terrace and, in the evening, the sweet fragrance of the *riccasperma* plant as we dined on the terrace and saw the lights of the city spread below us.

June is sweet wherever it is experienced, but Rome was particularly prodigal in occasions for feasting—not only the national holiday to celebrate the birth of the republic, but saints Anthony, John the Baptist, Peter, and Paul. On June 2, 1946, the year following the end of World War II, the Italian republic was proclaimed by public referendum, marking the end of the monarchy in Italy.

Annually on June 2, the president of the republic hosts a great party in the gardens of his Quirinale residence, with guests from every walk of life. Antonio, as one of the representatives of the arts, and I were invited. It was a short walk from our place to the president's. Everyone was there: farmers and workers; the famous, like Gina Lollobrigida and Elizabeth Taylor (who, one unforgettable year, appeared wearing the same designer dress); politicians; soldiers and sailors; senators; journalists—a representative sampling from all over the country.

When we no longer lived in Rome, we still commemorated the day of the republic with a pasta called *pasta tricolore*, which incorporates the red, green, and white of the Italian flag. It is made of both spinach and natural pasta (known literally as hay and straw—*paglia e fieno*—though grass and straw would be more apt), which are cooked together and topped with the red of the classic tomato sauce.

The thirteenth of June marked a very important feast day in our family—that of Saint Anthony of Padua, the namesake of my father and brother and husband, along with cousins and nephews and grandnephews as well. Saint Anthony of Padua (to distinguish him from the hermit Saint Anthony, who lived in the desert subject to the temptations of the devil and the subject, too, of much literature and art) was an extremely learned preacher who had been deeply moved by Saint Francis at the great gathering in Assisi of 1221. He was known for the fluency of his tongue and his singular knowledge of scripture and became identified with Padua, where he preached in the last years of his life and died in 1231. He was canonized within a year, and immediately work was begun on the great edifice known as the Saint's Basilica in the Piazza del Santo. Reminiscent of Saint Mark's in Venice, the imposing structure is rich in art, including Donatello's bronze bas-reliefs recounting the life of the saint.

Antonio told of being taken on a pilgrimage to the great basilica of his patron saint as a boy, and still today one sees youngsters dressed in Franciscan robes, like little monks, who are brought to the shrine to dedicate their lives to the saint. In 1946, Saint Anthony of Padua was declared a Doctor of the Church. Before that he was more humbly known as "the Wonder-Worker." As recorded in Butler's *Lives of the Saints*, he is a saint of paradox—though militant in his activity and travels, he somehow entered tradition as a contemplative, depicted with a lily in hand and the Holy Babe on his arm. Born a Portuguese aristocrat, he was monopolized by Italians and became the special advocate of the poor so that alms given in his name are called "Saint Anthony's Bread." Educated and eloquent, "he has become the patron of the illiterate, the finder of lost trifles, the saint of the trivial appeals. One of the most effective preachers the world has ever known is now invoked against the petty, almost the comical, little ills of life." But then, forebearance and humor is also a trait of the saints.

Far from Padua, in upstate New York, the Italian-American community in and near Syracuse also kept the saint's day. From my childhood I can recall my grandfather coming each June 13 with a box of cigars for my father, whose name is Anthony. As a young boy, my father had played the clarinet in a marching band that was part of the Italian social club *Società De Amicis*, which played at all the saints' festivals and holidays. During the early years of this century, June 13 had become a big event in upstate communities, at times surpassing even the annual county fair for crowds.

The feast day of Saint John the Baptist, which falls on June 24, is unique because it commemorates the date of his birth; usually saints are honored on the date of their death, which marks their birth to eternal life. Saint John the Baptist, however, was sanctified in his mother Elizabeth's womb and came into the world not only sinless but as the herald of Christ—the morning star who ushers in the sun of justice and the light of the world. He died at the behest of Salome, who asked for his head on a platter and was given it by King Herod. (This head was said to have been conserved for many centuries in Rome's church of San Silvestro in Capite, built in 752 on the remains of a temple to the sun.)

Saint John is often pictured as a kind of wild man, a bearded ascetic clothed in animal skins and living in the desert, where, according to Matthew, "his meat was locusts and wild honey." There is, though, the great exception of Caravaggio's famous portrait of him, which presents another vision altogether—sensual, playful, a plump and fair-skinned nude youth in a contorted position, with one arm around the neck of a barely seen goat and an impudent look toward the viewer, all highly reminiscent of graphic pagan portraiture.

In Rome, Saint John's night is celebrated with the eating of snails. That was not a custom I adopted into our home life, even though I was fascinated by the wording of a Veneto recipe for them (where they are called *bovoloni* and eaten Christmas Eve), which read, "Leave the snails for two days in a wicker basket lined with vine leaves and some pieces of bread soaked in water. . . ." The Romans take a less picturesque approach and, after purging them in a pail of water with salt and vinegar, simmer them slowly with garlic, anchovy, tomato, fresh mint, and pepper.

Saint John the Baptist is the patron and protector of Florence, and the Florentine cricket festa perhaps is associated with his fondness for locusts. In the very center of the city adjacent to the duomo is the baptistry named for Saint John and called by Dante, who was baptized there, *"il mio bel San Giovanni."* It is the oldest structure in the city, standing on even older pre-Christian ruins, and is renowned for the magnificence of its bronze doors, whose panels by Ghiberti recount the life of the saint. The whole edifice, inside and out, is a Renaissance masterpiece, and truly the heart of the city. In Florence on Saint John's feast day, the festivity includes a reenactment of a sixteenth-century procession in costume, which precedes a ball game in the Piazza Signoria. I remember from my student days in Florence the whole spectacle, and though Antonio, then my fiancé, scoffed at the masquerade as something spurious, to me it was a beautiful spectacle. It was followed by fireworks in the Boboli Gardens, a display that is probably related to the bonfires lit in parts of Europe on Midsummer Eve (June 23) and closely associated with pre-Christian sun ceremonies at the time of the summer solstice. "Gorgeous as the sun at midsummer," says Shakespeare in *King Henry IV*, to refer to the sun at its peak. The celebration of the summer solstice has deep pagan reverberations in human consciousness: Midsummer marks the passing of the sun's apex and is a reminder of approaching darkness and cold. The bonfires lit all through Europe were thought both to strengthen the weakening sun and to keep evil creatures at bay. Pagan practice at the summer solstice was transferred to the Christian feast of Saint John the Baptist, and the bonfires to the sun then supposedly honored Saint John.

In ancient times, at the point when the sun's power began to diminish, a time of uncertainty and danger prevailed—elves, fairies, and evil spirits were in the air—and it was thought that on Midsummer Eve witches held their sabbath and were abroad casting spells. Shakespeare, of course, devised his comedy of mischief-making sprites and confusion as *A Midsummer Night's Dream* and in *Twelfth Night* calls a vexed moment, "this very midsummer madness."

The common Saint John's wort, which springs into bloom

around Midsummer Day and brightens fields and roadsides the whole summer long, is steeped in the tradition and lore of this great observance. Named for the saint, the plant is a radiant golden yellow, and, it was thought, resembles a small sun. Druids were said to have used the flowers as sun symbols in their rites. It was also thought to repel evil spirits, to be effective against the evil eye and lightning bolts and, when applied to the mouths of accused witches, to cause them to confess. Hence, its other popular name of Devil's Bane, or the equivalent in French, *chasse-diable*, and in Italian, *caccia diavoli*. To complete the catalogue of properties of this pretty plant, it was also used in love charms, for a Saint John's wort picked before dawn on Saint John's Eve and placed under a girl's pillow that night would let her dream of the man she would marry. In addition, concoctions and tisanes that were made from it were curatives for melancholy, hysteria, and madness. As an ointment it was used for cuts and bruises. And, hung on doors on Midsummer's Eve, it protected homes from the witches flying about that night—such was the magic it evoked.

The herald of summer, Saint John the Baptist, is also the patron saint of love and marriage, and it was on the Saturday nearest his feast day that my eldest daughter, Linda, chose to be married. At the wedding feast, however, she forewent the stewed snails that Italian tradition calls for at celebrations on this day. We were living in the States then, and I prepared a splendid outdoor reception on that perfect rare day in June, incorporating the Italian custom of passing around white sugar-coated almonds called *confetti* (for fertility, since they simulate the bean shape), which may be where the custom of throwing paper confetti at newlyweds derives from.

Rome's own particular Christian festa is for saints Peter and Paul on June 29. The two great apostles were both martyred in Rome and have been linked since the earliest times, when their names were first joined together in crude scrawlings on catacomb walls. During my first visit to the catacombs of Saint Sebastian, there was nothing more moving and impressive to me than to decipher ancient graffiti appealing to "Petro" and "Paule." There are said to be about 650 graffiti, in both Latin and Greek, which are invocations to the apostles, all dated to the second half of the third century. Humble sentiments were scratched upon the plastered walls of the catacombs: "Peter and Paul, intercede for Victor"; "Peter and Paul, do not forget Antonius Bassus"; "I, Tomius Coelius, made a feast to the honor of Peter and Paul." And even today, the saints are remembered together when we say we shouldn't rob Peter to pay Paul.

Again it was Caravaggio who painted the most dramatic and vividly realistic portraits of the two saints, both works filled with powerful immediacy. So overwhelmingly grounded in the life force were Caravaggio's paintings that they were often rejected by those who had commissioned them because it was thought that their tough reality showed a lack of respect for divinity or saintliness; yet the artist's genius was in that very sense of vitality and expressive tension. Both his *Conversion of Saint Paul* and *Crucifixion of Saint Peter* hang in the little-visited church of Santa Maria del Popolo in Rome's Piazza del Popolo, superb renditions of two dramatic moments.

The *Conversion of Saint Paul* depicts Saul, as he was first known, on his journey to Damascus, where he was going to carry forward the persecution of the first Christians. On the road he experienced a devastating vision of Jesus, which left him blind. Caravaggio catches him, fallen from his horse, arms stretched upward, at that moment of revelation from which he will emerge as Paul, the missionary of Christianity and promulgator of the Church's theological doctrines. From his prison in Rome, shortly before his martyrdom at about the same time as Peter's, Saint Paul wrote those stirring words: "I have fought a good fight; I have finished my course; I have kept the faith."

After Antonio died and the older girls were off at school in the States, Niki and I lived in a small penthouse apartment near the

Vatican. On the feast of Saint Peter, when the dome of the basilica was illuminated, it became a gigantic globe filling the bathroom window with its glory. When we lived so near to Saint Peter's, one of our favorite outings was to go to its rooftop bar for ice cream and the views. The people who work at the basilica are a special work force permanently attached to Saint Peter's and are known as the *sampietrini*. They climb around the great dome with the balance and confidence of acrobats, and proudly hand down their skilled jobs from father to son.

Inside the great edifice we would visit the bronze statue of Saint Peter seated on a marble throne. He is robed in papal vestments, and his mantle is fastened with a broach set with garnets, zircons, crystal, and topaz and presented by Czar Nicholas I on June 29, 1851. The foot of the bronze statue is worn to a golden patina by the kisses of the faithful. Every visit to the basilica would inevitably remind me of the chance meeting there between Margaret Fuller and her future lover and husband, Marchese Angelo Ossoli; she, separated from her friends and lost; he, noting her predicament and offering help—a legendary meeting.

Simon the fisherman became the apostle Peter, whose symbol is the fish; he was also the first among the "fisher of men" and was given his new name by Christ, who addressed him with the Latin word for rock, "You are *Petrus*, and on this rock I will build my church." He is the prince of the apostles; the first bishop of Rome, from whom comes the succession of popes; the patron saint of fishermen; and the keeper of the gate to heaven to whom one applies for admittance.

Feast of the Republic
"Grass and Straw" with Basic
   Tomato Sauce
Stuffed Peppers
Zucchini-Endive Salad with Red
   Onion
Peaches in White Wine

Saint Anthony's Day
Summer Antipasto
Marinated Vegetable Salad
Tomatoes Stuffed with Orzo
   and Pesto
Cold Veal Scaloppine
Fruit Soup

*Midsummer Night—Saint
   John's Day*
Peperonata
Meat Ring
Berry Sauce for Ice Cream

Feast of Saints Peter and Paul
Black Olive Pasta
Saint Peter's Seafood Skewers
Summer Squash with Tomatoes
Linda's Lemon Dessert

Feast of the Republic

"GRASS AND STRAW" WITH BASIC TOMATO SAUCE
6 SERVINGS

> *½ pound fresh white fettuccine*
> *½ pound fresh green fettuccine*
> *1 recipe Basic Tomato Sauce (see recipe, page 55)*
> *Freshly grated Parmesan cheese, to pass at table*

1. In a large quantity of boiling water, cook white fettucine, then add spinach fettucine until both are al dente.

2. Meanwhile, heat the Basic Tomato Sauce.

3. Drain the pasta and put it into a serving bowl. Pour the sauce over it, and mix. Serve immediately, accompanied by a bowl of grated Parmesan cheese.

STUFFED PEPPERS
6 SERVINGS

   3 large, firm sweet peppers, red or yellow
   ¾ cup soft fresh breadcrumbs
   1 clove garlic, minced
   3 tablespoons minced parsley
   1 cup ground ham (about 5 ounces)
   1 teaspoon dry mustard
   3 tablespoons minced onion
   ½ cup grated Parmesan cheese
   Salt and freshly ground black pepper, to taste
   ½ teaspoon dried sage, or 5 fresh leaves, chopped
   2 to 3 tablespoons olive oil

Preheat the oven to 350° F.

1. Remove the tops of the peppers; remove the seeds and membrane and discard. Cut the peppers in half lengthwise. In a large quantity of boiling water, parboil the peppers for 5 minutes

2. Mix the breadcrumbs with the garlic and parsley.

3. In a bowl combine the ham, breadcrumb mixture, mustard, onion, Parmesan cheese, salt, pepper, and sage. Place the peppers in an oiled baking dish just large enough to hold them comfortably, and fill them with stuffing. Trickle the olive oil over the peppers.

4. Bake the peppers 30 minutes on the middle rack of the oven, or until the stuffing is firm and the peppers tender. Serve at once.

ZUCCHINI-ENDIVE SALAD WITH RED ONION
6 SERVINGS

   3 or 4 medium zucchini, washed
   1 medium sweet red onion, peeled
   ½ cup olive oil

¼ cup red wine vinegar

2 tablespoons minced parsley

1 tablespoon chopped fresh basil leaves

2 cloves garlic, minced

½ teaspoon salt

3 medium Belgian endives, washed and separated
  into leaves

1. Cut the zucchini in long strips and the onion in thin rounds.

2. Combine the olive oil, vinegar, parsley, basil, garlic, and salt in a bowl. Add the zucchini and onion; toss together, cover, and chill for several hours.

3. Arrange the endive leaves on serving plates. With a slotted spoon remove the zucchini and onion from the dressing; divide them equally among the plates, arranging them on the endive leaves.

4. The remaining dressing can be served separately, if desired.

PEACHES IN WHITE WINE
8 SERVINGS

4 large peaches

½ cup macaroon or amaretti cookie crumbs

¼ cup Candied Orange Peel (see recipe, page 48)

4 teaspoons unsalted butter, cut into 8 dabs

8 toasted whole almonds

¼ cup dry white wine

Preheat the oven to 350° F.

1. Drop the peaches into boiling water for a count of 20, then immediately plunge them into cold water. The skins should slip off easily. Cut the peaches in half, and remove the pits. Scoop out about ¼ inch of peach pulp to enlarge the hollows. Put the pulp in a bowl, and mash it.

2. Add the cookie crumbs and Candied Orange Peel to the peach pulp.

3. Arrange the peach halves in a buttered baking dish, and pour enough water around them so the bottom of the dish is barely covered.

4. Divide the peach pulp–crumb mixture evenly among the peach halves, and top each with 1 almond and a dab of butter. Sprinkle the peach halves with the wine.

5. Bake the peaches on the middle rack of the oven until tender, 20 to 35 minutes, depending on the ripeness of the fruit. Check after 15 minutes to see if the filling is dry. If so, sprinkle with more wine.

6. Serve the peaches hot or at room temperature.

Saint Anthony's Day

SUMMER ANTIPASTO
8 TO 10 SERVINGS

*2 pounds fresh mozzarella cheese (from an Italian
grocery, if possible)
1 large bunch fresh basil*

1. Cut the mozzarella cheese into cubes. Put them into a large bowl.

2. Tear the basil leaves coarsely, and sprinkle over the mozzarella. Serve with toothpicks to spear cubes of cheese and basil.

MARINATED VEGETABLE SALAD
10 TO 12 SERVINGS

> 2 cups broccoli florets
> 2 cups (about 5 ounces) quartered mushrooms
> 2 cups red bell pepper strips
> 1½ cups cauliflower florets
> 1 medium cucumber, scrubbed and sliced
> ½ cup diagonally sliced scallions
> 1 cup olive oil
> ⅓ cup red wine vinegar
> 1 large clove garlic, minced
> 2 tablespoons minced fresh basil leaves or 1
>   tablespoon dried basil
> ¼ cup capers, not drained
> 1 teaspoon salt
> ¼ teaspoon freshly ground black pepper
> 2 teaspoons dry mustard
> 1 teaspoon lemon juice

1. Combine the broccoli, mushrooms, red bell pepper, cauliflower, cucumber, and scallions in a large bowl.

2. In a 2-cup measure, combine the remaining ingredients and blend well with a fork. Pour the dressing over the vegetables, and toss well.

3. Cover the salad, and chill for several hours before serving.

TOMATOES STUFFED WITH ORZO AND PESTO
8 SERVINGS

> 8 large ripe tomatoes
> 1 cup orzo (rice-shaped pasta)
> ½ cup Pesto Sauce (see recipe, page 77)

241

Salt and freshly ground black pepper, to taste
2 tablespoons minced parsley

Preheat the oven to 350° F.

1. Cut a large slice off the top of each tomato (about ⅓ of the tomato), and carefully hollow it out with a serrated spoon. Keep the shell intact. Remove the seeds from the pulp and discard. Chop the pulp, and let it drain in a sieve placed over a bowl; discard the liquid. Invert the tomatoes on paper towels, and let them drain.

2. Cook the *orzo*, drain it, and mix with the drained tomato pulp. Add the Pesto Sauce, salt, and pepper. Mix well.

3. Divide the tomato-*orzo* mixture equally among the tomatoes, and place them in an oiled baking dish.

4. Bake 15 minutes on the middle rack of the oven.

5. Sprinkle the stuffed tomatoes with the parsley, and cool before serving.

COLD VEAL SCALOPPINE
8 SERVINGS

¼ cup all-purpose flour
Salt and freshly ground black pepper, to taste
2 eggs
1 tablespoon water
2 cups fine dry breadcrumbs
16 thin veal scallops (about 2 pounds)
3 tablespoons unsalted butter
1 tablespoon olive oil
Lemon slices, for garnish
Small parsley sprigs, for garnish

1. On a large sheet of wax paper, combine the flour with the salt and pepper. In a small, shallow bowl beat the eggs with the water. Put the breadcrumbs on another sheet of wax paper.

2. Place each veal scallop between 2 sheets of wax paper, and pound it as thin as you can with a wooden mallet.

3. Dip each veal scallop into the seasoned flour, and shake off any excess. Next dip it into the egg mixture, let it drain a little, and then dip it in the breadcrumbs, covering both sides.

4. Put the butter and olive oil in a large skillet over medium-high heat. When sizzling, cook the veal until it is golden brown on both sides, turning once, approximately 3 to 5 minutes overall. Cook the scallops in batches; do not crowd the pan. (Add more butter and oil, if necessary.) Remove the cooked veal to a platter.

5. Let the veal cool. Serve garnished with lemon slices and parsley sprigs.

FRUIT SOUP
12 SERVINGS

> ½ canteloupe, scooped into balls
> ½ small watermelon, scooped into balls
> ¼ honeydew melon, scooped into balls
> 1½ cups seedless green grapes
> 2 ripe peaches, sliced
> 2 ripe plums, sliced
> 2 cups mixed berries, including sliced strawberries
> 2 kiwi, peeled and sliced
> ½ cup white wine
> ½ cup honey
> 2 cups low fat vanilla yogurt
> ¼ teaspoon ground ginger

1. In large glass bowl blend together yogurt and ginger. Add fruit.

2. Blend together wine and honey and pour over the fruit, mixing well.

3. Chill the fruit soup for at least an hour before serving.

Midsummer Night—Saint John's Day

PEPERONATA
6 servings

> ¼ cup olive oil
> 3 cloves garlic, minced
> 1 cup onion, sliced thin
> 4 peppers, green, yellow, and red, cut in strips
> 3 ripe tomatoes
> 1 teaspoon red wine vinegar
> ½ teaspoon salt
> 1 tablespoon minced parsley
> pepper to taste

1. Heat olive oil in a deep skillet over moderate heat. Add onions and garlic and sauté until translucent and golden.

2. Remove stems, seeds, and membrane from peppers and cut into thin strips. Add pepper strips to skillet, reduce heat and cook for 10 minutes, stirring occasionally.

3. Plunge tomatoes into boiling water for a minute. Cool under cold water, and peel. Seed tomatoes, and cut into chunks.

4. Add tomatoes, vinegar, salt, and pepper to skillet. Cover and cook over low heat 30 minutes. Sprinkle with parsley and serve hot as a vegetable dish, or chill the *peperonata* and serve cold as an antipasto with crusty bread.

MEAT RING
6 TO 8 SERVINGS

3 tablespoons unsalted butter
¾ cup minced onion
½ cup minced celery
½ cup minced carrot
½ cup minced red pepper and green pepper,
    combined
2 teaspoons minced garlic
1½ pounds very lean ground beef
½ pound ground pork
½ pound ground veal
2 eggs, slightly beaten
1 teaspoon soy sauce
½ teaspoon white pepper
1 teaspoon chili powder
½ cup wheat germ
2 tablespoons tomato paste dissolved in ½ cup water
8 watercress sprigs
4 scallions, slivered

Preheat oven to 350° F.

1. Melt butter in a large skillet over moderate heat. Sauté the onion, celery, carrot, peppers, and garlic until soft, about 10 minutes. Let cool in the skillet.

2. Put the beef, pork, and veal in a large bowl. Add the eggs, soy sauce, white pepper, chili powder, wheat germ, and tomato paste dissolved in water, and incorporate these ingredients into the meats. Add the sautéed vegetables to the meat, and mix together well.

3. Pack the mixture into an ungreased ring form (6-cup capacity) to create the ring shape. Then turn the packed mix out of the form into a shallow baking pan. Bake 45 minutes. Cool.

4. Fill the center of the ring with sprigs of watercress and slivered scallions. Serve at room temperature.

BERRY SAUCE FOR ICE CREAM
4 TO 6 SERVINGS

> 2 cups ripe blueberries, strawberries, or raspberries
> 1/2 cup sugar
> 1 tablespoon fresh lemon juice or fruit liqueur

1. Partially crush the berries in a heavy nonaluminum saucepan. Add the sugar and lemon juice.

2. Cook over moderate heat until the sugar has dissolved and formed a sauce with the juices. Stir occasionally. Cool.

3. Serve over vanilla ice cream.

BLACK OLIVE PASTA
4 TO 6 SERVINGS

> *1 pound* fischietti *"whistle" pasta (short tubes)*
> *5 tablespoons olive oil*
> *1 large clove garlic*
> *4 to 5 tablespoons olive paste (available at Italian*
> *   groceries and specialty shops)*
> *2 tablespoons minced parsley*
> *Freshly grated Parmesan cheese (optional)*

1. In a large quantity of salted boiling water, cook the pasta al dente. Drain it, and put it in a bowl. Toss with 1 tablespoon of the oil.

2. Pour the remaining oil in a small skillet over moderate heat. When it is sizzling, add the garlic clove and cook until golden, stirring constantly. Discard the garlic.

3. Pour the garlic-flavored oil on the pasta; add the olive paste and parsley. Mix well.

4. Serve immediately, accompanied by grated Parmesan cheese, if desired.

SAINT PETER'S SEAFOOD SKEWERS
6 TO 8 SERVINGS

> *3 branches fresh rosemary*
> *8 tablespoons softened unsalted butter*
> *2 tablespoons minced fresh parsley*

1½ tablespoons mixed minced fresh herbs, such as
chives, thyme, oregano, dill, rosemary, or basil
(or 1 teaspoon dried herbs)
1 teaspoon lemon juice
1 pound swordfish, salmon, or tuna steak cut into
1-inch cubes
1 pound (about 40) peeled, deveined medium
shrimp
1 pound whole sea scallops
1 cup fresh sage leaves

Prepare a charcoal fire. Toss moistened fresh rosemary branches onto moderately hot coals just before cooking the skewered seafood.

1. Combine the butter, parsley, herbs, and lemon juice in blender or food processor. Beat until fluffy.

2. Arrange seafood on skewers, alternating each variety with a leaf of sage.

3. Brush the seafood with the herb butter, reserving some herb butter for basting.

4. Place seafood skewers on a well-oiled grill, about 4 to 6 inches from the heat.

5. Cook, brushing with extra herb butter, allowing 3 to 4 minutes to a side, for not more than 8 minutes total.

6. Serve the seafood with the remaining herb butter.

SUMMER SQUASH WITH TOMATOES
6 SERVINGS

5 medium yellow summer squash
3 to 4 ripe tomatoes, peeled
¼ cup olive oil

2 cloves garlic
1 medium onion, sliced
Salt and freshly ground black pepper, to taste

1. Scrub the squash, and cut it into 1-inch cubes. Seed the tomatoes, cut them into chunks, and let them drain in a sieve set over a bowl. (Discard the liquid.)

2. Pour the olive oil in a large, heavy skillet, over moderate heat. When it is sizzling, add the garlic and onion. Cook, stirring, until the onion is soft and translucent. Discard the garlic.

3. Add the squash cubes, cover the skillet, lower the heat, and cook gently for 10 minutes, stirring occasionally.

4. Remove the lid, raise the heat, and add the tomatoes, salt, and pepper. Cook 5 minutes, stirring constantly. Serve immediately.

LINDA'S LEMON DESSERT
8 SERVINGS

5 eggs, separated
Juice and grated rind of 3 large lemons
1 cup sugar
2 envelopes unflavored gelatin
½ cup cold water
⅛ teaspoon cream of tartar
1 cup heavy cream

1. In the top of a nonaluminum double boiler over hot water, place the egg yolks, lemon juice, lemon rind, and sugar. Cook to thicken, stirring constantly.

2. Soften the gelatin in the water, and add to lemon mixture. Stir until dissolved. Cool.

3. Beat the egg whites with the cream of tartar until stiff.

4. Whip the cream, and fold it into lemon mixture.

5. Fold the beaten egg whites into the lemon mixture.

6. Pour into a 2-quart soufflé dish or mold. Refrigerate, covered, for at least 2 hours.

Eight

JULY

July in Italy meant the great outdoors, moving out into summertime, whether at the sea at Maratea, in the Marche countryside, or into the piazzas and streets of Spoleto at the Festival of Two Worlds.

When our Australian friend Essie Lee still had her place at Porto Ercole, we would drive up from Rome for a weekend of bathing and visiting. I remember being introduced to stacks of the new magazine *New York* on Essie's patio and absolutely devouring them for their cheeky, slick lingo and the connection with home. Essie made a fresh tomato soup, which she called *"contadina* style," perhaps because her tomatoes were always delivered fresh and sun-soaked from the vine by the peasant woman down the road. Essie peeled five or six tomatoes, mixed them with basil and garlic and three tablespoons of olive oil, and then poured the mix over thick slices of Italian bread in a casserole. She added a little stock and cooked it slowly for a half-hour, then served it with grated cheese.

In Rome in July, the *Festa di Noantri* ("Our Very Own Festa") is held in the Trastevere quarter at the same time when, in antiquity, a festival for Neptune was held to invoke the god of the sea to increase the River Tiber's water supply during the summer drought. For the Trastevere celebration, counters are set up featuring neighboring Ariccia's famous whole stuffed and roasted pig, whose exact seasoning is still secret—and sublime. Or challenges are given to see who can gobble the most spaghetti the fastest at the spaghetti counters. The festa overlaps the feast of the *Madonna del Carmine* on July 16 but is celebrated right through July 31 and has become associated with the *trasteverini*, literally those who live on the other side of the Tiber. It is still a folk festival with dances, songs, floats, processions, and fireworks, and is popular with Italian-Americans whose roots go back to Naples, where the Madonna of Carmine is patroness. In New York's Little Italy, the day is a pushcart vendor's paradise for selling specialty foods.

Earlier than my experience of Italian festivals is the memory of the family festa. This took the form of a picnic; we gathered in a meadow at Cazenovia Lake, near Syracuse, around the black-garbed figure of our grandmother, an old immigrant woman, to celebrate ourselves with abundant good food and good feelings. One part of our group came from Syracuse, the other from Utica, and we joined together in that upstate New York locale, spreading our blankets and sharing all the food. This memory is primeval.

In our family this annual summer picnic, willed by our grandmother, was the event that pleased her most—more than Christmas, Easter, or any of the saints' days—for it came at the peak of summer when the bounty of her backyard garden was in evidence and the days and evenings long and easy. All through the long winters, she lived with the memory of each summer's picnic, and by spring she was out in the backyard starting the first crops of peas and greens, putting in rows of lettuce and herbs, setting the stakes for the pole beans and, later, the tomatoes. The memory of that family picnic remained a fixture for me, and in Italy it was always evoked with our al fresco dining. It was as if I had been prepared as a child in the meadow of Cazenovia for all those Italian gatherings under arbors, at seasides, or on hillsides where we ate out.

I remember the Spoleto Festival of Two Worlds in 1966, during our first summer back in Italy after we moved there from Shady Lane Farm. While we were in Westchester, Antonio had come to know Gian Carlo Menotti, who then had a house with Samuel Barber in Mt. Kisco, not far from us. In the early sixties Menotti had asked Antonio his opinion of a festival of two worlds—a gathering of performing artists in opera, ballet, chamber music, drama, and film, with the participation also of writers and poets, painters and sculptors, in the unique setting of some unfrequented but beautiful Italian town that Menotti was then engaged in searching out. Antonio did not think it would work. It did. And it worked so well that Menotti has since gone on to found a second Festival of Two Worlds in Charleston, South Carolina, and now a third in Melbourne, Australia.

That summer of 1966, Antonio had been asked to read from his work at the festival's poetry session. We drove to Spoleto from Rome, and the city literally burst upon our view as we made a turn in the curving roadway and suddenly saw it in its setting. The towers and walls of the town on one side of the road were linked by a high aqueduct bridge (emanating from heights dominated by an old castle-fortress, once the seat of Lucrezia Borgia's duchy) to the other side, which consisted of open grain fields and a winding road, through woods, to Monte Luco. Banners of all nations fluttered at the turn into town. In the main square, the Piazza della Libertà, posters announced the maestro's fifty-fifth birthday. Called in jest the duke of Spoleto, Menotti had truly become the modern-day eminence of that town, as important in his own way as the legendary Renaissance figure, Lucrezia Borgia, who had been given the town as her fief and with it the title of duchess of Spoleto by her father, Pope Alexander VI.

La Rocca, the fortress on the heights, still looming over the town, had been her residence. In more recent times it was a government prison. Only recently, in 1984, was it returned to the town to be restored to its former glory. I was in Spoleto again in 1984 and enjoyed once more the noonday concerts at the delicious Teatro Caio Melisso under the direction of Charles Wadsworth, the American impresario who has guided these successful events from the very beginning, establishing a casual, warm, and popular tone that still charms audiences and intrigues the more formal Italians. On this occasion, chatting affably, Wadsworth pointed up from the stage to a box at his left, and there was the maestro himself. It was déjà-vu; I had just seen Menotti seated in a box in a similar setting in May at the Dock Street Theater in Charleston, uncannily reminiscent of the Spoleto theater.

Eating was chancey in Spoleto when there were great crowds of people on hand for the festival. Some of the best food I had was in out-of-the-way places, like the inn halfway up Monte Luco, where we once found rooms when everything in Spoleto was taken. There, on a terrace overlooking the town, in utter peace and with a rainbow arching over the castle towers, I had *caccioto ai ferri* for the first time: a dish of cheese grilled over an open fire, served with an anchovy sauce and sopped up with the garlic toast called *bruschetta*. Another time, at the noontime concert, a tasty local speciality, black olive paste on *crostini*, was served as an hors d'oeuvre, and this acquaintance led me to concoct a superb cold pasta salad made with the same olive paste.

But best of all were the fresh trout taken from the spring waters of the Clitunno for grilling over an open wood fire. The classical source of the spring, *Fonti del Clitunno*, is not far from Spoleto. It is a few kilometers down a roadway laid over one of the great Roman roads, the ancient Via Flaminia. I first traveled it during my student days in Perugia, when I'd go down to Rome by bus and Clitunno was a stop on the bus route. Just a year or so earlier, in Latin class at Wells College, I had been reading the odes of Propertius, in which he spoke of the sacred font and the procession of garlanded oxen that paid tribute to the gods at Clitunno. It appears as a spring within a pool of marvelously clear water, a peaceful little oasis just off the roadway, sheltered by weeping willows and graceful poplars. It was a sacred spot and animals were purified in its waters before being sacrificed. In a different era Lord Byron, in the fourth canto of his long poem *Childe Harold*, described the locale thus:

"But thou, Clitumnus! in thy sweetest wave
Of the most living crystal that was e'er
The haunt of river nymph, to gaze and lave
Her limbs where nothing hid them, thou dost rear
Thy grassy banks whereon the milk-white steer
Grazes; the purest God of gentle waters!
And most serene of aspect, and most clear:
Surely that stream was unprofaned by slaughters,
A mirror and a bath for Beauty's youngest daughters!"

About the same time as Byron's visit, the French painter Jean-Baptiste Camille Corot, noted for his classical evocations, visited the spot and captured it in a poetically rendered landscape. Just a half-mile away from the source is a charming fifth-century Christian building known as the little temple, or *Tempietto*.

As often as possible, we'd cross the Appenines to get to our little farmhouse in the Marche region. We had favorite stopping places along the way, and one was the humble little trattoria all by itself about midway in the mountains, where we had wonderful fresh-water fish cooked over embers and basted with an oil-garlic-rosemary sauce. At Amatrice, an out-of-the-way mountain village, we would sample the peppery pasta with *pancetta* and *pecorino* cheese, which is renowned in the outside world as *spaghetti all'amatriciana*. Or sometimes we'd hold out until we got to Ascoli Piceno, noted for its speciality of huge deep-fried olives stuffed with a meat and cheese filling. Or, just a bit farther on, out of the mountains and off the Adriatica highway, which skirts the sea, there was La Stalla, a former farmhouse turned trattoria and offering its famous home-made *tagliatelli* made on the *chitarra* and served with a ragù sauce.

Summer days had a special rhythm in the country. Our little farmhouse was up in the hills some 10 kilometers from the sea. We would naturally head for the beach each morning, usually going to Porto San Giorgio, sometimes to neighboring San Benedetto del Tronto, or Sant'Elpidio. There we'd enjoy the sunbathing and swimming until noon, when we'd either go to the shadowy arbor at Fefe's eating place, within walking distance of the beach, or get in the car to drive up to the little hamlet of Torre di Palme, set on a high promontory overlooking the water. We'd park and walk through that miniature habitation to Nino's, where we would eat, say, a three-course fish fry dinner at the fixed price of 1,000 lire, then equivalent to $1.60. There was no menu; Nino and his wife would be at the stove when we entered through the kitchen; we could see and smell what was being prepared, and it was always wonderful.

Then we went home and spent the afternoons working around the place, going into Monterubbiano for supplies, walking in the country looking for wild rughetta which is called arugula here or fennel, or exploring the neighboring towns. The country is beautiful, all rolling hills, with walled towns on the heights. Off in the distance was the blue expanse of the Adriatic and, beyond that, Yugoslavia. We went down into the valley from our own hills of Monterubbiano and then up again in the hills of Montefiore to find the painter Domenico Cantatore. We found him at home, an affable and gentle man of the South noted for his strong and passionate canvases, alive with color and boldness, recording the gorgeous scenes of what lay before his eyes—the fields, the sea, the sky, the peasants at work and rest. It was Cantatore who recommended that we drop in the church at Montefiore and see the Carlo Crivelli triptych, which depicts six saints and is stylish with Renaissance elegance, all the more appealing for being found so unexpectedly in that remote village.

Montefiore, like Monterubbiano and Moresco and Fermo and Cossignano and all the other hill towns in the Marche, glows with the rosy hue of brick. They are all brick towns, each clean and wind-swept and each once a fortified castle held by the local lord. Now, however, the bastions are softened by ivy and tufts of flowering plants; houses have been built in or on them, balconies spilling over the riot of red geraniums and blue plumbago. In Offida, where there is a superb sixteenth-century municipal building, lace is still made by hand, and the speciality of the place is a curious sweet called *funghetto*, which is hard as a rock when made but turns soft after 4 or 5 days. It's made with a kilo of sugar mixed with a kilo of flour and flavored with a dash of anise. Each of these little towns has some speciality—a cheese, a wine, a sweet, a local product. We could never run out of places to see and visit.

From our own little Monterubbiano, we could see the nearest large town, Fermo; in other directions were the villages of Altidona, Lapidona, and the unbelievable fairy-tale vision of Moresco, whose crenellated castle towers rise above the walls and filled the window I opened each morning with that sight.

The *monterubbensi* and the *fermani* have a long-standing rivalry, and the story is told that in centuries gone by, those of Monterub-biano, offended because Fermo became the provincial capital, declared war on their neighbors. They built a cannon in Monterub-biano and faced it in the direction of Fermo. But a cannonball was needed to shoot from it, so the self-appointed cannoneers went

257

through town rounding up all the pots and pans they could commandeer. They melted down the metal, made a cannonball of sorts, and set it off—whereupon it blew up around them and killed fifteen *monterubbensi*. "Beh," said a survivor, "if it killed fifteen of us here, imagine how many it must have killed over there in Fermo!"

The little farmhouse in the Marche was sold a few years after Antonio's death, when I came back to the States. Our daughter Susanna, however, married a *marchigiano* of Urbino in the late seventies, so she still has a foothold in the region. She was born in Milan and, taking her first breath of Italian air, must have decided she was forever after an Italian. She is an innovative cook and an intrepid character. When we had our farmhouse, she participated in the local marathon, which is called the *Marcialonga*, and which is a real test of endurance, extending from the town of Fermo, up and down hill and dale, for 26 kilometers. While Susi ran, Linda was back at the farmhouse baking an apple pie for her sister.

Susanna's birthday is July 17, and we have always celebrated that day rather than her name day. The latter falls in August and honors Santa Susanna, a young Roman woman who was martyred at the end of the third century for wishing to remain a virgin. In Rome the church of Santa Susanna on Via XX Settembre was just around the corner from where we lived and is designated the American church.

When I last visited Susi and her husband, Nevio, an artist, it was in July, so I brought a packaged chocolate cake mix in order to make her a birthday cake on the spot, knowing she would not have all the ingredients on hand for American-style baking. Italians like a different texture to their cakes—firm, dry, low, and less sweet than ours, not high and airy, and often flavored with a liqueur. The cake from the mix was, as the package promised, moist and fudgy and two layers high. Susi said she could never serve it to Nevio's parents, who were coming that night to help her celebrate—they'd think it was a disgrace of a cake. So I said, that's all right, we'll just call it a *budino*, a pudding, and serve it in bowls with whipped cream. Which we did, with great success and to my relief.

Once, at Shady Lane Farm, Linda made a very special lemon icing topped with chocolate leaves for the angel food cake I had prepared for Susi's birthday. Linda had collected leaves from our gingko tree and patiently coated them with chocolate (according to a recipe she had found in a birthday book), then stripped each leaf from the chocolate, which remained impressed with the leaf prints, and used the chocolate leaves to decorate the cake.

July 26 is the feast of Saint Ann, and when I lived in Rome, that date was a reminder of elegant Renaissance evenings. With the fifteenth century's elation in the newly rediscovered classical world, the humanists and intellectuals of the day (and the courtesans who were their companions) used as their particular center of worship the Rome church dedicated to Saint Augustine. Cesare Borgia's mistress, the beautiful Fiammetta, also had her own chapel in the church, and other famous members of her profession were once buried there. As Georgina Masson says in her guide to Rome, the church was built between 1479 and 1483 of travertine plundered from the Colosseum and is one of the few of that period still to be seen in Rome. Raphael, Castiglione, Cardinal Bembo, and other *illustri* belonged to the circle of friends who met at the church. They also used to dine out on summer nights in the gardens of their friends, extemporizing verses and engaging in witty conversations in the company of beautiful women.

The most celebrated dinner always took place every year on the feast of Saint Ann, when, Masson writes, "verses were hung on the garden trees and statues. Today these poems read as the most extraordinary mixture of paganism and Christianity, with the Virgin and saints apostrophised as classical goddesses. . . ."

The Sansovino Madonna and Child, known as the Madonna of Birth, which is housed in the church of San Agostino, has a marked affinity with the mother cult of antiquity. As Masson says, "the cult of the mother strikes some deep atavistic chord in the Roman mind."

Mother, parents, family—they all merge in the festas that are so much a part of Italian life.

Festa di Noantri—Our Very Own Festa
Shells with Fresh Tomatoes and Basil
Veal Arcobaleno
Filled Zucchini Blossoms
Cantaloupe Cream

Susi's Birthday
Cold Zucchini-Rice Soup
Turkey Fillets with Balsamic Vinegar Sauce
Tomato Salad
Apple Torte

Festa di Noantri—Our Very Own Festa

SHELLS WITH FRESH TOMATOES AND BASIL
6 SERVINGS

4 to 5 ripe tomatoes (about 2 pounds)
½ cup olive oil
4 cloves garlic
¼ cup chopped fresh basil leaves
Salt and freshly ground black pepper, to taste
1 pound conchiglie *(shell-shaped pasta)*
2 tablespoons minced parsley

1. Plunge the tomatoes into boiling water for a count of 20. Rinse them under cold running water to cool, and slip off the skins. Seed the tomatoes. Chop them coarsely, and let drain in a sieve set over a bowl. Discard the liquid, and put the tomato chunks in the bowl.

2. Blend the olive oil, garlic, basil, salt, and pepper in with the tomatoes.

3. Let the mixture marinate 1 to 2 hours at room temperature.

4. Cook the pasta al dente. Drain it, and put it in a serving bowl.

5. Remove the garlic, and pour the tomato mixture over the shells. Toss. Sprinkle with parsley, and serve immediately.

VEAL ARCOBALENO
6 TO 8 SERVINGS

12 to 16 veal scallops (1½ to 2 pounds)
6 tablespoons olive oil
1 medium zucchini, diced into ½-inch pieces
1 red bell pepper, diced into ½-inch pieces (or
  substitute ½ cup diced carrot)
½ pound mushrooms, sliced
1 cup pearl onions, cooked
¼ cup all-purpose flour
Salt and freshly ground black pepper, to taste
½ cup dry white wine
½ cup chicken broth
½ cup whipping cream

1. Place each veal scallop between 2 sheets of wax paper, and pound it as thin as possible with a wooden mallet. Pound evenly.

2. Pour 3 tablespoons of the olive oil into a large, heavy skillet over medium-high heat. When it sizzles, add the zucchini and peppers or carrot. Cook, stirring frequently, until tender. Add the mushroom slices, and cook another 3 minutes. Add the cooked onions. Set aside on a warmed platter.

3. Lightly flour the veal scallops on both sides. Pour the remaining oil in a large, heavy skillet over medium-high heat. When it sizzles,

cook the scallops until golden, turning once, approximately 2 minutes overall. Cook the scallops in batches; do not crowd the pan. Season with salt and pepper. (Add more oil, if necessary.) Transfer the browned veal to a heated platter.

4. Increase the heat to high. Add the wine to the skillet; bring it to a boil, and cook for about 50 seconds, scraping the bottom of the pan. Add the broth, and continue cooking and stirring until the sauce begins to thicken, about 3 minutes. Return the scallops to the pan, and spoon the sauce over them.

5. Return the cooked vegetables to the pan, stir in the cream, and heat through. Serve immediately.

FILLED ZUCCHINI BLOSSOMS
6 SERVINGS

> 1½ pounds zucchini blossoms
> ½ pound mozzarella, cut into slivers
> Peanut oil for deep frying
> 1 recipe Pastella Batter (see recipe, page 162)
> Salt, to taste

1. Wash the blossoms, and gently pat them dry. Trim off the stems, and remove the small leaves at the stem ends of the blossoms. Remove the pistils.

2. Open the petals gently, drop a few mozzarella slivers into each blossom, then press the blossom closed.

3. Pour 4 inches of oil into a deep frying pan or deep-fat fryer, and heat.

4. Dip the blossoms quickly in the batter. Let excess batter drip off, and fry them, a few at a time, until golden brown. Remove them with a slotted spoon to drain on paper towels.

5. Serve the blossoms very hot, sprinkled with salt.

CANTALOUPE CREAM
6 SERVINGS

> ½ cup water
> ½ cup sugar
> ½ cup freshly squeezed orange juice
> 1 small ripe cantaloupe
> 1 tablespoon orange liqueur, such as Grand
>   Marnier
> ½ cup heavy cream, plus more for garnish
> Freshly grated rind of 1 orange

1. Combine the water, sugar, and orange juice in a small saucepan; bring to a boil. Cook 5 minutes, stirring often. Pour the mixture into a bowl, and set it aside to cool.

2. Cut the cantaloupe in half, and remove the seeds. Scoop out the pulp, and put it in the work bowl of a food processor equipped with a metal blade. Process until smooth.

3. Add the cantaloupe to the cooled orange juice mixture, and stir. Add the liqueur and stir.

4. Whip the cream until it forms stiff peaks; then fold it into the mixture.

5. Pour the cantaloupe cream into a 10 × 6 × 2-inch pan, and freeze until slushy, about 1½ to 2 hours.

6. Remove from the freezer, and process until smooth. Freeze again to the slushy stage, about 30 minutes

7. Process the cantaloupe cream once again. Freeze 2 to 3 hours, until firm.

8. Spoon the cantaloupe cream into dessert dishes, and garnish with additional whipped cream and grated orange rind.

JULY · *Festa di Noantri—Our Very Own Festa*

COLD ZUCCHINI-RICE SOUP
4 SERVINGS

> 4 cups chicken broth
> 2 tablespoons unsalted butter
> 2 tablespoons olive oil
> 1 medium onion, chopped
> 2 medium zucchini, sliced
> 2 medium ripe tomatoes
> 1 tablespoon chopped fresh basil leaves
> 1 tablespoon finely chopped parsley
> 3/4 cup rice
> Grated Parmesan cheese, to pass at table

1. Bring the broth to a boil. Meanwhile, put the butter and oil in a deep, heavy saucepan over moderate heat. When sizzling, add the onion, and cook until it is soft and translucent, stirring frequently. Add the zucchini to the pan and cook, stirring, until lightly browned. Set aside.

2. Plunge the tomatoes into boiling water for a count of 20. Rinse them under cold running water to cool, and slip off the skins. Seed the tomatoes, and cut them into small chunks to add to the zucchini. Mix well.

3. Pour the boiling broth into the vegetable mixture, along with the basil, parsley, and rice. Cook, uncovered, stirring occasionally, until the rice is cooked, about 30 minutes. Remove from the heat, and cool.

4. Serve accompanied by a bowl of Parmesan cheese.

TURKEY FILLETS WITH BALSAMIC VINEGAR SAUCE

6 SERVINGS

> 2 pounds turkey breast, cut into six ¼-inch-thick
>   fillets
> ¼ cup all-purpose flour
> 3 tablespoons unsalted butter
> 3 tablespoons olive oil
> Salt and freshly ground black pepper, to taste
> 1½ to 2 tablespoons balsamic vinegar
> 1 cup chicken broth

1. Lightly flour the fillets on both sides.

2. Put the butter and oil in a large skillet over medium-high heat. When sizzling, sauté the fillets 2 or 3 at a time, turning, until they are golden brown on both sides, 3 minutes in all. Remove browned fillets to a platter, and sauté the remaining fillets.

3. Return all the fillets to the skillet. Season with salt and pepper. Add the vinegar over medium heat, and cook until most of it is absorbed.

4. Add the broth, a bit at a time, and cook after each addition until it is absorbed, about 5 minutes overall.

5. Put the fillets on a serving platter, and pour the pan juices over them.

TOMATO SALAD
6 TO 8 SERVINGS

> 6 large ripe tomatoes, sliced
> 1 to 2 teaspoons sugar
> 1 tablespoon red wine vinegar
> 2 tablespoons water
> 6 large fresh basil leaves, torn into pieces

1. Arrange the tomato slices on a serving platter. Sprinkle with the sugar.

2. Mix the vinegar with the water; pour it over the tomatoes. Top with the basil pieces, and serve.

APPLE TORTE (*Crostata*)
8 SERVINGS

> *1 recipe Sweet Pastry Dough (*Pasta Frolla*) (see recipe*
> *below)*
> *1 cup apricot jam*
> *1 tablespoon brandy or applejack*
> *8 tart apples*
> *2 tablespoons unsalted butter, cut into small pieces*
> *1 egg, beaten*

Preheat the oven to 350° F.

1. Lightly butter and flour a 10-inch or 12-inch pizza pan.

2. Peel and core the apples, then cut them into ¼-inch slices. To keep them from turning brown, put the slices in a bowl of acidulated water until you are ready to use them.

3. Cut off ⅓ of the Sweet Pastry Dough, which has been chilled, and set it aside. On a floured work surface, roll out the larger piece of dough into a circle about ¼ inch thick, to fit the pizza pan. (You may find it easier to roll it out between 2 sheets of wax paper.)

4. Transfer the dough to the prepared pan. If you have used wax paper, pull off the top sheet. Lay the pizza pan on the dough. Flip it over, and pull off the second sheet of wax paper.

5. Mix the jam and brandy together, and spread evenly over the dough, leaving a ½-inch border around the edge. Dry the apple slices, and arrange them in concentric circles on the dough in several layers. Dot with the butter bits.

6. Roll out the remaining dough in a rectangle ⅛ to ¼ inch thick. Cut it into thick strips with a scalloped pastry wheel. Lay the strips over the torte in a crisscross pattern. Arrange any remaining strips around the edge to make a border, wetting them lightly to make them stick.

7. Brush the pastry strips and border with the beaten egg.

8. Bake 25 to 30 minutes in the upper third of the oven, until the pastry strips are golden.

SWEET PASTRY DOUGH (PASTA FROLLA)

> *2 cups unbleached all-purpose flour*
> *8 tablespoons unsalted butter, chilled*
> *3 egg yolks*
> *Freshly grated rind of 1 lemon*
> *½ cup superfine sugar*

1. Place the flour in a large bowl. Cut the butter into small pieces. Using a pastry blender or 2 knives, quickly cut the pieces into the flour until the mixture forms pea-size pellets.

2. Add the egg yolks, lemon rind, and sugar, and combine thoroughly with a wooden spoon.

3. Turn the dough out onto a floured work surface. Knead briefly, using the heel of your hand, until the ingredients are thoroughly blended. Wrap in wax paper or plastic wrap, and chill for 1 hour.

Nine

AUGUST

August is the month when all of Italy seems to close down. Tourists in Rome are seen forlornly wandering around looking for shops and restaurants that might be open; the great piazzas return to their original glory, emptied of parked cars. All factories and industries are closed to business in August; bonuses and extra payments are given out, and everyone, worker and boss, goes on vacation. It's not a time to count on seeing anyone. Everyone's gone from the city, to the sea or the mountains. Mere business interests and material gain have not yet prevailed over the custom of *Ferragosto*, the August State holiday.

Ferragosto derives from the Latin *Feriae Augustae*, and is deeply entrenched in Italian life, rooted there from the days of the emperor Augustus, when a festival was declared in his honor on the first of the month named for him. The Roman *feriae* (holidays) numbered over a hundred, always including the first of every month. Among the August festivals was one to Ops, an abstract divinity of abundance and resources, whose very name means wealth and from which comes the word *opulence*. When I first arrived in Italy, there were a multitude of *feriae*, including Befana and Saint Joseph's Day, which are no longer legal holidays; in fact, the official list is now down to nine, the same number as in the United States.

With the Christian era, August 15 became the day to celebrate the Feast of the Assumption of the Virgin Mary, almost as if to replace the festival of the goddess Diana, which had been observed on August 13. According to Catholic tradition (reaffirmed as dogma by Pope Pius XII in 1950), Mary ascended, in body and soul, to heaven on August 15 in A.D. 45 at the age, it's believed, of seventy-five. The assumption is not only a great church feast, but a grandiose idea in itself for believers—a kind of evocation of things to come, an anticipation of the general resurrection, when all mortals will be restored in body and soul. Certainly, the idea of resurrection or reincarnation has a great hold on humankind.

The Feast of the Assumption is also the titular feast of all churches dedicated to the Virgin Mary, and in Rome the foremost of these is Santa Maria Maggiore, one of the great basilicas and one of the seven churches (again, that magical number) that since earliest times have been the goal of pilgrimages. Saint Mary Major, to give it its English name, was built on one of the seven hills of Rome, the Esquiline, by Pope Sixtus III. Its eighteenth-century exterior encases a far older basilica, the only one, indeed, in the classical style to have kept its original integrity among Rome's major church edifices.

Rows of magnificent classical columns line the nave, giving an impression of classical harmony to the whole building. The Renaissance ceiling is said to have been gilded with the first gold brought from the New World; the style of the superb pavement is known as "cosmatesque" after the Cosmati, a family of craftsmen who excelled in mosaic work and after whom the whole school of Roman mosaicists was called. The mosaic panels and friezes recounting the story of Christ's divinity and the Virgin as Mother of God are the great glory of Santa Maria Maggiore.

Preceding the Feast of the Assumption is the remembrance of Saint Lawrence who, on the tenth of August in 258, was martyred in Rome, possibly by beheading, as was the customary punishment for Roman citizens. But by the following century, it was firmly believed that the saint had been slowly roasted to death on a gridiron. Still later the story was embellished by adding that Lawrence had asked his torturers to turn him over, "for that side is quite done." Out of deference and courtesy to his memory and respect for his horrible martyrdom (possibly also because of the season), it is the custom not to cook on Saint Lawrence's feast day and to serve only cold foods.

A story which in my mind relates him to Cornelia, the mother of the Gracchi (whose sons were her jewels), tells that as deacon to Pope Sixtus II, Lawrence was keeper of the official books of the Roman Church and holder of the ecclesiastical purse, charged with the care of the poor, the orphans, and widows. During Valerian's persecutions of the Christians, Pope Sixtus was one of the first victims. Foreseeing confiscation of Church funds, Lawrence hastened to change the property he administered into cash and pass it out as alms. When he was summoned and ordered to deliver up the treasure of the Church, Saint Lawrence produced a crowd of beggars and unfortunates, saying, "These are the Church's treasure."

Because he kept the books, Saint Lawrence is the patron of librarians, as well as of bakers and cooks. He is also invoked as a helper against injuries from burns or fever and all diseases connected with a burning sensation; this includes the cleansing fires of purgatory, for he is, appropriately, the patron of the souls temporarily detained there. In Rome's centrally located titular church of San Lorenzo in Lucina, the alleged gridiron of the saint's martyrdom is said to be conserved in a closed recess behind the main altar.

My mother's birthday falls on August 16, which is the feast day of Saint Roch (San Rocco in Italian), the patron saint of wool carders and, again, cooks. My mother's maiden name was Cardamone, which designates one who cards wool, and she has enjoyed a long life as a memorable cook—it is her way of giving pleasure and uniting family—so her saint is uniquely appropriate. One August we were all together when she and my father joined us in Italy, and we spent *Ferragosto* at the Lido of Venice in a comfortable pensione named Mabapa—an acronym for mama, bambini, papa. That was a lovely, leisurely month. The children went to Lido beaches with their grandparents; I investigated the Renaissance Aldine press in Venice; Antonio worked on a new book; and we all got together in the evenings for al fresco meals in the pensione gardens.

Assumption Day I remember as a day of intense heat that drove everyone out on the lagoon—virtually all of Venice seemed to be navigating the waters in observance of the holiday: people in rubber life rafts; whole families in rowboats equipped with outboard motors; sailboats; fishing craft; designer motorboats. The next day, on my mother's birthday, we took the *traghetto* (water bus) into Venice. Our first stop was the famous Harry's Bar for one of bartender Ruggiero's special concoctions, the fabulous Bellini cocktail, which so pleased my mother, she had him write down the recipe:

Put several ripe and pitted but unpeeled peaches in a blender.
To 2 oz. of the peach puree add 2 oz. gin, 1 oz. orange juice,

and 1 oz. lemon juice for each drink. Blend together with several ice cubes and serve chilled.

Perhaps I should add that the secret of this drink is the inimitable Verona peaches—they are pink-toned, juicier, and more delicate than our American yellow-fleshed variety.

Following the stop at Harry's Bar was a meal at Trattoria Madonna near the Rialto Bridge, where gift-shopping had first been attended to. The Madonna not only is a wonderfully apt Venetian trattoria (complete with a statuette of the Madonna and a vigil light over the entrance) for an outing on the Feast of the Assumption, but it is filled with lively Venetians who come for the superb fish and seafood risotto. The meal was followed by a visit to the magnificent Scuola San Rocco. Since it was the saint's feast day and my mother's birthday, I thought they should become acquainted.

The *Scuole*, or Schools, were a typical Venetian institution—like the doge, the gondola, and even the ghetto. There were six *Scuole*, one in each city quarter, and they were used as meeting places by the nobles. Later they were turned into benevolent societies whose task was to educate poor and orphaned girls. Vivaldi was music master to the girls of one of these Schools. The Scuola degli Schiavoni contains an oratory adorned with Carpaccio's exquisite paintings of the *Legend of St. George* and the *Story of St. Jerome*.

The Scuola San Rocco dates from the sixteenth century. The incredible Venetians, on one of their "saint-naping" missions, had stolen the body of Saint Roch from Montpellier in France and brought it back to Venice. Thereupon the Franciscans built the Church of San Rocco as a shrine to house the saint's relics, and attached to it was the Scuola. In our own time, Pope John XXIII was part of this confraternity when he was Patriarch of Venice, and a plaque recording this can be seen on the entrance floor. The Scuola's magnificence, however, lies in its great hall, which contains the work of Tintoretto in the many huge canvases he worked on for eighteen years. No other nativity scene has ever moved me as much as Tintoretto's *Presepio* at San Rocco—the dramatic technique, the lighting, and the humanity of the figures are perfect.

John Ruskin, whose *Stones of Venice* I was reading that summer, called the Scuola di San Rocco one of the three great buildings of Italy—the others being the Sistine Chapel in Rome and Pisa's Camposanto. With San Rocco I had now seen all three. I can remember only one depiction of Saint Roch in painting—a Lorenzo Costa portrait that shows him as a pretty youth pointing a slender-fingered hand toward a sign of plague on his trim leg, sleek in its tight hose. His attribute is, in fact, the leg, and like the physician saints, Cosmas and Damian, he's invoked against plague and contagious diseases because he devoted himself to tending its victims. In Calabria, where my mother's parents came from, the feast day of Saint Roch is celebrated with Italian gingerbread figures called *panpepati*, which represent various parts of the body and are ex-votos for people whose arms, legs, or various organs are protected by the saint and to whom they offer the baked symbols.

August is also the month of figs. When served with the sweet prosciutto of Parma, there is no choicer dish in the world, in my view. Eaten outdoors on a summer evening, overlooking the sea— what could be better? When we spent three summers in Maratea, we were in the realm of the fig, which was the sign, for me, of paradise found.

The first plant mentioned in the Bible is the fig, when its leaves served to hide the nakedness of our errant progenitors. Biblical references seem to make it a symbol of what is good and aspired to: "a land of wheat, and barley, and vines and fig trees. . . ."

"Every man under his vine and under his fig tree" may be the ultimate statement of the good life.

Wasn't the fig, then, the forbidden fruit? This would certainly be in keeping both with its delectableness and its suggestive appearance. In Greek mythology Dionysius is credited with creating the fig, and it became the symbol of fecundity and procreation; during revels it shared the honors with the grape and was the fruit sacred to Juno, the presiding divinity over marriages. D. H. Lawrence has a verse about the fig that minces no words—or, as the ancients put it, he calls a fig a fig:

> The Italians vulgarly say, it stands for the
> female part; the fig fruit:
> The fissure, the yoni,
> The wonderful moist conductivity towards
> the centre.

The fig is also entwined in Roman legend. The Romans believed a fig tree to have been connected with the founding of Rome, for the cradle in which Romulus and Remus were floated down the Tiber became lodged in the roots of a fig tree on the riverbank, which then became the site of the city. More likely the fig tree was the one in the Roman Forum under which the she-wolf was said to have suckled the twins, for that tree survived into historical times, where it was honored by annual sacrifices.

Figs were highly regarded in the classical world, and Apicius, the prototypical gourmet, was said to have fed expensive imported Syrian figs to his hogs to improve the flavor of their meat. In the excavated ruins of ancient Herculaneum is a wall painting of a round loaf of bread and two figs. Elizabethan times gave rise to England's "figgy pudding." And though the value of a fig today has been reduced to mean "the least bit, the merest trifle" according to the dictionary, in the Victorian language of flowers, the fig stands for "being prolific."

As with anything that is perfect in itself, I prefer the fig as it is, au naturel, with no tampering. There is, however, a wonderful Calabrian confection for which I make exception: these are the *ficchi Girotti*, which I found on Rome's Via della Croce at Christmas time. They are stuffed with a mixture of almonds, candied orange peel,

275

and cloves and baked and then rolled in a mix of cocoa and sugar. Exquisite!

August 18 is my name day, for it's the feast of Saint Helen, mother of Constantine the Great, the Roman emperor who in 313 became the first emperor to adopt Christianity and opened the way for it to become the official religion of the empire. Before a battle at the Milvian Bridge over the Tiber, still one of Rome's busiest crossings, Constantine saw a cross in the sky bearing the famous words, *in hoc signo vinces*—"by this sign you will conquer." Later he chose Byzantium as his new capital, and changed its name to Constantinople after himself.

The Church of Aracoeli, rising above the ruins of a temple dedicated to a pagan mother-goddess and then consecrated to the Madonna, is one of the most venerable in Rome and certainly one of the most splendidly placed, rising as it does on the hill above Piazza Venezia and adjacent to the Capitol buildings. In a porphyry urn resting upon the thirteenth-century altar are enclosed the remains of Saint Helen, who died in Rome in 328. Another Rome church, Santa Croce in Gerusalemme, was once part of an imperial palace owned by Saint Helen between the years 317 and 322 and then donated by Constantine to the Church. The mosaic-decorated chapel dedicated to her is associated with the tradition of her discovery of a relic of the true cross, thus giving name to the church.

Saint Helen, or Helena, is always represented in royal robes, wearing an imperial crown, for she was an empress. Sometimes she carries in her hand a model of the Church of the Holy Sepulcher, which she had built over the tomb traditionally known as the burial place of Christ; sometimes she bears a large cross or the three nails by which Christ was affixed to the cross. To complete her association with emperors, the island named for her—Saint Helena—was the exile of one—Napoleon—who lived out his last years there.

But more beguiling is the legend of Saint Helen's vision, which told her she would find the true cross in a place where the air was sweet with perfume. And, in fact, she is said to have discovered it in a patch of basil. Christian tradition thus fell into line behind the many pagan cults that attributed a religious character to the herb whose very name, from the Greek, means "kingly." The Greeks associated basil with death and mourning; the Romans classed it with jasmine and the rose as lovers' emblems. It flourishes in August and is beautifully married to that other August triumph, the fresh tomato.

August is the climactic month of fruits and vegetables in which I always prepare a vegetable dish that comes to me from my mother through her mother. It is known as *la giardiniera*, the gardener's dish, and is a gathering of fresh produce—tomatoes, zucchini, summer squash, peppers, onions, and fresh herbs all simmered together until those diverse sun-soaked flavors marry and merge. This we eat cold or warm with huge hunks of Italian bread. It's perfect for *Ferragosto* and relies on the absolute freshness of everything.

We had this dish often in Maratea, when Vincenza, a peasant woman and purveyor of everything that grew there, would come by our place bearing baskets of produce covered with vine leaves to protect it against the sun. Our neighbor in Maratea was a signora from Naples. Once I asked her about her way of preparing uncooked tomato sauce in order to compare her method with mine. Eyeing me suspiciously, she asked *"Ma, l'ha mangiata in Italia?"*—"But is it something you ate in Italy?" Versed only in her experience of Naples and knowing only its traditional sauce, marinara, she must have thought uncooked tomato sauce an American concoction. I wonder if she knew that tomatoes themselves originated in America and though brought to Italy in 1554, weren't consumed there until the eighteenth century because they were thought to be poisonous.

I still have some souvenirs from Maratea, tiles from Mount Biagio, where the sanctuary to San Biagio was being redone and they were discarding the antique squares of the old pavement for new ones. Don Domenico Damiano, the priest, also gave me the head of a plaster angel lying in the heap of discarded tiles. That angel head Susi now has in her Urbino garden.

It was Don Domenico, an antiquarian and collector, who gave me a curious explanation as to how Maratea got its name. In ancient Greece and particularly in the part of southern Italy known as Magna Graecia, the fennel plant, finocchio, was much esteemed. In Greek it was called *maratron*. It is probable, the priest concluded, that Maratea was first Maratona, a derivative from the word for fields of fennel.

The most congenial etymology, however, and the one used in tourist brochures, is that Maratea comes from *Dea Maris*, goddess of the sea. Whatever the origin of its name, it was a place of fertile imagination. One of the butcher shops in the upper village was owned by Salvatore, who used to hang out verses extolling the cuts of his meat to entice customers:

Solo da Salvatore,
prezzo qualità sapore;
taglio perfetto, pulizia,
Salvatore è garanzia.

Desiderate un buon "girello"
Salvatore vi dà quello;
se volete più "fettina"
ne trovate ogni mattina.

Preferite del "tritato"?
Ecco, presto, accontentato;
è il "ragù" che vi fa gola?
Salvatore vi consola.

Le persone buon buongustaie,
specialmente le massaie,
le trovate a tutte l'ore
a comprar da Salvatore.

(Only at Salvatore's—
price, quality, flavor;
perfect cuts, spotless shop,
Salvatore is the guarantor.

Want a good round roast?—
Salvatore gives you the perfect cut;
or, if you want choice slices
you'll find them here any morning.

Prefer chopped meat?
Here you are, to your heart's content;
is it stew meat you're hankering for?
Salvatore to the rescue.

People of good taste,
and especially housewives,
can be found any time at all
buying here from Salvatore.)

Sometimes, we'd go up to Giorgio Bassani's home in the upper village for drinks on his terrace. At sunset the sweeping view was truly marvelous, embracing town, mountain, sea, and sky. As evening came on, lights would flicker on, and the belfry of Maratea's Santa Maria Maggiore would strike its mellifluous notes every quarter-hour. Having become very financially successful with his books, and knowing the region through his travels as president of Italia Nostra, the association for preservation of the environment, Bassani had bought two adjoining houses in upper Maratea. Preserving their exterior to retain the authentic village look, he had gutted the insides and reconstructed a very smart three-floor townhouse complete with modern kitchen, maid's quarters, bathrooms, closets, and laundry room. It was a pioneer showplace in the sixties, but Maratea has now been discovered by land speculators, and a building boom has reached even that part of Italy, which once was totally ignored.

When I was in Maratea, it was still a southern village, and the

Ferragosto procession was an old-style pageant. The ritual procession in upper Maratea featured a peasant-faced statue of the Madonna wearing dangling gold hoop earrings and cloaked in a silk moiré mantle, which was carried up and down the village streets. A drum major boy carrying a banner led the procession, followed by little girls wearing their First Communion veils; then little boys with ribbons across their chests, choirboys in red gowns and lace carrying armfuls of hefty carved cherubim, a censor-swinging priest, and finally the Madonna on her lurching platform. After that came crowds of giggling young women in their Sunday best, gossiping middle-aged women, and, trailing behind, the old women in black. The bells were incessant as the straggly procession filled the whole main street on its way to the church of Santa Maria Maggiore.

Later that evening there was the Festa of the Madonna del Porto in Fiumicello: lighted archways were set up over the street, the flutter of colored banners was everyplace, and stands were selling nougat, peanuts, *mostacciuolo calabrese* (a tough honey sweet), bread and cheese. The band and singers were imported from the big city, Naples. The Mass, which was said in the main square, was "attended" by people sitting at their ease at café tables. There were fireworks, strolling crowds, the air of holiday. Capping the whole event was the much enjoyed *Sagra di Pesce*, Fish Festival, which has become traditional for *Ferragosto*. A huge frying pan was set up on the sandy shore of Maratea Porto, and all the fish that were fried in it were distributed to the crowds of onlookers.

A friend who knows the area well tells me it's all changed, but I rest with my memories of an earthy paradise.

Saint Lawrence's Day
Cherry Tomatoes with Basil
Vitello Tonnato
Rice Salad
Watermelon Ice

Ferragosto
Figs with Prosciutto
Baked Fillet of Sole
Vegetables Giardiniera
Pears Helene

Saint Lawrence's Day

CHERRY TOMATOES WITH BASIL
6 SERVINGS

24 ripe cherry tomatoes, stemmed and washed
6 large fresh basil leaves, washed and patted dry

1. Put the tomatoes in a serving bowl. Tear the basil leaves into small pieces, and sprinkle over the tomatoes.

2. Spear the tomatoes with toothpicks, and serve from the bowl.

VITELLO TONNATO
6 TO 8 SERVINGS

10 oil-packed anchovy fillets, drained
3-pound boneless veal roast, securely tied
2 whole cloves
1 small onion, peeled
1 small carrot, pared
1 small celery stalk
4 sprigs parsley
One 6½-ounce can oil-packed tuna, drained
1 teaspoon capers, drained
2 tablespoons fresh lemon juice
Freshly ground black pepper, to taste
½ cup olive oil
Capers, for garnish
Finely chopped parsley, for garnish

1. Cut 6 of the anchovies into 1-inch lengths. With a small, sharp knife make incisions along the length of the veal. Insert the cut anchovies into the slits.

2. Stick the cloves into the onion. Put the veal in a heavy pot just large enough to hold it comfortably. Surround it with the onion, carrot, celery, and parsley. Add water to cover, and bring to a boil; reduce the heat to low and simmer, covered, for 1½ hours.

3. Drain the veal, pat it dry, and allow it to cool.

4. Put the tuna, the remaining anchovy fillets, the capers, lemon juice, and pepper in the container of a blender. Blend to a smooth purée. Slowly add the olive oil until the sauce is smooth and the consistency of cream; add more oil, if necessary.

5. Put the veal in a deep bowl, and pour the sauce over. Cover the bowl, and let the veal marinate in the refrigerator for 2 days.

6. To serve, slice the veal very thin, and arrange it on a platter.

Cover the slices with the sauce, and sprinkle with the capers and parsley.

RICE SALAD
4 TO 6 SERVINGS

> 1 cup rice
> ½ cup diced red and green bell peppers
> 1 cup julienned celeriac
> 1 cup sliced marinated artichoke hearts (about 1
>   jar), drained
> 1 cup sliced mushrooms
> 1 6½-ounce can tuna, drained and flaked
> 1 cup diced tomatoes (1 to 2 ripe tomatoes, peeled
>   and seeded)
> ½ cup pitted and sliced black olives, preferably
>   imported
> ¼ cup drained chopped anchovies
> ¼ cup olive oil
> ½ teaspoon freshly ground black pepper
> ½ teaspoon salt
> 1 tablespoon capers, drained
> 1 red onion, thinly sliced

1. Cook the rice in salted water until tender but firm and dry.

2. Cool the rice, then toss it with a fork to separate the grains. Add the peppers, celeriac, artichoke hearts, mushrooms, tuna, tomatoes, olives, and anchovies. Toss together with two forks. Add the olive oil, pepper, salt and capers. Toss again.

3. Heap the rice salad on a serving plate, and arrange the onion slices over it.

WATERMELON ICE
6 SERVINGS

> *2 to 3 pounds ripe watermelon (to yield 2 cups*
> *juice)*
> *¼ cup sugar*
> *3 tablespoons cornstarch*
> *¼ cup mini chocolate chips*
> *Pinch ground cinnamon*

1. Scoop out the watermelon pulp, remove the seeds, and reduce to a liquid in a blender or food processor.

2. Put the 2 cups of watermelon juice, the sugar, and the cornstarch in a saucepan, and stir until the cornstarch is completely dissolved. Bring to a boil over moderate heat, and cook, stirring constantly, for 5 minutes or until the mixture thickens.

3. Pour the mixture into a bowl, and chill for at least 2 hours. Stir in the chocolate chips. Spoon into dessert dishes, and keep refrigerated until you are ready to serve. Just before serving, dust each portion with a tiny bit of ground cinnamon.

Ferragosto

FIGS WITH PROSCIUTTO
6 SERVINGS

> *12 ripe figs*
> *12 very thin slices prosciutto*

1. Prepare the figs by trimming off the stems, then making 4 equidistant incisions from stem end to base. Carefully peel the skin open to form "petals."

2. On each plate place 2 figs, petal side up, and 2 slices of prosciutto, 1 draped over each fig.

BAKED FILLET OF SOLE
6 SERVINGS

> *3 tablespoons olive oil*
> *1 small onion, sliced*
> *1 clove garlic, minced*
> *1 cup tomato sauce or 3 large peeled tomatoes,*
>   *chopped*
> *Salt and freshly ground black pepper, to taste*
> *⅓ teaspoon chopped fresh rosemary*
> *2 pounds fillet of sole*
> *1 teaspoon minced parsley*

Preheat the oven to 325° F.

1. Place the olive oil in a medium skillet over moderate heat. Sauté the onion and garlic for 5 minutes, stirring frequently. Add the tomato sauce or tomatoes, salt, pepper, and rosemary. Reduce the heat to medium-low, and cook 20 minutes, stirring occasionally.

2. Put the fish in a baking dish just large enough to hold it comfortably, and pour the sauce over it. Cover with aluminum foil.

3. Bake on the middle rack of the oven until tender, about 15 minutes.

4. Remove the aluminum foil, and let the fish stand 5 minutes. Sprinkle with the parsley, and serve.

VEGETABLES GIARDINIERA
6 SERVINGS

> *3 tablespoons unsalted butter*
> *3 tablespoons olive oil*
> *2 cups chopped onions (about 1 pound)*
> *2 zucchini, cut in ¼-inch slices*
> *1 yellow summer squash, cut in ¼-inch slices*
> *½ cup chopped celery (about 2 stalks)*
> *2 green bell peppers, membranes removed, cut into*
> *rings*
> *4 large basil leaves, chopped*
> *3 large ripe tomatoes, peeled, seeded, and lightly*
> *chopped*

1. Put the butter and oil in a large saucepan over moderate heat. When sizzling, add the onions. Cook, stirring, until they are translucent but not brown.

2. Add the remaining ingredients. Cover, and lower the heat to medium. Cook for 20 minutes, until the vegetables are tender but still crisp. Serve warm.

PEARS HELENE
6 SERVINGS

> *2 cups water*
> *¾ cup sugar*
> *One 3-inch strip lemon peel*
> *6 large ripe pears, peeled, cut in half lengthwise, and*
> *cored*
> *1½ cups milk*
> *2 ounces unsweetened baking chocolate*
> *½ cup superfine sugar*
> *1 tablespoon all-purpose flour*

Pinch salt
2 tablespoons unsalted butter
1 tablespoon cream sherry or brandy
1 pint vanilla ice cream

1. Combine the water and sugar in a large, heavy saucepan over moderate heat, stirring until the sugar is dissolved. Add the lemon peel and the pears. Reduce the heat to medium-low, and poach the pears in barely simmering liquid, about 10 to 12 minutes. Let the pears cool in the liquid.

2. Place the milk and the chocolate, broken into pieces, in a small saucepan over medium-low heat. Cook together, stirring, until the chocolate is melted.

3. Mix together the superfine sugar, flour, and salt. Stir slowly into the chocolate milk. Cook 5 minutes over low heat, stirring constantly.

4. Stir the butter and sherry or brandy into the chocolate mixture.

5. Place 2 drained pear halves, flat side up, in each individual dish. Place small scoops of vanilla ice cream on each pear half, and drizzle with the chocolate sauce. Serve immediately.

Ten

SEPTEMBER

My most important arrivals in Italy, from when I first got there as a young student, seem always to have been in September. The second time was when Antonio and I were returning from the States, where he had been the Italian consul in Syracuse during the year our first daughter was born. That time we returned with nine-month-old Linda, disembarking at Genoa and touring Liguria in those soft September days of late summer before heading north to the Piedmont region and our country life in Strambino. The third September arrival happened after our move from Shady Lane Farm when I sailed aboard the ocean liner *Michelangelo*, with three daughters, to join Antonio, who had preceded us to Rome.

September is a wonderful time to be in Italy. The summer hordes are gone, the lazy vacation period of August is over, the towns are filled with work and purpose and the beginnings of the rich calendar of cultural events—and it's still warm enough for a getaway swim outside Rome at Fregene.

The Nativity of the Virgin, which is celebrated on the eighth day of September, is the name day for all Marias and a former church holiday. It is the day to have blueberries in some form for breakfast—blueberry muffins or pancakes or just plain on cereal, for the color is symbolic of the Virgin in her blue mantle. Now September 8 is even more significant in our family annals as the birthdate of Susi and Nevio's first son, Beniamino, my first grandchild. One year, Benji was with me at Cape Cod, and we went out to pick wild blueberries. Born under the sign of Virgo, he is very prudent and exacting, and I had to assure him that yes, these berries were good to eat, because he had never seen them in his part of Italy and was showing a true country caution before trying them.

In Venice the first Sunday of September is the occasion for the historic regatta, a brilliant affair during which all the palaces overlooking the Grand Canal display their most costly tapestries from windows and balconies. These become the background for the procession of decorated gondolas, led by the replica of the doge's *Bucintoro*, the gilded state galley. The *gondolieri* compete in regatta races, wearing colored shirts and sashes with their white trousers; the important personages in the state barge are all in costume, and by night all of Piazza San Marco and the Grand Canal is illuminated.

A story was often told of the bell tower of Piazza San Marco, which was the first thing Antonio's grandmother saw each morning as she flung open the shutters of the windows to a new day. But then came the day when his grandmother opened the shutters only to sense that something was missing. She had an eerie feeling and

290

leaned out the window to look more carefully, then shouted, "It's gone!" And, in fact, during that night in 1902, the famous landmark tenth-century campanile had quietly collapsed and lay in a pile of bricks in the square. It has, of course, been skillfully rebuilt.

Antonio knew Venice intimately, and many of his stories centered around it. Once he took me to the church where a seafaring ancestor had hung a votive painting depicting the miraculous apparition of the Madonna who appeared to him as he was praying for help during a tremendous storm at sea.

Antonio knew everything about his family and who they were: solid tradition went back and back and back into the recesses of time and documented history, effecting for him an ease with life that was built upon foundations of long experience and well-being, and a tolerance toward the unforeseen that comes with a firm grasp of human values. My past, in a sense, did not exist beyond the grandparents who came to America, so I delighted in Antonio's family stories.

In September 1967, Antonio's Italian publisher, Feltrinelli, gave him a magnificent party at the Casino Valadier in Rome on the occasion of the publication of his novel *Le Notti della Paura*. Casino Valadier is a mansion of several floors, plus penthouse, at the height of the Pincio, a public park. It was named for the nineteenth-century architect and urban planner, Giuseppe Valadier who, despite his French surname, was Roman born and did his work in Rome, including the enhancement of Piazza del Popolo. The Pincio affords an inimitable view over Rome to the dome of Saint Peter's, which is particularly grandiose at dusk, when Rome's own distinctive golden film of light is further heightened. What did we eat that evening? Wonderful things! A magnificent buffet table with artistically prepared hors d'oeuvres of all varieties and other foods presented in a blend of Italian art and artfulness made the occasion indelible. It was as close to a Renaissance banquet as I'm likely to get.

The feast day in September that had some resonance in my own family was that of the physician saints, brothers Saint Cosmas and Saint Damian, the so-called *Medici*, who are celebrated on the twenty-seventh of the month. This is an important festival in my mother's hometown of Utica, New York, but strangely enough, it was not her family who participated in it (because, my mother explained, her mother was "not big on saints") but my father's family from Syracuse. Each fall my Syracuse grandfather would make the trip to Utica with his youngest child, my uncle Ben, to celebrate the pair of saints. Grace Pizzuto Fahey also remembers being taken on the trip as a child in order to clear up some illness she had. The brother saints, as physicians and the patrons of doctors, were powerful interceders—prayers, in effect, being doubled because there were two of them.

Grace has described the occasion as a special treat—there were spits of lamb in the restaurants and special pastries at Utica's renowned (and still existing) Florentine Pastry Shop on Bleecker Street. She also remembers busloads of people coming from as far away as Canada and New Jersey for the festa, which actually is celebrated in and around the church of Saint Anthony of Padua, sponsored by the Saints Cosmas and Damian Society at Saint Anthony's. It is like a gigantic party, with crowds sometimes of over 5,000 people. Eating, dancing, and singing go on continuously after the formal procession, masses, and novenas. The gathering includes those who may have prayed to the saints for healing and then have come to the festival in thanks because their prayers were answered, as well as those who have come to ask for intercession. Two huge statues of the saints on the church grounds are regularly adorned with dollar bills pinned to their robes by the pilgrims.

The festival was brought to Utica at the beginning of the century by immigrants from Bari and Alberobello in southern Italy, where the *Medici* are particularly venerated. A recollection in the Utica *Observer* related how the Utica families would entertain relatives from all over the state who had come for the September festa, an event almost as big as Christmas. Families and guests would go to church for the special blessings, march in the processions, return home for a huge midday meal (that always seemed to start with chicken soup with greens and tiny meatballs), and then go back to the street festival to listen to the various band concerts and sample pastries from the red, white, and green stands. And every year representatives from Utica and other American communities are sent to participate in the even more grandiose festivities that take place at Alberobello.

The saints, who were born in the Arabian town of Egea, studied at the University of Alexandria in Egypt and practiced their medicine in the eastern Mediterranean countries, effecting miraculous cures. It is said that years before, their father had been put to death as a Christian, and they were warned against practicing the religion— to which they replied, "We are doctors, and we are Christians." They were martyred in the persecutions of the emperor Diocletian toward the end of the third century, and their earliest cult can be traced to Cyr, in southern Syria. Word of the holy doctors, or *Santi Medici* as they are known, was based on the cures of those who had invoked their aid, and when the emperor Justinian showed his own gratitude for a cure, their fame spread throughout the church. A church dedicated to them stands in the Roman Forum; it was built there in the sixth century in what had been part of Vespasian's library and is adorned with mosaics that are considered some of Rome's finest and earliest examples.

Some exquisite scenes of the miracles of the two saints, as well as their burial, are depicted in beautiful predellas or altarpieces by Fra Angelico in Saint Mark's Museum in Florence. One shows a famous miracle in which a man with a diseased leg went to sleep in a church dedicated to Saints Cosmas and Damian. He dreamed that the saints had cut off his bad leg and given him a new one, and when he awoke, he was healed.

A particularly sweet and poignant recurrence in Rome was the day that truly marked the end of summer, the feast of Saint Michael the Archangel on September 29. It was the true end of summer because in Italy school began for all the vacationing children on October 1, and because the warmth of summer was still in the air by day, but mornings and evenings were getting chilly. In the fields the brilliant yellow flowers (like the last burst of sun and the harbinger of fall days to come) are called Michaelmas daisies since they come into bloom around Saint Michael's Day. I used to pick these flowers on the beaches near Rome, and, appropriately, sometimes made a yellow sponge cake called "Margherita" (the Italian word for daisy) on that day.

Once Italian name-giving reflected more than it does now the importance of saints in family life—when one was born often determined one's name. Antonio's sister, born in September, was named Mariarcangela to honor both the Nativity of the Virgin Mary and Saint Michael the Archangel.

Various sayings of forecast are attached to Saint Michael's Day, especially clues to the coming weather, as, for instance: "If Michaelmas Day be fair, the sun will shine much in the winter, though the wind at northeast will frequently reign long and be very sharp and nipping. . . . If, on the other hand, the day be dark, look for a light Christmas."

Saint Michael's Day is also a time when one might extend the hours of sleep, hence this nursery rhyme:

> Nature requires five,
> Custom gives seven,
> Laziness takes nine,
> and Michaelmas eleven.

From the daisies and the doggerel about extra sleep that are associated with Saint Michael, the fact that he is the stern-countenanced "prince of angels," often depicted in armor and bearing a lance and shield with which he combats a dragon, might somehow be overlooked. In the Old Testament he was the guardian angel of Israel; he is also the patron of the Catholic Church, of the holy souls in purgatory, and of Christian soldiers, and he was supposed to have appeared to Joan of Arc. He is the first of the seven archangels, the leader of God's celestial armies against the rebellious angels who will be cast into hell with the Devil, and the one to whom Milton, in *Paradise Lost*, gives the charge:

> Go, Michael, of celestial armies prince,
> And thou, in military prowess next,
> Gabriel; lead forth to battle these my sons
> Invincible; lead forth my armed Saints
> By thousands and by millions ranged for fight.

Saint Michael was said to have appeared on the site of Mont-Saint-Michel in Paris and thus gave the place his name. He is also said to have brought the gift of prudence to mankind, and in the final judgment he will sound the trumpet and balance the good and evil of the souls of the risen dead on his scales.

Feast of Saints Cosmas and Damian
Mother's Chicken Soup with Greens and
   Tiny Meatballs
Cleofe's Skillet Rabbit
Herbed Baby Carrots
Chocolate Cream with Croccante Topping

Michaelmas
Passatelli in Broth
Susi's Chicken Breasts
Stewed Mushrooms
Grape Dessert

Feast of Saints Cosmas and Damian

MOTHER'S CHICKEN SOUP WITH GREENS AND TINY MEATBALLS
8 SERVINGS

> *1 3-pound stewing fowl or 2 turkey wings (2 to 3*
>   *pounds)*
> *1 small onion, peeled*
> *5 or 6 parsley sprigs*
> *2 or 3 celery stalks with tops*
> *1 medium carrot, pared*
> *1 medium ripe tomato, peeled, seeded, and chopped*
> *Salt and freshly ground black pepper, to taste*
> *½ pound ground veal*

1 small clove garlic, minced
1 tablespoon grated Parmesan cheese
1 egg yolk
¼ cup cracker meal
1 head washed and shredded escarole

1. Put the fowl or turkey wings in a soup kettle, and cover with water, at least 3½ quarts. Bring slowly to a boil. Adjust the heat so the liquid just bubbles gently. Skim off the scum from the top.

2. Add the onion, 3 sprigs of the parsley, the celery, carrot, tomato, salt, and pepper. Simmer 3 hours, partially covered.

3. Remove the fowl or turkey and vegetables, and strain the broth. Leave the fowl and vegetables in a quart of broth for use at another time.

4. Cool the broth, then refrigerate it, uncovered.

5. Chop fine the remaining parsley sprigs. Mix them together with the ground veal, garlic, Parmesan cheese, egg yolk, and salt and pepper. Add just enough cracker meal to bind the mixture.

6. Bring 2 quarts of the broth to a boil. Roll the veal mixture into balls the size of marbles, and drop them into the broth. Stir in the escarole. When the soup returns to a boil, lower the heat and simmer it uncovered for 20 minutes. Serve immediately.

CLEOFE'S SKILLET RABBIT
4 TO 6 SERVINGS

1 2- to 3-pound rabbit, defrosted if frozen
Salt and freshly ground black pepper, to taste
½ cup olive oil
3 cloves garlic, minced
2 to 3 tablespoons fresh rosemary leaves
½ teaspoon fresh thyme
1 teaspoon fresh lemon juice

2 tablespoons unsalted butter
1 cup dry white wine
1 cup light cream

1. Rinse the rabbit, and cut it into serving pieces. Sprinkle with salt and pepper.

2. Mix the olive oil, garlic, rosemary, thyme, and lemon juice together in a bowl for a marinade.

3. Put the rabbit pieces in the marinade, and leave for 2 hours at room temperature, turning several times.

4. Heat the marinade and the butter in a skillet. Add some of the rabbit pieces and sauté about 5 minutes, turning, until browned. Remove the browned pieces to a platter, and brown the remaining pieces. Return the previously browned pieces to the skillet.

5. Add the wine to the skillet, turn up the flame, and cook rapidly until the alcohol evaporates. Reduce the heat to low, pour the cream over the rabbit, and cover.

6. Cook on low heat for 1 hour. Serve with the cream sauce.

HERBED BABY CARROTS
6 TO 8 SERVINGS

1½ pounds baby carrots, scrubbed
3 tablespoons unsalted butter
1 teaspoon fresh lemon juice
Salt and freshly ground black pepper, to taste
2 tablespoons chopped fresh mint or parsley

1. Place the carrots in a steamer basket over ½ cup boiling water. Cover, and steam 5 minutes over medium-high heat, or until barely tender.

2. Melt the butter in a saucepan over medium-low heat. Add the carrots, and sprinkle with the lemon juice and salt and pepper. Cook 5 minutes, stirring constantly.

3. Remove the carrots to a serving bowl, and sprinkle with the mint or parsley. Serve immediately.

CHOCOLATE CREAM WITH CROCCANTE TOPPING
4 SERVINGS

> *2 cups milk*
> *2 eggs*
> *5 tablespoons sugar*
> *2½ tablespoons all-purpose flour*
> *2½ tablespoons unsweetened cocoa*
> *½ teaspoon vanilla extract*
> *1 tablespoon unsalted butter*
> *2 tablespoons Croccante Topping (see recipe, page 00)*
> *Whipped cream (optional)*

1. Scald the milk in a small saucepan over moderate heat.

2. Put the eggs, sugar, flour, cocoa, and vanilla in the top of a double boiler over simmering water, and mix. Slowly add the scalded milk. Cook, stirring, until the mixture is thick; stir in the butter.

3. Cool the mixture, stirring it occasionally.

4. Serve in dessert bowls, sprinkled with Croccante Topping. Pass the whipped cream separately.

PASSATELLI IN BROTH
8 SERVINGS

> 6 cups breadcrumbs
> 1 cup grated Parmesan cheese
> 5 eggs
> ¼ teaspoon freshly grated nutmeg
> ½ teaspoon grated lemon rind
> 2 quarts chicken broth
> 1 tablespoon minced parsley

1. Heat broth to just under a boil.

2. Put the breadcrumbs, Parmesan cheese, eggs, nutmeg, and lemon rind in a large bowl, and mix by hand until well blended.

3. Pass mixture through the large-hole disk of a food mill onto a sheet of waxed paper to make the *passatelli*.

4. Bring the broth to a boil. Add the *passatelli*, then lower the heat to a simmer, and cook 5 minutes.

5. Add a sprinkle of parsley to each serving.

SUSI'S CHICKEN BREASTS
4 SERVINGS

> 3 tablespoons unsalted butter
> 1 tablespoon olive oil
> 6 fresh, large sage leaves
> 4 skinless, boneless chicken breasts
> Salt and pepper, to taste

1 cup broth

2 tablespoons cream

1. Heat butter and olive oil in a skillet, and add the sage leaves; do not let brown.

2. Salt and pepper the chicken breasts, and add them to the skillet, heating through on both sides for a few minutes.

3. Add the broth and let the chicken absorb it, cooking 10 minutes on low heat. Mix in the cream, and cook another 10 minutes. Serve with the pan juices and Stewed Mushrooms (see following recipe).

STEWED MUSHROOMS
4 to 6 SERVINGS

1½ pounds mushrooms

⅓ cup olive oil

2 cloves garlic, crushed

1 tablespoon tomato paste

6 to 8 fresh mint leaves, chopped

Salt and freshly ground black pepper, to taste

1. Wipe the mushrooms with a cloth. Trim off the stem ends, and slice the mushrooms thinly.

2. Put the olive oil in a large, heavy saucepan over moderate heat. When it is sizzling, add the garlic cloves. Cook for about 2 minutes. Discard the garlic.

3. Add the mushrooms, turning to coat them with the oil. Reduce the heat to medium-low, and cook until the mushrooms give off their liquid, about 5 minutes.

4. Stir the tomato paste into the liquid. Sprinkle the mushrooms with the mint, salt, and pepper.

5. Serve over chicken breasts, or as an accompaniment to other dishes.

GRAPE DESSERT
8 SERVINGS

5 cups Concord grapes
4½ cups water
2 envelopes unflavored gelatin
1½ cups sugar
Whipped cream, for garnish

1. Combine the grapes and 4 cups of the water in a large, heavy saucepan. Bring to a boil over high heat. Reduce heat, and simmer for 40 minutes.

2. Strain the cooked grapes, pushing down with a wooden spoon. Discard the skins and seeds. Return the grape liquid to the saucepan.

3. Combine the gelatin with the remaining ½ cup water. Stir the softened gelatin into the grape liquid. Add the sugar, and bring the mixture to a boil over high heat. Reduce the heat to medium-low and simmer, uncovered, until the sugar is dissolved. Cool until the mixture begins to set. Turn it into a glass bowl.

4. Chill until firm. Garnish with whipped cream, and serve.

Eleven

OCTOBER

I first went to Italy to learn the language; by October I found myself settled into Italian life in Perugia, where I had enrolled at the University for Foreign Students. There, among many nationalities, an ex-GI and I were the only Americans. Through the university I found a nearby room in a dank and foreboding medieval structure at #13 Via Ulisse Rocchi, with Count Lorenzo Beni-Fabiani and his florid, Boccaccio-character countess, who were taking in paying guests because they, like everyone, were impoverished during that period following the war. For warmth in those austere days, we sat together in the log-filled kitchen under festoons of grapes drying on clotheslines strung crisscross through a room redolent with the aromas of the count's fabulous cooking. There I learned about *minestrina* and *minestrone!* And stews—they have variations and can be called a *stufato*, a *stracotto*, or an *umido* but are always rich and delicious. Because of the long cooking, the Italian expression for being "burned up" or "sick and tired" over something that's gone on too long is *sono stufato*—literally, I'm stewed.

In the Beni-Fabiani kitchen, I savored the infinite variety of pastas and sauces, which made the routine spaghetti of my childhood diminish forever. There I began to learn about Italian cheeses— not the strong Romano of my childhood, but the fabulous asiago, fontina, gorgonzola, cacciotto, and delicate mascarpone. The count showed me how good an accompaniment a piece of Parmesan was for a ripe pear, intoning, *"Al contadino non far sapere/ Quanto è buono il formaggio con le pere."* This advice of keeping from the peasant (or anyone else) the knowledge of how delectable cheese is with a pear so that, presumably, there'd be more for the co-gnoscenti, was downed with the good wines of the region. And so my education began.

On Via Ulisse Rocchi, close by the ancient Etruscan arch that is one of the glories of Perugia, I got to know Italian more through listening to the count's stories and recipes than by going to class. When the countess wasn't engaged in her activity as a livestock broker, sometimes she would be there, too, up to her elbows in flour, making the week's supply of pasta, singing arias from *Norma* or *Madama Butterfly*, and often accompanied by the sounds of the count chopping wood for the stove, or the cackling of hens from a small cubby next to the kitchen. The hens were an important part of the household until the arrival of company or an important festa turned them into the dish of the day.

The countess introduced me to Italian festas, the first being the grape-gathering harvest, or *Vendemmia*, at the country place of one of the farmers she represented. It took place at the end of September, when the vines were heavy with the sweet grapes of Umbria, and we picked them swiftly, dumping our basketloads into huge wooden barrels, where they were pressed. After the picking, we spread blankets and ate in the vineyard. The farm women carried huge baskets of food on their heads from the farmhouse—baskets full of freshly roasted chickens still on the spit and discs of a regional flatbread called *cresci*, fragrant with oil, fresh herbs, and bits of pork.

From Perugia's Porta del Sole, the Sungate (mentioned in Dante's *Paradiso*, Canto XI, line 47), I could look off into the distance and see Assisi rising on its own hill. Not visible but not far from Assisi is the medieval town of Gubbio, whose name has rung in my ears since my Convent School days. The Convent School I attended in Syracuse was run by the Franciscan sisters, whose order descends from that founded by Saint Francis in 1209. How well I remember the school play dramatizing the story of Saint Francis going out to confront the terrible wolf who was terrorizing the citizens of Gubbio and, by talking to the beast, shamed him into meekness.

> Oh lupo!
> Oh mio fratello lupo
> Perchè mi guardi
> Così ombroso e cupo
> Perchè mi mostri
> quegli aguzzi denti?
> Ascolta, vieni qui
> Senti. . . .
>
> *(Oh wolf!*
> *Oh my brother wolf,*
> *why do you look at me*
> *with such dark and glaring eyes,*
> *why do you show me*

those pointed teeth?
Pay attention, come here
listen . . .)

October 4 is the feast day of Saint Francis of Assisi, patron of Italy and the most cherished of saints. He was also a poet, and the world knows him through his life as a symbol of holiness and sainthood. He is the beloved saint, famed for his joy in virtue, his love of all living things, and for having embraced poverty (which he called his beloved Sister) as a fundamental tenet of his beliefs. Dante (himself a lay Franciscan) immortalized this union in a canto of *Paradiso*, when he wrote, ". . . take now Francis and Poverty for these lovers. . . . Their harmony and happy looks moved men to love and wonder and sweet contemplation and led them to holy thoughts. . . ."

Saint Francis was born Giovanni Francesco Bernadone in 1182, the son of a prosperous Assisi merchant. At about the age of 26, after a brief combative career in local wars and a year of imprisonment in Perugia, he experienced a religious call and turned away from worldly things, embracing asceticism and mysticism. This he made clear when he stripped himself naked before his bishop and formally renounced, in his father's presence, all claim to his father's wealth. Francis henceforth devoted himself not only to prayer but also to the care of the poor, the sick, and the unfortunate.

Yet his approach to religion was more than mystical withdrawal; it was also characterized by joyousness, innocence, and a love of nature. All of creation, both animate and inanimate, were brothers and sisters to him. After fasting forty days, as had the Lord, Francis received on his body the stigmata of Christ's wounds. He died in 1226 and was canonized as a saint two years later. The legends and anecdotes about his life, along with his sermons and sayings, were collected and written down as *Fioretti di S. Francesco d'Assisi*—"The Little Flowers of Saint Francis." The most celebrated of his writings is the "Canticle of Created Things," the hymn of praise to all living creatures that the saint is said to have composed as he lay dying:

> Be praised, my Lord, for earth, our mother and
>   our sister;
> by thy power she sustains and governs us,
> and puts forth fruit in great variety,
> with grass and colorful flowers.

From my sun- and light-filled room in Perugia, I wrote poetry, induced by feelings of the specialness of being in Italy. It was a rare and privileged time, a time of discovery and exploration, of finally feeling at one with my surroundings and a growing awareness of my *italianità*. Everything was wonderful, including the Italian language. I was moved to write a verse in Italian, a playful limerick about my doubts as to the wolf of Gubbio, in which I described myself as the obtuse girl from Perusa (the old spelling of *Perugia*):

> C'era una fanciulla di Perusa
> che amava la vita diffusa.
>   Ma nel lupo di Gubbio
>   aveva gran dubbio
> questa fanciulla ottusa a Perusa.

Obtuse, perhaps, because I hadn't yet found the way to accommodate belief in what can't be proved; that came later. But legends of the kindly wolf, embodying the ambivalence of much wolf folklore, abound; and when saints are involved, the stories are parables setting forth the importance of Christian compassion toward all of creation—toward animals as well as humankind.

In 1986, many years after my first arrival in Italy, I was back in Assisi with my daughter Niki on a beautiful October 4 for Saint Francis's feast day. In 1945, Saint Francis had been designated the patron of Italy, and each successive year an Italian region has been honored in Assisi on his feast day. Representatives of the honored region come in their traditional costume, bearing oil to give the Franciscan brothers for keeping the flame on the saint's tomb lit. Auspiciously, when Niki and I were there, Saint Francis was being honored by a special delegation from Calabria, and it was like seeing a procession of our relatives doing the tarantella down the narrow and winding medieval streets of Assisi, so close were the facial characteristics to our family look.

The day before, at Santa Maria degli Angeli (site of the church of that name, which encloses the Porziuncola chapel, where Saint Francis constructed the first *presepio*, or manger scene, and where he would die), there was a massive traffic jam of sightseeing buses. The faithful were converging from all over Italy on the vigil of the saint's day. Two hundred years earlier almost to the day, when Goethe arrived there on his first trip to Italy, he let his coachman go at Santa Maria degli Angeli and noted in his diary entry of October 26, 1786, "I was longing to take a walk by myself in this silent world and climbed the road to Assisi on foot. . . ." Scorning the Basilica of Saint Francis, with its great treasure of Giotto frescoes, Goethe rather close-mindedly went on to view the ancient temple of Minerva, reconsecrated to the Virgin Mary in the usual overlay of Christian Madonna over pagan goddess, which is in the town's upper piazza and which Goethe esteemed the only thing worth seeing in Assisi.

Giotto is still in Assisi, and so is the ancient temple, but gone forever is Goethe's silent world! Santa Maria degli Angeli, now the station stop for those traveling to Assisi by train, is busy with tourists and pilgrims. Niki and I found Assisi sold out—there wasn't a room to be found for us, and we were advised to drive off to some nearby mountaintop resort to try for rooms. But that sounded expensive and out of the way, so we drove to the outskirts of Assisi and found a little settlement called Palazzo with a sign on the main road saying *"Camere Linda"*—"Linda's Rooms." That's where we stayed, escorted to our room through a delicious grape arbor from which signora Linda herself invited us to pick. From our window we could see the farm fields reaching to the very edge of the dwellings. On the through road, which is also Palazzo's main street, a small-town circus was being set up in connection with festivities for Saint Francis.

Although the festa is rigorously religious, it is combined with a lot of good spirits and fun. Another interpretation of Saint Francis (called *il poverello*, the poor one, by Italians) has been picked up in modern times by the Italian left. The "saint of the marginal," of "the least," is seen as having an affinity for the political left, and this is made vivid by the mingling of communist political posters with the religious symbols.

Another saint of the same name, and the one from whom I most probably get my middle name, Frances, is the Calabrian Saint Francis of Paola, who lived in the fifteenth century and founded the order of Minimum Friars. I have a friend, Orlando Giacinto, a recent Italian immigrant, who came from Calabria. He is proud of his hometown, Paterno Calabro, which he told me, has the second church founded by Saint Francis of Paola and the one in which a miracle was recorded. It seems that the keystone over the church portal was a mammoth block of stone that somehow split during the building process. The miracle is that the church did not collapse and is still standing today, and this is attributed to its having been blessed by the saint.

Assisi was thronged for the feast of Saint Francis—everyone buying food from the vendors, or filling the souvenir shops. I found a health food store beautifully named, in the Franciscan manner, Sorella Terra—Sister Earth. From the shop I purchased a balsamic vinegar at a bargain price compared to what was asked at the Wine Museum in Torgiano. In a pastry shop with a window of beckoning delectables, I saw the honey-almond cookies called *mostacciuoli* (and the same cookie that we have at Christmas and on Saint Blaise's Day), which the dying saint asked be prepared for him although "he ate little thereof, because he grew continually weaker and drew near to death."

We drove to the top of the mountain where Saint Francis had often gone in retreat, passing along the way the more devout, who were making the trip by foot—some barefoot. Known as Eremo Carceri, the "hermitage prison," it had been used to house prisoners from World War I, who, in turn, had reforested the slopes of Mount Subasio. Signs reminded us where we were: *Posto Sacro: Silenzio. Rispetto. Decoro* —"This is a Holy Place: Silence, Respect, Decorum." It was indeed holy and very suggestive—braced against the winds, the very olive tree under which Francis had preached to the birds was pointed out to us by one of the brothers who live up there in the sanctuary.

That story of Saint Francis preaching to the birds is often depicted in art, the most sublime rendition being the frescoes painted in the basilica over 700 years ago in Giotto's *Life of Saint Francis* cycle. Olivier Messiaen's contemporary opera *Saint Francis of Assisi* has a great number of authentic bird songs, which the composer has incorporated into the music: the *capinera* "blackcap," which is a typical Umbrian bird, as well as other birds noted in the environs of Assisi and in other parts of Italy—the song thrush, skylark, blackbird, golden warbler, nightingale, turtledove, and even those foreign to Italy. It is a most complex and compelling opera, which I saw in its American premiere performance at Carnegie Hall in New York on an April evening in 1986. Long before that, however, Franz Liszt had already composed his tone poem, *Saint Francis Preaching to the Birds*.

On the way down the mountain, we stopped at La Stalla, an open-air restaurant that has modernized itself into self-service while still keeping the antique air of a farmhouse with tables out under the arbor. Already on the feast of Saint Francis, the waiters were speaking among themselves of the coming feast of Saint Martin—

Saint Martin's Day, on November 11, is synonymous with winetasting at nearby Torgiano.

October days in Rome were delicious, too. Every Roman October was mild, delightful, sunny, and dry. And each October the Romans would congratulate themselves, saying to one another, "What an exceptional October! Here we are in mid-October, and look what weather!" as if it were not the norm. By fall the glare of summer is softened into a warm, golden pall over the city. On the city edifices all the tawny and orangish and umber tones—what I think of as the real hue of Rome, and an autumn one—are heightened. October is a time for excursions into the country, called appropriately, *ottobrate*, "October outings," to nearby Veio or Bracciano or to towns like Viterbo, Orvieto, and even the Etruscan sites of Cerveteri and Tarquinia. It is another time of *sagre*, those country festivals that celebrate harvests of everything from grapes to mushrooms to truffles to chestnuts to snails and skylarks. I can recall, in little Tuscan towns outside Florence, festas for a particular kind of fennel-seasoned salami—*la finocchiona*—or a special sausage of wild boar called *cinghiale*. The earth's bounty is always cause for celebration and in Italy is not limited to one day of thanksgiving; each marvelous fruit of the earth is given due attention. But preeminent in Italy are those staples of the diet—olives, grapes, and wheat, which become, in turn, oil, wine, and bread.

In Venice in October 1986, I saw the local *sagra*, or festival, for bread given a broad, universal tone. The bread bakers, on their own initiative and with the endorsement of the European parliament, put up stands under the slogan, "From a grain of wheat, life for all," at the focal points of Venice, and from them bread was given out to passersby in return for a donation to combat hunger in the world. I bought a bag of bread, and Niki and I ate the *panini all'olio* as we wandered through the Venetian passageways called *calli* toward the water bus for the island of San Giorgio. The crusty

311

yet delicate bread rolls made with oil were superb and we relished every crumb. I kept the bag they came in, for it bears in print a canon of my belief, *Il pane è vita, civiltà, e pace*: "Bread is life, civilization, and peace."

Years before, when I lived in Rome, I had gone to the grape harvest, or *Vendemmia*, at San Marino, one of the towns in the outlying hills, which are called collectively the Castelli Romani. It's a famous festa that still endures. Exuberance reigns, and all the wine shops in town are adorned with branches signifying that the new wine is available. In front of every *osteria* on the main street, wooden tables and benches are put out. Some people bring their own food and order liters of wine; others buy delicious hunks of roast pork, peasant bread, olives, and cheese from vendors, again accompanied by copious wine. The mood is certainly one of bacchanale, or as close as we get to it in our time. The town fountain flows with red wine, and a huge effigy of Bacchus, god of revels, presides over the main piazza, where he pours wine from an immense bottle. Balconies are entwined with grapevines from which bunches of grapes, or an occasional bottle of wine, are thrown down to the people in the street. Later comes the parade of pretty girls in regional costume followed by decorated carts loaded with barrels of wine, wine presses, and bushels of grapes.

The old Italian immigrants to America brought their love of wine and skill at wine making with them. Even in upstate New York, with its inhospitable weather that hardly seems congenial to the grapevine, my father remembers going to the grape-picking festivals in the Finger Lakes region as a dashing young man on a motorcycle. As a child I well remember the acrid smell of Uncle Joe Maio's cellar, where he had his press and wine barrels.

Something new to me on my most recent trip to Italy was the Wine Museum at the lovely Umbrian town of Torgiano between Perugia and Assisi—well worth a detour for a few hours' visit. Located in the stupendous *cantina*, or basement, of the Baglioni Palace, it is a veritable showpiece of Italian civilization as manifested in the making and purveying of wine. The museum fulfills my own personal requirements for a museum: it is small and it is local. There, without tourist crowds and droning tour guides, Niki and I could savor at our leisure the magnificently laid out displays detailing the history and techniques of wine making, its traditional overtones, its ramifications in art and in associative crafts. From the wine amphoras of the classical world through the room of awesome and enormous wine presses, to the step-by-step depiction of modern wine making, it is a rich and beautifully organized exhibit, detailed with samples of ancient, medieval, Renaissance, and baroque majolica and glass vessels used for wine. Wine in medicine, wine in Church functions, wine in mythology, wine making depicted in ancient manuscripts—the whole panorama of this ancient art of civilization is here unfolded. And one is reminded that the ancient Greeks' name for the Italian peninsula was Oenotria, "the Land of Wine."

All that seemed to be missing was some mention of Antonio's eccentric cousin Lisetta and her grape cure. Lisetta Barolini was a stunning woman of indeterminate age who married, late in life, a much younger man. When she died in 1984, she was revealed to have been ninety-four years old to her husband's fifty-seven years. Each year at the height of the grape season, Lisetta arrived in Vicenza to stay with Antonio's mother and sister and to follow her grape regime. She ate nothing but grapes during this period, kilos of them per day. Was it to this, we all wondered, that she attributed her beautiful skin, her longevity, her special cachet?

In the wine museum I was particularly interested in seeing examples of the ceramic vessel called *albarello*, which was used for storing pharmaceutical herbs or spices or, in this instance, medicinal wine. Albarello is the family name on Antonio's mother's side and gives further substance to his claim that we were made for each other through the meshing of our separate family names—

he the wine (the linkage from Albarello and Barolini), I the bread (Mollica). The links to Dionysius, god of the vineyard, were every-where depicted in ceramic art; one in particular seemed to highlight the omnipresent pagan link with the Christian world: depicted on a Renaissance plate is a monk genuflecting before a barrel from which wine is flowing into a bottle.

Rather than making wine, my daughter Susi and her husband, Nevio, harvest the fruit of their vines to keep as table grapes. They cut them with a T-shaped piece of the vine still attached so that they can be hung in clusters from their storeroom rafters. Kept this way, they will be good right up to Christmas. There is an inimitable taste to the Italian grape—I think it is the sun, not to mention the gor-geous scenery it grows in; all I know is that when I saw a plate of those grapes on Susi's table during my last visit, I became ravenous. "Take them," she said. And I did.

Columbus Day is a transcultural festa in our family, bridging old world and new and incorporating strands from both the Italian and American heritages. Columbus was himself influenced by the semi-legendary Saint Brendan, the Irish abbot who died in 577 at the age of 94 and who was called "The Navigator." In popular medieval lore Brendan is supposed to have set out on an Atlantic voyage in search of an earthly paradise, or "land promised to the saints," to be found on an island in midocean. Columbus was so persuaded that Brendan did indeed reach an unknown country far west of Ireland that he took a Galway seaman with him on his first voyage. Columbus's son testified as to the effect the legend had on him: Columbus spoke of Saint Brendan's Islands, also known as the For-tunate Islands, which lie west of the Azores, for they supported his concept of circumnavigation. Later Columbus argued that the so-called paradise would be found up the Orinoco River.

While a meal of symbolic food might easily have included pesto, which is a speciality of Genoa and thus would honor Columbus's birthplace, Columbus Day for me has always been associated with the preeminent new world food, corn. Corn, or *grano turco* (Turkish grain) as it is known in Italy, is not eaten as it is in the States, but is ground into cornmeal for polenta, which is a word of ancient origin. The name of the staple food for Caesar's legions was *pulmentum*, a type of porridge or mush made of cereal grains such as millet or chickpea flour. The Roman legions conquered the known classical world on that field ration. With time, and with the major innovation of replacing grain with corn from the New World, *pulmentum* became polenta, an important ingredient in the basic diet of the Veneto region, where the Barolini family comes from. It is still cooked today much as it was in the bygone centuries and can be eaten as the Romans did—either soft like a gruel, or firm and sliced.

Traditionally for the *veneti*, polenta is served *con uccelli*, with songbirds, but this is something I absolutely forego. Antonio, in one of his Veneto stories, "The Great Bird Barbecue of Cousin Canal" from *Our Last Family Countess*, tells of my horror at seeing strings of larks or thrushes or blackbirds, plucked and skinny and still with their heads on, hung up at market stands in Vicenza's magnificent Piazza delle Erbe, where market has been held for centuries. We were all going that fall evening to dine on spitted birds at a market trattoria, for as he wrote in that story, "A good *arrosto* of birds of passage is the expression of high civilization and delicate cuisine in our tradition."

But how could he have ever thought that I, American, and educated in a Franciscan convent school, could ever swallow a bite of a lark! All I could think of was the gentle Saint Francis, who loved as his brother, not as his meal, the crested lark, which reminded him of a good friar in a hooded brown habit. Legend has it that on the evening of Saint Francis's death, a cloud of larks wheeled over his resting place and sang their farewells to him. Even though I cannot eat songbirds, I recognize that it is a squeamishness that may be thought foolish. Italians eat birds with equanimity, considering them all part of nature's bounty for human well-being. The English cookbook writer Elizabeth David seems to have reached this stage of equanimity and gives her bird recipes in *Italian Food* without apology. And in his classic *Italian Family Cooking*, Ed Giobbi, as renowned a cook as he is an artist, has said of the Italian taste for birds: "This attitude differs a lot from our own violent society, which cannot stand seeing a rabbit hanging in a market but which commits daily crimes of violence at home and abroad."

But the best story about eating birds comes from Grace Pizzuto Fahey. Although Grace married a man of Irish descent, her five daughters retain a great deal of Italianness in their ways because of the presence in the home of Grace's Italian grandmother. Donna, the eldest Fahey daughter, still has and uses the original pasta-making machine (called the *chitarra*) made by her great-grand-father, and a handsome hand-carved breadboard. As a child, Donna once found a hurt bird in the backyard and rather than taking it home to bandage and nurse along as children often do, she brought it to the old Italian grandmother and asked her to cook it for her.

The feast day of Saints Simon and Jude falls on October 28, just before All Hallows' Eve on the last night of October. Both saints were among the twelve disciples, and Saint Jude is also known as Thaddeus to distinguish him from Judas. According to tradition, Saint Simon was one of the shepherds to whom angels revealed the birth of Christ. He and Jude joined together in preaching the gospel in Syria and Mesopotamia, and both were martyred in Persia. Not much is known about either saint, but Saint Jude has become particularly popular in our times as "patron of hopeless cases." This patronage is said to have developed because in ancient times no-body invoked him for anything—his name too closely resembled that of the traitor disciple, Judas. Consequently, grateful for any notice from the faithful, he favors even the most desperate situations of those who pray to him, and newspaper personal columns, often after death notices, are filled with testimonies to his efficacy: "Thank you, Saint Jude, for answering my prayers," they read, or "Thanks be to Saint Jude." The practical Tuscans honor Saint Simon by eating chestnut dishes on October 28. In England, it's dirge cakes or, as they're known here, doughnuts.

We've moved doughnuts along to All Hallows' Eve, or Halloween. And it's said, though long forgotten, that the doughnut, as a version of the dirge or soul cake, symbolizes eternity in its continuous circular shape without beginning or end. Apples are also very traditional at this time—as cider, or in the Halloween game of bobbing for apples, or in the practice of divination. Dickens, for one, described apple divination as peeling the fruit in one long strip and tossing it over the left shoulder in order the get the initial of one's future sweetheart.

The use of apples in Halloween celebrations is as ancient as the Roman holiday for Pomona, goddess of orchards and fruit, whose festival fell on November 1. (Halloween is the vigil eve of the festival.) In pre-Christian times wild masquerades were held on that night in order to frighten away the demons at the approach of the dark evenings of winter. And in many European countries the custom survives of eating apples, or giving away dishes made of apples, on this night. I certainly remember ducking for apples at every Halloween party I ever went to as a child, and when we went trick or treating, we always seemed to be given apples.

In the old calendar, October 31 was the last day of the old year. That night was the time when all the witches and evil spirits were thought to be abroad, holding their wicked revels. With Christianity, it was taken over as the Eve of All Hallows, meaning the sainted ones. All Saints' Day, which is celebrated on November 1, was introduced in the seventh century to commemorate the saints and martyrs of the Christian church, thus overlaying the original ancient festival of the dead and the powers of darkness.

For the pagan Celtic tributes, the eve was a great fire festival held to mark the beginning of winter. In *The Golden Bough*, Sir

317

James Frazer remarks: "Throughout Europe, Hallowe'en, the night which marks the transition from autumn to winter, seems to have been of old the time of year when the souls of the departed were supposed to revisit their old homes in order to warm themselves by the fire and to comfort themselves with the good cheer provided for them in the kitchen or the parlour by their affectionate kinsfolk."

The macabre witch and skeleton outfits with which we garbed ourselves for "Halloweening" are a throwback to the grotesque masks and costumes of old, meant to keep demons and hobgoblins at bay. It's said that the food offerings now given to the trick or treaters are relics of the food offerings once given to the dead. In the Piedmont region, where we once lived, chestnuts are ritually served to commemorate All Hallows' Eve, and they are said to keep away the souls of the dead if left out on the table overnight. Chestnuts are the sign of fall and as old as Apicius, who gave a recipe for them (with lentils) in his cookery notes of imperial Rome. But chestnuts also have other properties, and on my last visit to Strambino in the Piedmont, an old friend, Piera Massetto, gave me a chestnut to put in my coat pocket—to keep you healthy, she said, and to keep away colds. Some beliefs endure forever.

Saint Francis of Assisi's Day
Fettuccelle with Artichokes
Chicken Valdostana
Plum Tartlets

Columbus Day
Mushroom Salad
Polenta Cakes with Sausage
    Sauce
Pears Stuffed with Cheese

Halloween (All Saints' Eve)
Beef Stew in a Pumpkin Shell
    with Potato-Pumpkin Purée
Apple Fritters
Chestnut Fritters
Italian Doughnuts

Saint Francis of Assisi's Day

FETTUCCELLE WITH ARTICHOKES
6 TO 8 SERVINGS

> 2 pounds small, very fresh young artichokes or 2
>   packages frozen artichoke hearts, thawed
> 1/2 lemon
> 1/2 cup olive oil
> 1 teaspoon minced garlic
> 1 1/2 tablespoons minced Italian parsley
> Salt and freshly ground black pepper, to taste
> 1/2 cup light cream
> 1 1/2 pounds fresh or dried fettuccelle (flat noodles)
> 1/2 cup freshly grated Parmesan cheese

1. If you are using fresh artichokes, prepare them by washing them, cutting off the sharp tips of the leaves, cutting off and discarding

the large leaves at the base, and cutting 1 inch from the tops.

2. Bring a large pot of lightly salted water to a boil. Squeeze the ½ lemon into the water, and drop in the rind. Immerse the artichokes, and keep them immersed with the aid of a wooden spoon. Cook until tender, about 10 minutes for fresh artichokes and 6 minutes for packaged ones.

3. Drain the artichokes in a colander. When they are cool enough to handle, shake the water out of them. Cut them into bite-size pieces. If you are using fresh artichokes, remove the chokes and discard.

4. Put the olive oil in a large, heavy skillet over moderate heat. When it is sizzling, add the artichoke pieces and cook, stirring, 1 to 2 minutes. Add the garlic, parsley, salt, and pepper. Cook, stirring, another 2 minutes. Add the cream and mix thoroughly. Set aside.

5. Have ready a large pot of lightly salted boiling water. Cook the *fettuccelle*, about 3 minutes if fresh, 5 to 7 minutes if dried. Drain and transfer to a serving bowl. Add the artichoke sauce a little at a time, mixing well.

6. Serve accompanied by the Parmesan cheese.

CHICKEN VALDOSTANA
6 SERVINGS

> *3 whole chicken breasts, cut in half*
> *¼ cup all-purpose flour*
> *2 eggs, beaten*
> *4 tablespoons unsalted butter*
> *4 tablespoons olive oil*
> *Salt and freshly ground black pepper, to taste*
> *¾ cup diced lean boiled ham*
> *3 tablespoons tomato paste*

1 teaspoon dried marjoram leaves, crumbled
1/4 cup dry white wine
6 slices Italian fontina cheese
1/2 cup chicken broth, hot

Preheat the oven to 400° F.

1. Remove the skin and bones from the chicken breasts. Wash them and pat them dry with paper towels.

2. Put the flour on a sheet of wax paper. Dip each chicken piece in the beaten egg, let the excess drip off, then coat on both sides with flour. Put the butter and oil in a large skillet over moderate heat. When sizzling, add the chicken; cook for 3 minutes, turn, and cook another 3 minutes.

3. Transfer the chicken to a baking dish just large enough to hold the pieces comfortably. Season with salt and pepper.

4. Mix the ham, tomato paste, marjoram, and wine in a small bowl.

5. Place a slice of fontina cheese on each piece of chicken, then top with the ham-tomato mixture.

6. Gently pour the hot broth onto the bottom of the pan (not over the chicken). Cover the pan with aluminum foil.

7. Bake 15 minutes on the middle rack of the oven.

PLUM TARTLETS
8 SERVINGS

1 recipe Sweet Pastry Dough (see recipe, page 268)
1/2 cup plum jam
16 Italian prune plums, pitted and cut into halves
Juice and freshly grated rind of 2 lemons
1/4 teaspoon freshly grated nutmeg
3 tablespoons unsalted butter, cut into small pieces

Preheat the oven to 375° F.

1. Prepare and chill the Sweet Pastry Dough. On a lightly floured work surface, roll it out into a rectangle about ¼ inch thick. Trim the dough to line eight 3-inch tartlet forms. Press the dough gently against the forms, and prick lightly with a fork. Wrap any remaining dough, and refrigerate.

2. Spread a little plum jam on each tartlet shell.

3. Arrange four plum pieces in each shell. Sprinkle with the lemon rind, juice, and nutmeg. Dot with butter pieces.

4. Set the tartlets on a baking sheet, and bake 20 to 25 minutes on the middle rack of the oven, until the plums are cooked and the pastry is golden.

Columbus Day

MUSHROOM SALAD
6 TO 8 SERVINGS

> *1 pound thinly sliced fresh mushrooms*
> *1 tablespoon fresh lemon juice*
> *½ cup thinly sliced scallion greens*
> *1 tablespoon chopped chives*
> *¼ cup olive oil*
> *½ teaspoon salt*

1. In a serving bowl, toss the mushrooms with the lemon juice until the slices are moistened.

2. Add the scallion greens.

3. Cover the bowl with plastic wrap and chill for at least an hour.

4. Before serving, sprinkle the salad with chives; add the olive oil and salt, and toss again.

POLENTA CAKES WITH SAUSAGE SAUCE
6 SERVINGS

> *4 cups water*
> *1 teaspoon salt*
> *1½ cups coarse cornmeal*
> *1 tablespoon unsalted butter*
> *½ cup Parmesan cheese*
> *1 egg, beaten*
> *2 cups Sausage Sauce (see recipe below)*

1. In a large, heavy saucepan, bring the water to a boil. Add the salt. Stirring constantly with a wooden spoon, pour the cornmeal into the water in a very thin stream. Reduce the heat to low, and cook for 30 minutes, stirring frequently.

2. Remove the saucepan from the heat, and stir in the butter and ¼ cup of the Parmesan cheese. Combine thoroughly; stir in the egg.

3. Preheat the oven to 400° F. Put the mixture in a buttered baking dish, about ½ inch thick, and spread with the Sausage Sauce. Sprinkle with the remaining cheese.

4. Bake on the middle rack of the oven for 15 minutes.

SAUSAGE SAUCE

> *1 ounce dried mushrooms*
> *3 tablespoons olive oil*
> *1 clove garlic*
> *¾ cup chopped onion*
> *1 celery stalk, chopped*
> *1 carrot, chopped*
> *½ pound sweet Italian sausage, casing removed*
> *One 28-ounce can peeled Italian plum tomatoes*
> *Salt and freshly ground black pepper, to taste*
> *6 large basil leaves, chopped*

1. Soak the mushrooms 15 minutes in warm water. Drain.

2. Put the olive oil in a large skillet over moderate heat. When it is sizzling, add the garlic; cook until golden, then discard. Add the onion, celery, and carrot to the seasoned oil, and cook until soft.

3. Crumble the sausage meat into the mixture. Add the mushrooms, tomatoes, salt, pepper, and basil leaves. Simmer 45 minutes, partially covered.

PEARS STUFFED WITH CHEESE
6 SERVINGS

> 6 ripe medium Bartlett pears
> 1 tablespoon fresh lemon juice
> ¾ cup crumbled gorgonzola cheese
> 6 tablespoons heavy cream
> 2 tablespoons Cognac or grappa
> ½ cup chopped walnuts

1. Peel the pears, and cut them in half from top to bottom, leaving the stem attached to one half. Scoop out the seeds and some of the pulp to make a hollow for the filling.

2. Brush the insides of the pears with the lemon juice.

3. With a wooden spoon, cream together the gorgonzola cheese, cream, and Cognac. Stir in the walnuts.

4. Divide the filling among the pears. Put 2 halves together to form a whole pear. Chill 1 hour before serving.

Halloween (All Saints' Eve)

BEEF STEW IN A PUMPKIN SHELL
WITH POTATO-PUMPKIN PURÉE
6 SERVINGS

> 1 medium pumpkin (about 6 pounds)
> Salt, to taste
> ½ onion
> 4 slices bacon
> 1 stalk celery
> 1 carrot, pared
> 4 tablespoons unsalted butter
> 3 tablespoons olive oil
> 2 pounds lean beef cut into 1½-inch cubes
> ¼ cup seasoned flour (flour mixed with salt and
>   pepper to taste)
> ½ cup dry red wine
> 2½ tablespoons tomato paste
> 2 cups beef stock, hot
> 1 bay leaf
> 1 whole clove
> Freshly ground black pepper, to taste
> 6 small whole onions, peeled
> 2 carrots, cut in strips
> 1 pound boiling potatoes
> 2 tablespoons grated Parmesan cheese

Preheat the oven to 350° F.

1. Cut off the top of the pumpkin, and set it aside for a lid. Scoop out all the seeds. (They can be dried, roasted on a baking sheet, and eaten as a snack.) Salt the inside of the pumpkin, replace the

325

top, and wrap it securely in oiled aluminum foil. Bake about 2½ hours.

2. While the pumpkin is baking, chop together the bacon, celery, and carrot. Put 2 tablespoons of the butter and all the olive oil in a large, heavy skillet over moderate heat. When oil mixture is hot, add the bacon-vegetable mixture, and cook until lightly browned.

3. Roll the beef cubes in the seasoned flour. Add them to the pan, and cook over medium-high heat, turning to brown on all sides.

4. Add the wine. Cook over high heat until the alcohol evaporates.

5. Dissolve the tomato paste in 1 cup of the hot beef stock. Add the bay leaf, clove, and pepper. Pour the liquid over the meat, cover, reduce the heat to medium-low, and simmer for 2 hours, or until the meat is tender. Add more hot stock as needed.

6. About 30 minutes before the beef is done, add the 6 small onions and the carrot strips to the pan.

7. Peel the potatoes and, in another saucepan, cook them in lightly salted water until tender, about 20 minutes. Drain well, and push them through a food mill into a larger saucepan.

8. Scoop out the pumpkin pulp, and push it through the food mill into the saucepan with the potato. If the mixture is too liquid, dry it somewhat by placing the saucepan over low heat and cooking, stirring constantly, for 2 to 3 minutes. Remove it from the heat, and stir in the remaining butter, the Parmesan cheese, and more salt. Put the purée in a warmed serving dish.

9. Put the pumpkin on a serving platter; remove the bay leaf and clove from the stew, and put the stew in the pumpkin. Replace the lid, and bring the pumpkin to the table. Serve the purée on the side.

APPLE FRITTERS

> *6 large apples*
> *7 tablespoons rum*
> *2 tablespoons sugar*
> *1¼ cups sifted all-purpose flour*
> *⅔ cup water*
> *Pinch salt*
> *1 egg, separated*
> *1 tablespoon finest grade light extra-virgin olive oil*
> *Peanut oil for frying*
> *Confectioners' sugar*

1. Pare, core, and slice the apples into ½-inch-thick rounds. In a large bowl combine 4 tablespoons of the rum with the sugar. Marinate the apple slices in the liquid 1 hour.

2. In a wide, shallow bowl, beat together the flour, water, salt, and egg yolk. Add the remaining rum and the olive oil. Mix well and let stand 1 hour.

3. Beat the egg white until stiff but not dry. Fold into the flour mixture.

4. Drain the apple slices, and pat them dry.

5. Pour 4 inches of peanut oil into a deep skillet or deep-fat fryer. Heat oil to 375° F on a deep-fat frying thermometer.

6. Dip the apple slices in the batter with tongs, and fry them, a few at a time, until golden brown, 3 to 5 minutes. Remove them with tongs and drain on paper towels. Serve hot, sprinkled with confectioners' sugar.

CHESTNUT FRITTERS
6 SERVINGS

> ½ *pound chestnut flour (available at Italian*
> *groceries and specialty shops)*
> *1 cup water*
> *Pinch salt*
> ½ *cup seedless black raisins*
> ½ *cup chopped pistachio nuts*
> *1 tablespoon finest grade light extra-virgin olive oil*
> *Peanut oil for frying*
> *Confectioners' sugar*

1. Put the chestnut flour in a bowl, and slowly stir in enough water to make a thick paste. Stir in the salt, raisins, pistachio nuts, and olive oil. Mix well.

2. Pour 4 inches of peanut oil into a deep skillet or deep-fat fryer. Heat oil to 375° F on a deep-fat frying thermometer.

3. Drop the dough by the tablespoonful into the oil, and fry the fritters, a few at a time, until golden brown. Remove them with a slotted spoon, and drain on paper towels.

4. Serve hot, sprinkled with confectioners' sugar.

ITALIAN DOUGHNUTS (*Ciambelle*)
YIELD: 20

> *2 cups all-purpose flour*
> *5 tablespoons sugar*
> *Pinch salt*
> ½ *cup dry white wine*
> ½ *teaspoon anise seeds*
> ½ *cup finest grade light extra-virgin olive oil*
> *1 egg, beaten*

1. Sift the flour into a medium bowl. Add the sugar, salt, wine, anise seeds, and oil. Mix to a dough and, on a floured work surface, knead the dough with the heel of your hand for several minutes until smooth.

2. Put it back in the bowl and cover. Let stand 1 hour.

3. Preheat the oven to 425° F. Lightly oil a baking sheet.

4. Divide the dough into 20 pieces. Roll each piece into a cylinder the thickness of a finger, then shape it into a ring. Arrange the rings on a baking sheet, and brush them with the beaten egg.

5. Bake 20 minutes on the middle rack of the oven, or until lightly browned.

Twelve

NOVEMBER

The first day of this month is dedicated to the memory of the holy dead—those legions of anonymous saints who are not named individually in the official calendar with a feast day during the year but who nonetheless deserve remembrance. There have always been saints without official sanctification, and they are feted on All Saints' Day. Such a collective feast day originated when Pope Boniface IV rededicated the Pantheon (a pagan temple whose very name means "to all the gods") to the Blessed Virgin Mary and All Holy Martyrs in 610. The November 1 Feast of All Saints is a major day

331

of observance in the Church as well as an official Italian holiday.

The Pantheon, also known as the Rotonda from its circular shape, is a perfectly preserved construction of antiquity, as majestic and harmonious today as when it was completed during Hadrian's reign in A.D. 125. I lived in its immediate neighborhood for a year or so, and it was my pleasure each day to walk through the Piazza della Rotonda (where the obelisk of Rameses II rises from a bevy of café tables) and see this wonderful building. Until this century, its magnificent dome was the greatest in the world, surpassing even Saint Peter's. As a temple in classical times, the Pantheon held statues of all the great gods prominently displayed in the middle area, with the minor ones located in recesses. Today the Pantheon contains the tombs of two kings of unified Italy and the artist Raphael, as well as some other artists of lesser note.

On All Saints' Day, when prayers are said for all the saints but especially for family ones, chestnut dishes are traditional and seasonal. In Italy these dishes can be of many sorts—stuffings for roasts, a puréed side dish, sweet fritters, cakes, and creams. Among my favorites was the Tuscan *castagnaccio*—a flat, peasant kind of cake made from chestnut flour, which I first had in Lucca.

The chestnut is said to have arrived in western Europe from Castan, a town in eastern Thessaly, which gave the nut the generic name Castanea, whence Castagna, the Italian word for chestnut and the name of the Calabrian town, surrounded by chestnut forests, from which my maternal grandparents came. From the crude chestnut flour that the poor used for bread making, to the extreme refinement of candied *marrons glâcés* (the elaborately made sweet identified with voluptuousness and said to have been invented for Louis XIV, but actually mentioned 150 years earlier by Aretino, the Renaissance writer), chestnuts run the gamut from humble fare to luxury dishes.

Immediately after All Saints' Day comes All Souls' Day, on November 2, so I make a culinary combination of the two feast days although they have distinct identities as remembrances. All Souls' Day, officially called the Commemoration of All the Faithful Departed, is popularly known as the Day of the Dead, a time for visiting and decorating graves. In Rome I often visited one of my favorite spots, the Protestant cemetery near the pyramid of Gaius Cestius, where Keats and Shelley are buried and where in February 1971, the one hundred and fiftieth anniversary of Keats's death was observed.

The countess with whom I boarded when I was a student in Perugia made sure I became acquainted with that annual Perugian phenomenon known as the Fair of the Dead, which extended all up and down Corso Vannucci the first week of November, commemorating All Souls' Day and the dead in general—but not mournfully! Each year the city takes on a carnival atmosphere for a festival that has its origins in the Middle Ages. The main street and the grand central square, which is the heart of medieval Perugia and one of the finest in Italy (overlooked by the Priors' Palace and Cathedral and containing the Great Fountain), fill with vendors. They come from all over Italy to set up their booths and sell everything from rolling pins and pasta-making machines to winter underwear, eight-way food choppers, costume jewelry, fine old books, crockery, Florentine silver, gaudy neckware, and everything else an exuberant market offers to crowds. Food stands are everywhere, selling hot sugared *bombe* (which are like jelly doughnuts) and the confections known as "dead bones," which are the specialty of the occasion. I still have my precious purchases from the Fair of the Dead I attended in 1948: one is *Le Avventure di Pinocchio*, the first book I read in Italian, and the other is *La Divina Commedia* with the Doré illustrations. (As a Christmas gift, I once received a promissory note for a close reading of the latter from my eldest child, the Dante scholar, but she has yet to deliver.) I got my copies from a dealer in second-hand books at the low prices that were common just after the war, when people were selling many of their treasured possessions for whatever they could get.

During the festival all kinds of morsels (known as *calia*—a word indicating "shavings" or "gold dust" but that has come to mean trifles to nibble or chew on) are to be found. Some of them seem strange to an American palate, but then again, wouldn't our junk food of today have appeared odd to former civilizations? The vendors display neatly arranged piles of beans and seeds—pumpkin, sunflower, calabash, chickpeas, and lupines; there are all kinds of nuts, including, of course, roasted chestnuts and peanuts, which are known as American nuts; vats of olives, green or black, briny or sweet; strands or lumps of licorice; heaps of nougat called *torrone*; and all kinds of nut brittles (*croccanti*).

The speciality food for All Souls' Day is ground-almond cookies, called either *fave dei morti* or *ossi dei morti*—"Fave of the Dead" (for the fava bean, because of their oval shape), or "Bones of the Dead." Artusi, the master, says that the association of the bean with the dead goes back to remote antiquity. The Egyptians thought that the souls of the dead were enclosed in the beans. The association with death bothers some visitors to Perugia, including the eminent poet Paul Valéry, who called the delicious cookies "this horrible confection" and attributed them to the Umbrian reputation for ferocity. What would he have made of the still prevalent Sicilian custom of fashioning vividly decorated sugar confections in the shape of skulls for All Souls' Day?

On the other hand, when Plutarch wrote, "Abstain from beans," he was not referring to them as a food associated with the dead but in their political use as a voting token, so his meaing was: Keep out of politics. The bean is one of the world's most venerable foods, going back to prehistory, and certainly a staple of the common diet of the ancient world. That the Romans honored the various peas and beans is demonstrated by the surnames of several of the most patrician families of Rome, which derived from them. And perhaps, in the ultimate connection, in England the broad bean, which is the Italian fava, is called the Windsor bean.

The custom of naming cookies *fave dei morti* originated when fava beans (greatly esteemed in the ancient Roman world) were offered to Pluto, lord of the underworld, and his wife Proserpina, and to the three Fates—the *Parcae*—who controlled human destiny. In Venice on November 2, the long tradition continues with a different twist, for it is a day on which couples announce their engagement. In an old and charming practice that is still observed, the suitor sends his fiancée a box containing oval-shaped *fave* cookies tinted white, pink, and chocolate. Amidst the cookies, in its own separate case, is the engagement ring.

In pre-Christian times food was put on the graves in November, when the spirits of the dead were believed to roam the earth. From this came the Christian custom of baking special breads, known as All Souls' breads, for the family table. In addition to the bread, other "soul food," like lentils and beans, was served. Since it was thought that the dead returned to earth on November 2, windows were kept open as people prayed so that the souls in purgatory could hear the prayers for their special intention and be consoled. In some parts of Italy, food is placed on the table at an empty place in remembrance of the departed and subsequently given to the poor.

Observance of All Souls' Day emphasizes praying for the souls in purgatory, and one of the charming tales in *The Little Flowers of Saint Francis* is titled "How Friar John of La Verna, while saying mass on All Souls' Day, beheld many souls set free from Purgatory" when he saw "a multitude of souls, well-nigh infinite, come forth from purgatory, after the manner of countless sparks issuing from a fiery furnace." But the remembrance of the dead goes back in time far earlier than Christian belief, for all primitive cultures honored and remembered the dead (and feared them, and therefore appeased them, primarily with food offerings).

But all is not beans and bones. The fall is also truffle season in Italy, and my daughter Susi has the good fortune to live in one of Italy's two white truffle areas, the part of the Marche region around Urbino. In Umbria I have had the *tartufo nero*, or black truffle, as an antipasto spread on *crostini*, or cooked into a fragrant sauce served with delicate meats like chicken or veal. The black truffle, different from the white, has its own mystery and mystique and, being denser and less perishable, can be cooked. Whites are better savored without cooking. Each in its own way is superb. But my gastronomic memory is precise: it is the white truffle that entices me.

The "white" truffle looks like nothing more prepossessing than a knobby brown golfball. But the fragrance! A *tartufo* has an aroma—distinctive, unforgettable, penetrating—that for me is paradisiacal, an aroma with woodsy and earthy overtones that makes the truffle an object of mystery—what has been described in *Le Monde* as "a wild and fantastic food whose underground growth escapes all observation and defies all prediction."

In 1986 Niki and I were at Susi's during truffle season. We laid our plans: the secret was to get the truffle as fresh as possible and use it immediately. Instead of our making the *tagliatelli* that the occasion demanded, we decided to buy them freshly made at the pasta shop so that we could give our time to hunting down the tuber.

We set off for Fermignano, a little country town of five thousand people in the plain below Urbino, one of those usual, pleasant, but unremarkable places one passes through quickly, not thinking twice of it. But in this case it merited a second thought, for it was the birthplace of the great Renaissance architect Bramante. A long, tree-lined approach fronted by small homes in gardens led us into a colonnaded piazza. On this day the main square was filled with country carts festooned with wayside flowers, both the wild purple asters called *settembrini* in Italy because they bloom in September and the tall golden coreopsis that dots the countryside. It was the *Mercato Micologica*, the mushroom market, in full sway, featuring exhibits of mushrooms from all of Italy. Hundreds of varieties, the deadly and the edible, all awesome, filled the tables in the arcades; coupled with the mushroom fair was a display of *Apicultura*, bee-hives and honey, and sweets made with honey. It was a charming scene of country life in a small-town market square and the sort of thing I love about Italy, but we were on a serious mission, and there wasn't time to linger over mushrooms.

Nevio spotted a man in the piazza who was known as a *tartuffaio*, a truffle hunter. In fact, the man told Nevio, he had just dug up *tartufi* that morning. *Benissimo!* We followed him to his home on the outskirts of town. He invited us into his silent, dimly lit house. We went into a darkened sitting room off the entry hall and stood there waiting. A round table was in the center of the room and on it a scale. The man, who had disappeared, came back into the room carrying something wrapped in a handkerchief. As he unfolded it, an unforgettable aroma filled the place: it was certainly a truffle. "It stinks in here," said Niki. "How much?" I breathed to Susi, who passed it on to Nevio, who asked the man. Forty thousand lire an *etto* (hectogram), the man said. I couldn't believe the bargain—$35 for 3½ ounces. But, from my years of marketing experience in Italy, I knew I shouldn't show my eagerness.

"How do we know it's fresh?" I asked to show I was no novice.

"Ma, signora, non si sente?"—"Well, can't you smell it?" he retorted more than reasonably.

That night we prepared the *tagliatelli*, and as soon as they were about to be drained, I got the truffle out, gently wiped it with a slightly damp cloth to remove any earth that might still cling to it, and grated the precious tuber over the pasta. But wait!—it wasn't white. Somehow my memory had tricked me into thinking the truffle would look like paper-thin slivered almonds, even though I'd been reassured by no less an authority than Elizabeth David that white truffles "are in reality a dirty brownish colour on the outside, beige inside."

But it didn't disappoint: it was a magnificent truffle, and, I'm persuaded, the only way to have them is by going in person to where they are found.

In mid-November, a fine mild time in Italy that is called Saint Martin's summer and that would correspond to our somewhat earlier Indian summer, there falls the feast of Saint Martin of Tours. He died in 397 and is commemorated on November 11, in antiquity the Roman feast day of Bacchus, god of wine and revels. This coincidence has made Saint Martin the patron saint of drunkards and has given rise to the phrase that someone thoroughly intoxicated is "Martin drunk." It is still customary to taste new wine on Saint Martin's Day, and the wine tasting at Torgiano, which is promoted by the Wine Museum there during the week of November 11, is evidence of the continuing custom.

Saint Martin is not only associated with drunkards but, according to Susi's father-in-law, with cuckolds as well. The occasion for my learning this intriguing nugget of hagiology was a Christmas holiday I spent with Susanna and her family at Urbino. We were invited to her in-laws' home for Christmas dinner, and after mother-in-law Cleofe's exquisite handmade *cappelletti* course, there arrived on the table a roast capon whose castrated condition led father-in-law Peppino into an unexpected explanation of why November 11, the day of San Martino, was the feast day of cuckolds. "It was our little king's birthday, you know," Peppino began, referring to Italy's last ruling monarch, Vittorio Emmanuele III, known for his diminutive stature. "Since he was married to a very tall and attractive woman, Elena of Montenegro, no one could believe that he wasn't being replaced in his husbandly duties. In fact, Crown Prince Umberto was a tall, strapping young man not at all like the king but more like the captain of the horse guards. So that's how San Martino, by having his feast day on the king's birthday, got to be the patron of cuckolds."

Though the popular imagination sees him one way, historically the saint seems to have been otherwise. Saint Martin was born in that part of the Roman Empire which is now Hungary, during the reign of Constantine. He joined the imperial cavalry and was stationed in France, where he underwent his conversion to Christianity. It is also said that after his conversion, Martin refused to fight further in the Roman legions and was imprisoned by the emperor Julian. He preached pacifism and so is known as the first conscientious objector. Eventually he was released, and he settled in France, where he founded that country's first monastery.

Known as a saintly man of God, Saint Martin tried to follow a contemplative life, but the legend has it that when the citizens of Tours were seeking him out to be their bishop, a goose revealed his hiding place, whereupon he had to put up with being the bishop of Tours for thirty years. His most famous legend, and one often pictured in art, is of an event that occurred when he was still a military tribune in Amiens. One winter, meeting with a scantily dressed man who was begging alms (or, in another version, who was a drunkard who had given away his garments in order to buy wine), Saint Martin had pity on the shivering man and took out his sword, divided his cloak in two, and gave one half to the stranger. That night, Christ himself appeared to Martin in a vision, dressed in the very cloak, and said, "What thou hast done for that poor man, thou hast done for me."

In Europe, Saint Martin's Day was the last religious feast day before the beginning of Advent, which in earlier times was a fast period. To mark the occasion, goose, the last of the fresh-killed meat before winter, was eaten on November 11. Another explanation for the goose's association with Saint Martin is that he was once annoyed by a goose, which he ordered to be killed and served up for supper. He died from the repast, and so a goose is "sacrificed" to him on each November 11.

Actually, the day was generally observed as a thanksgiving day, a day to celebrate the harvest home before the coming of winter. Saint Martin's feast, called Martinmas, closed the series of harvest celebrations associated with each festival, or *sagra*, of particular foods. As such it became the main thanksgiving and was brought by the Pilgrims to the New World.

Since biblical times, when the Lord gave the commandment to "keep . . . the Feast of Ingathering which is in the end of the year when thou hast gathered in the labors out of the field," autumn has been a time of thanksgiving for harvest safely gathered. The Succoth Festival of the Jews is this Feast of the Ingathering, and it is observed in October with booths or tabernacles covered with greens and the season's produce.

The harvest is laden with associations—ensuring rain for the next year's crops, offerings for ensuring new life, rituals at the cutting of the last sheaf, propitiating the power that was thought to reside in crops and the earth's fertility, and appeasing the underworld gods (for crops came from under the ground, where the dead reside), and honoring the strength of new growth.

If I had remained in Italy, leading the country life we had in Strambino, I might have observed harvest thanksgiving with a goose on Saint Martin's Day rather than the Puritan Thanksgiving of my American life. Rosetta of our Strambino days, who now lives in the nearby village of San Martino Canavese, has an enormous celebration on her village's feast day—relatives from all over come to her on November 11, and she in turn visits them on the occasion of their village festivities.

The first year of my Strambino life, however, I insisted that we have a turkey, and to ensure that it would be a proper, well-fatted turkey, Antonio got one at a poultry market and farmed it out at signor Ghiggia's barnyard. Every so often during the fall, I would walk baby Linda over to see our turkey. Antonio's sister Arcangela came from Vicenza to visit us in Strambino that fall, and she still remarks on the succulence and goodness of our turkey when it was served up, stuffed, for Thanksgiving dinner.

Since I couldn't grow or find native American cranberries in Italy, I used Swedish lingonberries for their color and appearance and closeness in taste. I learned a new use for pumpkin when I first had *ravioli di zucca*—pumpkin ravioli at the Dodici Apostoli in Verona.

What always remains the same is a custom I started at a long-ago Thanksgiving—that of inviting to our family dinner anyone who happens to be alone on a holiday. It has remained a tenet of my holiday observance. I find it impossible to understand people who think they are keeping Thanksgiving or Christmas by eating a meal at a restaurant, rather than being with family or sharing festivities with other couples or singles or anyone alone. For what is important is the ritual, the symbolic activity of the gathering, the renewal of ties and loyalty in the celebration with food and drink.

All is as old as the world and as enduring as people's place in it.

NOVEMBER RECIPES

All Saints' and Souls' Days
Vermicelli with Truffles
Stuffed Veal Breast
Torgiano Salad
Dead Bone Cookies

Thanksgiving (Saint Martin's Day)
Robiolo Cheese with Olive Paste
Pumpkin Gnocchi
Roast Turkey with Chestnut-Sausage Dressing
Potato-Celeriac Purée
Broccoli Timbale
Baked Apples in Wine
Honey-Nut Crostata

All Saints' and All Souls' Days

VERMICELLI WITH TRUFFLES
4 TO 6 SERVINGS

1 pound vermicelli (thin pasta)
2 tablespoons unsalted butter
3 ounces gruyère cheese, cut into slivers
Salt and freshly ground black pepper, to taste
¼ cup, or more, chicken broth
1 white truffle (1 ounce)

1. Cook the vermicelli in lightly salted boiling water.

2. While the pasta is cooking, melt the butter in a saucepan over moderate heat. When the butter is melted, add the cheese, stirring until it melts. Season with salt and pepper. Add broth to thin the mixture to the consistency you wish.

3. When the sauce is blended, thinly slice ½ of the truffle into it.

4. Pour the sauce over the cooked and drained pasta. Divide the pasta among the serving plates, and slice the remaining truffle directly over each portion, also adding a dab of butter to each serving.

STUFFED VEAL BREAST
6 SERVINGS

> 1 pound hot Italian sausage
> ¾ cup chopped onion
> 3 tablespoons grated Parmesan cheese
> 3 tablespoons minced parsley
> 1 cup dry breadcrumbs
> 2 eggs
> 1 teaspoon dried oregano
> 1 cup cooked rice
> One 6-pound veal breast, with a deep pocket cut in
>   large end
> 1 clove garlic, peeled and cut in half
> 2 tablespoons olive oil
> Salt and freshly ground black pepper, to taste
> 2 teaspoons dried rosemary
> 2 cups chicken stock or canned broth
> 4 slices bacon

Preheat the oven to 325° F.

1. Remove the casing from the sausage, and crumble the meat into a large, heavy skillet. Cook, stirring often, over low heat until the

meat is no longer pink. Stir in the onion, and cook until translucent and lightly colored, stirring often.

2. Put the sausage-onion mixture in a bowl. Add the Parmesan cheese, parsley, breadcrumbs, eggs, oregano, and rice. Mix well.

3. Stuff the veal pocket with the mixture. Close it securely with skewers.

4. Rub the breast with the cut garlic and then with the olive oil. Sprinkle with salt and pepper and the rosemary.

5. Put the stuffed breast in a baking pan. Pour the stock into the pan. Arrange the bacon over the veal breast. Roast uncovered for 2 hours and 40 minutes, or until the meat is tender when pierced by a fork. Baste it from time to time with pan juices.

6. Let the veal stand a few minutes before slicing.

TORGIANO SALAD
4 TO 6 SERVINGS

> *1 large bunch arugula (rughetta)*
> *1 medium head romaine lettuce*
> *1 pound firm white mushrooms*
> *1 lemon*
> *¼-pound chunk Parmesan cheese*
> *Basic Salad Dressing (see recipe, page 57)*

1. Wash the arugula well and dry it. Cut away any large stems, and discard them. Wash the romaine leaves, and dry them. Chop the arugula and lettuce, and toss them together in a salad bowl.

2. Wipe the mushrooms, trim off the stem ends, and discard. Slice and sprinkle with juice of half or whole lemon. Add the mushrooms to the salad greens.

3. Using the largest holes of a hand grater, slice slivers of cheese directly over the salad bowl.

4. Dress the salad, toss, and serve immediately.

DEAD BONE COOKIES (*Ossi dei Morti*)
YIELD: 4 DOZEN

⅔ cup sugar
8 tablespoons unsalted butter
2 eggs
2 cups sifted all-purpose flour
1 teaspoon pure vanilla extract
1 cup ground pistachios

Preheat the oven to 400° F.

1. Lightly grease 2 baking sheets.

2. Cream the sugar, butter, and eggs together in a small bowl. Add the flour gradually, beating until smooth with each addition. Add the vanilla and nuts, and blend well.

3. Break off small pieces of dough (about 1 teaspoon), and form them into kidney bean shapes. Place them 1 inch apart on the baking sheets.

4. Bake 10 minutes, or until the cookies are lightly browned. Remove to a rack to cool.

ROBIOLO CHEESE WITH OLIVE PASTE
8 SERVINGS

> *½ pound robiolo cheese (creamy, soft, cow's milk*
>   *cheese)*
> *⅓ cup olive paste (available at Italian groceries and*
>   *specialty shops)*
> *One 6-ounce can pitted black olives, preferably*
>   *imported, drained*

1. Cut the cheese in half horizontally. Spread the olive paste on the bottom half, and replace the top half.

2. Cut the olives in half from top to bottom, and press them, shiny side showing, into the sides of the cheese.

PUMPKIN GNOCCHI
6 TO 8 SERVINGS

> *2 cups freshly cooked pumpkin pulp, well drained,*
>   *or one 16-ounce can*
> *¾ cup grated Parmesan cheese*
> *2 eggs, slightly beaten*
> *¼ teaspoon grated nutmeg*
> *¼ teaspoon marjoram*
> *¼ teaspoon sage*
> *¼ teaspoon thyme*
> *¼ teaspoon celery seed*
> *¼ teaspoon white pepper*
> *1¼ cups flour*
> *4 tablespoons butter*

1. Bring salted water to a boil in a large pot.

2. In a bowl combine the pumpkin, ½ cup of the Parmesan cheese, the eggs, nutmeg, herbs, and white pepper.

3. Add flour (up to 1 cup) to the pumpkin mixture until it is thick enough to hold its shape on the spoon.

4. Put ¼ cup flour on a wooden board. With floured fingers pick off a small amount of the pumpkin mixture; shape it into a small ball. Roll it lightly in the flour, and put it aside on waxed paper, using all the pumpkin mix to make about 48 gnocchi.

5. Butter a large baking dish. Melt the butter over low heat.

6. Immerse the gnocchi, a dozen at a time, in the boiling salted water. When they float to the surface, in about a minute, skim them out of the water and put them in the baking dish; keep the baking dish warm in a 200° F oven.

7. Cover all gnocchi with the melted butter, sprinkle with the remaining ¼ cup grated Parmesan cheese, and serve immediately.

ROAST TURKEY WITH CHESTNUT-SAUSAGE DRESSING
12 TO 16 SERVINGS

2 pounds dried chestnuts
One 10- to 15-pound turkey, with giblets and neck
1 carrot, chopped
4 large onions, peeled
3 stalks celery
2 teaspoons salt
10 tablespoons unsalted butter
1 pound sweet Italian sausage
1½ pounds seasoned croutons
1 teaspoon dried sage

1 teaspoon poultry seasoning
4 fresh sage leaves
2 teaspoons fresh rosemary leaves
1 lemon, cut in half
¼ cup olive oil
1 cup dry white wine
1 tablespoon all-purpose flour

1. Soak the chestnuts overnight in water to cover. To cook, put them in a large pot and cover with about 5 inches of water. Bring to a boil, lower the heat, and simmer 5 minutes, until the chestnuts are tender and puffed up. Drain. When they are cool, cut them up coarsely.

2. Put the turkey giblets and neck, carrot, one of the onions, one of the celery stalks, and 1 teaspoon of the salt in a medium, heavy saucepan. Cover with water and bring to a boil. Reduce the heat to low and simmer 30 to 45 minutes. Strain the broth, and set it aside.

3. Finely chop the remaining celery and onions. Put 2 tablespoons of the butter in a large, heavy skillet, over moderate heat. When it is sizzling, add the celery and onions and cook, stirring, until the onion is soft and translucent. Remove the casing from the sausage, and crumble the meat into the skillet. Cook over low heat, stirring often, until the meat is no longer pink.

4. In a small saucepan bring ½ cup water to a boil. Add the remaining butter. Have the croutons ready in a large bowl. When the butter is melted, pour mixture over the croutons and toss. Add the sausage mixture, chestnuts, dried sage, poultry seasoning, and the remaining teaspoon of salt. Mix well.

5. Preheat the oven to 325° F. Mince together the sage leaves and the rosemary leaves.

6. Rinse the turkey. Pat it dry, and rub the cavity with the cut lemon. Put the stuffing into the cavity and neck pouch, and secure with skewers.

7. Cut ¼-inch slits in the turkey wings, at the leg joints, and at several places in the breast. With the point of a small, sharp knife, insert some of the sage-rosemary mixture into the slits.

8. Put the turkey on a rack in a large roasting pan, breast side up. Cover the breast with a double layer of cheesecloth, and dribble the olive oil over the cloth.

9. Roast the turkey 40 minutes. Pour the wine over it, and continue cooking 4½ to 5½ hours, depending on the size of the bird, or until a meat thermometer inserted into the flesh registers 165 to 170° F.

10. As the turkey roasts, baste it 4 times with some of the giblet broth. Thirty minutes before the bird is cooked, remove the cheesecloth so the breast can brown.

11. Remove the turkey to a platter, and let it rest 20 minutes before carving.

12. As the turkey rests, skim off most of the fat from the roasting pan. Place the pan over moderate heat, add the remaining giblet broth to the pan juices, and scrape up the browned residue from the bottom and sides of the pan. Stir in the flour until smooth; cook, stirring, until the gravy thickens. Adjust the seasoning, if necessary.

POTATO-CELERIAC PURÉE
6 TO 8 SERVINGS

2 pounds boiling potatoes
2 pounds celeriac (celery root)
6 tablespoons unsalted butter, room temperature
½ cup heavy cream
Salt and freshly ground black pepper, to taste

1. Peel and dice the potatoes, putting them in a large bowl of acidulated water as you work. Peel and dice the celeriac, and put the pieces in a separate bowl of acidulated water.

2. Put the potatoes in a large saucepan, and cover them with lightly salted water. Bring to a boil over high heat; reduce the heat to medium-low and cook until tender, 15 to 20 minutes. Drain well.

3. Meanwhile, in a separate saucepan, follow the same procedure with the celeriac.

4. Put the potatoes in the bowl of a stationary mixer, or in a large mixing bowl. Cut the butter in small pieces, and add it to the potatoes. Beat with the stationary or hand-held electric mixer until fluffy; beat in the cream.

5. Put the celeriac in a blender container or the bowl of a food processor, and purée. (Work in batches, if necessary.) Add the celeriac to the beaten potatoes, and mix well. Season with salt and pepper.

BROCCOLI TIMBALE
6 SERVINGS

> 1 large bunch broccoli
> 2 cups milk
> 4 tablespoons unsalted butter
> 1/4 cup all-purpose flour
> 1/4 teaspoon nutmeg
> 1/4 teaspoon salt
> Freshly ground black pepper, to taste
> 2 eggs, lightly beaten
> 2 tablespoons grated Parmesan cheese

Preheat the oven to 350° F.

1. Butter a 6-cup mold.

2. Wash the broccoli well. Trim and peel the stalks, discarding any woody parts. Cut the broccoli into small pieces.

3. Put the broccoli in a steamer over ½ cup water, and steam, covered, 7 minutes, or until tender. Do not overcook.

4. Working in batches, put the broccoli and a small amount of cooking liquid in the container of a blender, and purée. Scrape the purée into a large bowl; you should have 2 to 2½ cups. Set aside.

5. Put the milk in a small saucepan, and scald it over moderate heat. In a larger saucepan, over moderate heat, melt the butter and stir in the flour. Whisk. Stir in the nutmeg, salt, and pepper, and reduce the heat to medium-low. Add the milk, a little at a time, stirring constantly, and cook until the sauce is thickened. Remove from the heat.

6. Add the eggs and cheese to the sauce; mix well. Pour the sauce over the broccoli purée and mix well.

7. Spoon the mixture into the prepared mold. Put the mold into a deep ovenproof pan and pour in enough boiling water to reach about ¾ of the way up the sides of the mold.

8. Bake 30 to 40 minutes on the middle rack of the oven, until a knife inserted in the timbale comes out clean.

9. Let the timbale stand 5 minutes. Run a knife around the inside of the mold. Place a serving dish over the mold, and invert it so that the timbale slides onto the plate.

BAKED APPLES IN WINE
4 SERVINGS

> ¼ cup raisins
> ¼ cup pine nuts (pignoli)
> ½ teaspoon grated lemon rind
> ¼ cup sugar
> 4 medium cooking apples
> 2 tablespoons unsalted butter, chilled
> ¾ cup dry white wine

1. Soak the raisins for 15 minutes in boiling water to cover. Drain.

2. Preheat the oven to 400° F. Butter a baking pan just large enough to hold the apples comfortably.

3 Combine the pine nuts, raisins, lemon rind, and sugar in a small bowl.

4. Core the apples to within 1 inch of the bottom. Starting at the top, peel the upper ⅓ of each apple. Divide the nut mixture evenly among them.

5. Place the apples in the prepared pan, and cover them with thin shavings of butter. Pour the wine over the apples.

6. Bake the apples 30 to 60 minutes on the middle rack of the oven, basting every 15 minutes; bake until tender but not mushy. (Timing will depend on the firmness of the apples.)

HONEY-NUT CROSTATA
6 SERVINGS

> *1 recipe Sweet Pastry Dough (see recipe, page 000),*
>   *chilled*
> *5 eggs, separated*
> *1 cup honey*
> *1⅔ cups finely ground walnuts*
> *5 ounces unsweetened baking chocolate, grated*
> *Grated rind of ½ lemon*

Preheat the oven to 375° F.

1. Roll out enough of the Sweet Pastry Dough to line a 9-inch pie plate.

2. With an electric mixer, beat the egg yolks with the honey until the mixture is fluffy.

3. Beat the egg whites until stiff but not dry.

4. Gently mix the walnuts, chocolate, and lemon rind into the egg yolk–honey mixture. Fold in the egg whites.

5. Pour the mixture into the pie shell. Bake 1 hour on the middle rack of the oven, or until the crust is golden and the filling set.

The place of ritual and allegory in life seems secure to me—it is the magic we rely on to soften the hardness; the routineness; the too-oft dreariness of facts, figures, and unceasing foolishness in high office and elsewhere. There is more to life than the measurable; more than the governance which everywhere regulates our existence on this earth.

"I do not think," said anthropologist Margaret Mead, "ritual can be relegated to the past. . . . Ritual is an exceedingly important part of all culture. . . . It is on ritual forms that the imagination of each generation feeds."

"Feeds," she said aptly, perhaps not by chance. And I agree.

As a woman, a writer, a mother, and a grandmother, I agree. I agree as a human being, for symbolic thinking is part of human existence. Rituals are joint symbolic actions. Most of all, they are fun and freeing, and often about feeding.

Whether it is the long-ago ancestor of Antonio Barolini adding an ex-voto to the wall of a church in Venice already bedecked with hundreds; or my daughters and myself preparing the seven-fish dinner of Christmas Eve while my 87-year-old mother in Syracuse again rolls out the ancestral cookies from Calabria; or my grandson in Urbino marching solemnly with the rest of his first-grade class into church on October 4 to honor Saint Francis of Assisi—wherever and whatever it is, ritual is in us, a needed part of our being.

Celebrating a festa is a form of devotion as well as a mode of pleasure. It is of primeval origin, and persistent in the collective human consciousness. Jung and Mead see ritual in our very souls—something we cannot get away from as long as we are human. In fact, it is human nature that makes ritual work. There is in human nature that which makes us express symbolically what is deep within us. The danger is not in ritual becoming superstition or mere formality, but in human beings becoming so depersonalized that they lose their need for the mysteries, and so their humanity. Ritualizing is not archaic, but a continuing renewal of the collective experience; ritualizing makes real to the participants who they are and where they come from. And since ultimately the meaning of ritual is festivity, it becomes joyousness.

In *The Meaning of Ritual*, Leonel L. Mitchell writes: "Probably the most important symbol is the meal," and he adds:

> Centuries of secularism have failed to transform eating into something strictly utilitarian. Food is still treated with reverence. A meal is still a rite—the last "natural sacrament" of family and friendship, of life that is more than "eating" and "drinking." To eat is still "something more" than to maintain bodily functions. People may not understand what that "something more" is, but they nonetheless desire to celebrate it.

In Russia, despite more than a half-century of official atheism, there is still a place in the souls of people for remembrance of their traditions. Easter has long ceased to figure on official calendars, but every year at Eastertime, bakeries fill up with traditional baked goods, and even though they're called spring cake, everyone knows them for the Easter sweet they are. So, too, with the Christmas tree, which Stalin, when he could not stamp it out, proclaimed it to be a New Year's tree. Thus does the old live on under the new façade or name. It's not much different from the Puritan attempt, and failure, to stamp out Christmas in England.

In Leningrad, as reported in December 1986, despite the official Soviet doctrine of atheism, people still come to the old Smolensk cemetery to pin their supplications to the fencing surrounding the chapel wherein lies Ksenya, a saintly woman who lived in the eighteenth century. The messages plead for her intercession: "Help me find a one-room apartment. . . ." "Blessed Ksenya, help me, a sinner, excel in deeds and in love. . . ." or even, "Help me finish fifth grade." It's not much different from the Sicilian fishermen who take their statue of San Francesco di Paola to the seashore and not only beseech him to favor their catch, but threaten him with a ducking if he doesn't. Nor from the poet Montale's worldly wife, who begs Sant'Antonio to help her find her mislaid umbrella.

On my visit to Italy in the fall of 1986, I found posters affixed to the city walls of Ravenna proclaiming the feast of the Guardian Angel. The guardian angel of each Italian child is a transformation of the Roman tutelary spirit and goes back millennia to the classical world, when such spirits were revered and devotions made to them. When Niki was in school in Rome with the Sisters of the Sacred Heart at Trinità dei Monti, this was her daily prayer to her angel:

> Angelo di Dio che sei mio custode,
> illumina, custodisci, regge governo
> a me che ti fu affidata dalla pietà celeste.
> Così sia.

> *Angel of God, my guardian,*
> *enlighten, look after, and guide me*
> *who was entrusted to you by divine mercy.*
> *Amen.*

The saints and angels, and the rites which honor them, are a lovely part of life and dreams. And nothing can be more modern, more relevant, as Gertrude Stein manifested in her collaboration with Virgil Thompson for the opera *Four Saints in Three Acts.* It is a playful, stately pageant that works; and what works is that Gertrude Stein takes the saints seriously in their dedication and their sense of removal from the workaday, material aspects of life. She honors the inner gaiety and tremendous strength of lives consecrated to nonmaterial ends. It is apparent that Gertrude and Virgil saw a parallel between the consecration of saints to their vision and creative artists to theirs. The lives of saints can be inspirational vehicles to all of us for channeling our visions.

And so it seems right that the saints are part of our festas. They are the light of the world, lit by the incandescence of their spirit, and they are necessary to our perception that life is good and blessed, as well as "real." Saints are the stuff of fantasy, an appeal to the unseen, the unknown, the bizarre, and the "otherness" of life. Every day, along with the heavy news of the world, every Italian newspaper includes in the vital notices of births and deaths the saint of the day. There are saints of all religions. The American Episcopal Church has published a list that includes not only the old standbys but such literary and humanitarian luminaries as John Donne, George Herbert, and William Wilberforce.

Phyllis McGinley wrote a book called *Saint Watching* in which she notes that during the process of canonization, the Church demands proof of joy in the candidate. I think of Saint Francis and the birds he preached to, the wolf of Gubbio whom he tamed, his Sister Earth and Brother Sun, his utter joyousness in all of creation. And then there were the *cafone* saints, the clods who were unlearned and clumsy but whose innocence was holy: the ones who, lacking Latin to say their prayers, turned somersaults or juggled balls in honor of the Lord. Or Saint Maria Bertilla Boscardin, known as "the Cinderella saint." Kept at first as a kitchen slavey in her convent, she learned to be a saint. And the saints of our day, in a direct line from Saint Francis, are Gandhi and Schweitzer and Mother Theresa.

Festa has been a great indulgence for me, a "Once upon a time . . ." tale. Festive reunions are harder to come by now that family is scattered, but they are still part of our lives and join me and the ones I love to the long, unfolding tale of humankind.

Index

365

Index